Credo

CREDO

A Catholic Catechism

Compiled by the
GERMAN CATECHETICAL ASSOCIATION

English translation and adaptation
Sister Benedict Davies OSU

GEOFFREY CHAPMAN
London

A Geoffrey Chapman book published by
Cassell Ltd.,
1 Vincent Square, London SW1P 2PN

Compiled by
Gottfried Bitter, Adolf Exeler, Wolfgang Hein, Günter
Lange, Wolfgang Langer, Maria Lorentz, Emil Martin,
Gabriele Miller, Dieter Wagner

assisted by
Rudolf Becker, Marie-Luise Fischer, Gotthard Fuchs

with valuable advice from
Edgar Bauer, Eleonore Beck, Maria Behnke, Wiltraut
Benz, Peter Eicher, Rudolf Englert, Klaus Fischer, Karl-
Theo Heil, Valentin Hertle, Hedwig Jarmußkiewicz,
Helmut Kurz, Klaus Kliesch, Albert Krauth, Anne
Mangold, Anna Miller, Franz W. Niehl, Josef
Quadflieg, Margot Saller, Arno Schilson, Otmar
Schnurr, Max Seckler, Günter Stachel, Oswald Traudes,
Veronika Wagner, Margarete Wolf, Alois Zenner

Production and design of German edition: Kösel-Verlag

Authorised by the Commission for Textbooks
of the German Bishops' Conference

First published in German as *Grundriss des Glaubens*;
© 1980 Kösel-Verlag GmbH & Co., Munich and Bernward Verlag GmbH,
Hildesheim

English translation © Geoffrey Chapman,
a division of Cassell Ltd. 1983

First published 1983
Reprinted 1983

This study edition first published 1984
ISBN 0 225 66403 8

Nihil obstat: Kevin O'Callaghan, SJ, *Censor*
Imprimatur: David Norris, *V.G.*
Westminster, 18 October 1982

The *Nihil obstat* and *Imprimatur* are a declaration that a
book or pamphlet is considered to be free from doctrinal
or moral error. It is not implied that those who have
granted the *Nihil obstat* and *Imprimatur* agree with the
contents, opinions or statements expressed.

British Library Cataloguing in Publication Data
Credo.
  1. Catholic Church—Catechisms—English
  I. German Catechetical association
  II. Grundriss des Glaubens. *English*
  238'.2   BX1961

Printed in Great Britain by
Biddles Ltd, Guildford, Surrey

Foreword

The original edition of *Credo: a Catholic Catechism*, compiled by the German Catechetical Association, translated and adapted by Sister Benedict Davies, OSU, has already proved successful in this country.

Nearly any book of instruction in the Faith will be useful, but this particular one will be of great benefit, not only to teachers, but also to older students and adults. It explains in a simple but scholarly way the teaching of the Church; it is up-to-date and accurate.

This new and cheaper Edition is to be welcomed by all who are interested in the Church.

Cardinal Basil Hume
Archbishop of Westminster

Translator's note and Acknowledgements

In translating *Grundriss des Glaubens* I have tried to keep closely to the German text. Where, in our countries, different conditions obtain from those in the German-speaking countries, the necessary adaptations have been made with the approval of the German authors, who have, at all times, shown an active interest in the work and given unstintingly of their time. In consultation with them some explanatory notes have been re-written.

The work has been done in close collaboration with Father Brian O'Higgins, Director of Brentwood Religious Education Services, to whom I am deeply indebted. I am grateful too to Father Pius Smart OFMCap., for his advice on technical points in Part IV of the book, and to Sister Clare Tanter OSU for reading the typescript.

Quotations from *The Psalms: A New Translation*, published by William Collins Sons and Company Ltd, are reproduced by permission of the Grail, England.

All other Biblical quotations are taken from *The Jerusalem Bible*, published and © 1966, 1967 and 1968 by Darton, Longman and Todd Limited and Doubleday & Co., Inc., and are used by permission of the publishers.

We are also grateful for permission to use the following quotations:

pp. 20, 38 and 138: reproduced by permission of the publishers: Mayhew-McCrimmon Ltd, Great Wakering, Essex.

p. 76: from Dietrich Bonhoeffer, 'Powers of Good', *Letters and Papers from Prison* (enlarged edition, 1971), published by SCM Press Ltd.

p. 102: by permission of A.R. Mowbray & Co. Ltd.

p. 114: from *An Duanaire: Songs of the Dispossessed*, published by Dolmen Press, by permission of Professor Thomas Kinsella.

pp. 131, 256: reproduced by permission of Kevin Mayhew Ltd.

p. 136: © 1969, James Quinn SJ.

p. 140: from *More Latin Lyrics*, published by Victor Gollancz Ltd, by permission of the Estate of the late Helen Waddell.

p. 243: © 1967 Franciscan Communications, Los Angeles, California 90015, U.S.A. All rights reserved.

Contents

II   The Creed

IV The greatest commandment

Preface

Many people regard the Christian faith as an old-fashioned building with many rooms, corridors, steps and corners, in which it is
easy to lose one's way. It contains such an abundance of statements about the faith, together with directives and advice for
personal behaviour, that it is difficult to know what is important
and what is not, what is central and what is peripheral. Even
people who grow up in the Church find it difficult to know which
way they are going. Many adults come across the Church and
begin to be interested in it as they search for a meaning to life: they
are likely to ask more insistently for more specific guidelines to
help them find their way.

Credo sets out to give such orientation. It provides, so to speak,
an architect's plan of the whole. It considers the Christian faith in
the context of Christian living in the Catholic Church and should
be regarded as an introduction into the life and tradition of this
church — for being a Christian always takes place within an
actual community: within a local parish and within the universal
church.

Built into this book are texts which are fundamental to being a
Christian in the Church:

- Christians pray to God as the Father of all: the basic text for
  this is the Lord's Prayer or the *'Our Father'* (Part I).
- Christians are accountable to themselves and to one another
  for what they believe: the basic text for this is the *Apostles'
  Creed* (Part II).
- Christians live and celebrate their Christianity in the
  community of the Church: the *Church* and her *Sacraments* are
  therefore treated in detail (Part III).
- Christians seek to put into practice the will of God: important
  foundations for this are to be found in the *great commandment*
  of love which is a summary of the ten commandments and
  other directives for Christian living (Part IV).

Although the book is intended to give orientation in outline,
the authors have another, more important purpose: they hope
that it will serve as an aid to decision-making and practical living.
It is therefore first and foremost an invitation: 'Come and see', so
that others too may be convinced that the message of Jesus is

'Good News'. It is a challenge to follow the path Jesus has travelled: the path of confidence, trust and faith.

Faith cannot be learnt by looking on or by powers of persuasion. Only one who is prepared to take risks can experience what is meant by faith.

Guidelines for the practical use of the book

- The book begins with an introductory chapter entitled: What do we mean by 'a Christian'?
- Each of the *four parts* of the book is preceded by an *introduction*: e.g. II means the Introduction to Part II.
- The four parts are divided into *thirty-nine chapters* which are numbered consecutively. Each chapter has several *lessons*: e.g. 18.4 means Chapter 18, Lesson 4.
- Each chapter has an introduction giving brief information about the content of the chapter. Above all it examines the relationship of the subject-matter to our daily lives.
- In each *lesson* there are three kinds of text: the *lesson* itself which forms the longest part; this is concluded by a *text to be learnt* (in **bold** print).
- *Explanatory notes* in smaller print, giving explanations and complementary information, generally conclude the lesson.
- The texts proposed for learning are usually prayers and hymns, texts from the Bible and the liturgy. Short explanations of concepts and answers to particular questions are in the notes, many of which are suitable for learning by heart.
- Under the headings preceding the lessons are *references* to other lessons. It would be helpful for anyone wishing to study a point in detail to follow them. The same holds good for the explanatory notes.
- The *index* at the end of the book includes all the notes in the book as well as the subjects treated in the lessons.
- In the lessons there are words in *italics*. They are the *keywords* of the lesson. With the help of the index it is easy to discover whether the concept is an important one and whether it appears in the notes. The italics occasionally used in the notes serve the same purpose there.

Planning Courses

Credo can be used as a text or resource book for a variety of courses and situations: directed individual study, adult group study, school and college courses, youth groups. The following suggestions for courses may be useful.

The liturgical year   The following sections in the book would be appropriate for study based on the liturgical year: Advent 18, 30.3; Christmas 14; Lent 1.2, 30, 9.2–4; Holy Week 15; Easter 16, 17, 27.2; Pentecost 19; Trinity 25.1, 25.2.

Another plan would be to take key ideas from the Lectionary readings throughout the year and consult the references in the *Credo* index; then follow cross-references, and references to other scripture passages. The use of a Concordance (Bible index) or the reference system in the standard edition of the Jerusalem Bible will help in exploring the scriptural background to a theme. These methods would be suitable for both private reading and group study.

A one-year course on Catholicism   The thirty-nine sections of *Credo* could be followed in the order given, shortening or selecting according to the time available. Or, the material could be re-arranged for three terms using the following sections:

Term 1   Faith and statements of belief 10; God, the Creator 11, 12, 19; the Incarnation 13–18; the Church 20–21, 25, 26;

Term 2   The Sacraments 27–33; Prayer 9, 2–6;

Term 3   The Church in the world 34, 39; Christian living 35–38.

Or, plan about thirty sessions, each taking as a starting point important issues in Christian living, e.g. person, freedom, love, marriage, family, sex, chastity, justice, laws, politics, the state, revolution, conscience, sin, forgiveness, evil, suffering and death, war and peace, hope, happiness, the future, poverty, possessions, power, work, leisure, creation. The index to *Credo* indicates sections on all these topics; the text then leads to doctrinal considerations and the cross-references indicate the place of these issues in Christian life and faith.

Another alternative is to take one key word or doctrine and explore related issues over a period of time. This is a good way to show the interaction of life and belief and the way Christian belief forms a coherent whole. Here is a sample diagram, but students could build up their own 'plan' on any theme as the term proceeds.

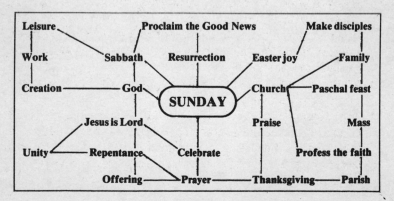

Rite of Christian Initiation of Adults   *Credo* makes an ideal handbook for the adult catechesis which forms a part of the newly revived RCIA. During the stage of formal catechumenate 'instructions should be given to the catechumens, showing them the whole Christian teaching. Thus their faith should be enlightened, their hearts should be directed toward God, their participation in the liturgical mystery should be encouraged, their apostolic action should be aroused, and their whole life should be nourished according to the Spirit of Christ' (RCIA Study Edition, 99).

In *Credo*, the Christian faith is explained according to the ancient tradition of using the Creed and the Lord's Prayer. This makes it particularly appropriate for the Presentation stage of RCIA where the catechumen hears a homily on the meaning and importance of the Creed in relation to the teaching he has received and is 'presented' with the Church's profession of faith (RCIA 186). Similarly 'The Lord's Prayer is also given to the elect. From antiquity it has belonged to those who have received adoption of sons in baptism. When the neophytes take part in their first celebration of baptism, they will say it together with the rest of the baptized' (RCIA 188). *Credo* could be used for private reading, group study or shared exploration between sponsor, catechist and candidate.

Sample questions

Any use of *Credo* for group or class study will benefit from suggested questions for discussion. With a little thought a teacher or leader can prepare these beforehand. Avoid questions which elicit a simple 'yes' or 'no' answer. Ring the changes on different *types* of question for any given topic, e.g. for study of the Eucharist suggest:

- questions which elucidate what has been studied, e.g. 'What are the ways in which Jesus is present in the celebration of the Eucharist?'
- questions which deepen understanding, e.g. 'Why is it important to "act out" what we believe?'
- questions which lead to connections with other topics, e.g. 'What are some practical implications of the doctrine of the Church as the Body of Christ?'
- questions which test a principle in a given situation, e.g. 'Why does the Church place restrictions on intercommunion with other Christians?'

Similar questions could be framed for other topics.

Other useful sample questions that could be framed about many topics are: (Some examples given in parentheses.)

- If you had to talk to . . . (non-Christians; children; school students) how would you explain . . . ?
- Plan a talk, a service, a homily on . . . (saints).
  Where would you deal with . . . in a course of study, or a book?
- What implications does . . . (belief in the Holy Spirit) have in your own life?
- Has your view of . . . (prayer) changed? If so, how?
- What does the Bible say about . . . (possessions)?
- Did anything in this section surprise you?
- If you asked a random sample of churchgoers about . . . (the Church and politics) what answers would you expect?
- How would you answer a person who says . . . (I can decide for myself)?
- What would you do if you were in charge of . . . (a parish ministry to the sick)?

- How can the Church keep a balance between believing . . . (in freedom of conscience and the role of authority)?
- If the Church discarded the doctrine of . . . (the resurrection of the body), what difference would it make?

Further reading

Richard P. McBrien, *Catholicism*, study edition (Geoffrey Chapman, 1984).
James J. Killgallon, Mary Michael O'Shaughnessy, OP, and Gerard P. Weber, *Becoming Catholic even if you happen to be one* (Geoffrey Chapman, 1980).
Monika Hellwig, *Understanding Catholicism* (Paulist Press, USA, 1981).
Tad Guzie, *The Book of Sacramental Basics* (Paulist Press, USA);
          Jesus and the Eucharist (Paulist Press, USA).

The Jerusalem Bible, standard edition (Darton, Longman and Todd, 1966).

John L. McKenzie, *Dictionary of the Bible* (Geoffrey Chapman, 1966).
Xavier Léon-Dufour (ed.), *Dictionary of Biblical Theology*, 2nd edition (Geoffrey Chapman, 1973).
Raymond E. Brown, *The Critical Meaning of the Bible* (Geoffrey Chapman, 1982).
Michael Fallon, *The Winston Commentary on the Gospels* (Geoffrey Chapman, 1984).
Robert C. Walton and others (eds), *Source Book of the Bible for Teachers*, new edition (SCM, 1975).
Etienne Charpentier, *How to Read the New Testament* (SCM, 1982).

1 Who is a Christian?

→ I Our Father; 36.1 necessary; 37.7 gift of oneself; 39.9 compassion

There are occasions when we ask ourselves: Who am I really? How do I differ from others? It is a good thing for us as Christians also to ask ourselves: Who am I? What is 'being a *Christian*'? What does it mean for me to believe in Christ? How can people tell I am a Christian?

At first it would seem simple enough to describe a Christian as one who models his life on Jesus, who lives as a *follower of Jesus*, or as one who, like Jesus, calls God 'Father'; one who strives to love God and man as Jesus loved them; or as one who knows that he has been redeemed by Jesus Christ; one who aspires to a life of close union with Jesus Christ.

It would not be difficult to formulate further statements of this kind. But to set about putting into practice such statements is more easily said than done.

However, since it is not thanks to our own efforts that we are Christians, none of us need be afraid of trying to become a Christian. We can be confident that we are guided, and that being a Christian is more a *way of life* along which one travels than a 'house' where one lives.

Along this way one does not always move forwards. Christians too can take wrong turnings because they are guilty, because they sin. As everyone therefore needs forgiveness, Christians trust in the forgiving *love of God* and of their fellow-men. This is why they celebrate the Eucharist, recall with gratitude what God has done for mankind and ask his pardon. When they say the Our Father they realise that it is as people in need of help that they make the petitions.

1.1 A Christian models his life on that of Jesus Christ

→ 28.2 member of the Church; 6.1 do not be anxious; 35.3 loving God

Each person tries to make his own way through our world. In doing so he is dependent on others and on his surroundings. Often his experiences as a child have exerted a powerful influence on him and are determining factors for his whole life.

Jesus Christ is the person whose influence is decisive for a Christian who believes that Jesus is the Son of God and that God himself is revealed in him. At the same time Christians are convinced that Jesus Christ is truly man. Therefore whatever Jesus says and does is *Good News* for human beings.

Jesus announces that God's kingship, the *kingdom of God*, is close at hand and this he shows in his words and deeds, in his life and death and in his resurrection. These events make it clear that God wills the good, the salvation, of everyone and that, because he is God, all that he wills can happen.

What then must a person do to turn towards Jesus? First, he must let himself be touched and guided by Jesus; he must become his *disciple*. This does not mean that new rules will be imposed on him, but it does mean that he will discover that his whole life takes on a different outlook. Because he knows he has received gifts from God, he can now give to others.

To be a Christian means to go the way of Jesus. In John's gospel Jesus says:
I am the Way, the Truth and the Life. *John 14:6*

Christians: The disciples of Jesus were first called·'Christians' in the town of Antioch (Acts 11:26).

Salvation (Hebr. shalom = well-being, peace): Collective term for all the good and the happiness that God intends for us and for which we long; experiencing God's loving attentions, his grace, his forgiveness, his adoption of us as his children, his sharing of his life with us. Salvation creates a relationship whereby we can live with one another and with God: complete, salvific, inviolable, fulfilled life for all (→ 22.2).

1.2 What does following Jesus mean?

→ 5.2 God's will; 37.2 loving in deeds; 37.3 taking the world seriously; 39.9 compassion; 28.3 way of life

Jesus invites his disciples to follow him, to tread the same path after him, to accompany him, to be closely united with him; he appeals to them to follow him. This *following* cannot be mere imitation: his disciples today live in conditions differing from those of the disciples in the lifetime of Jesus. But even their following could not be taken to mean slavishly 'copying' Jesus. The disciples of whom the *gospels* tell us were not obliged literally to do all that their Master did. According to everything in the New Testament and from what we are told by those who have had experience, following Jesus means to commit oneself wholly to God and to see people and the world as Jesus did.

Therefore following Jesus means: being pledged to the *service of God* and thus becoming the *servant of one's fellow-men*. Following Jesus means above all a total commitment, no 'half measures', i.e. not being selective in one's commitment. The texts in the New Testament relating to this commitment leave no doubt: it is a question of single-mindedness, an undivided heart, of *'all or nothing'*. But at the same time there is the sure hope that Jesus Christ will attract to himself anyone who dares to do this. Paul does not tire of speaking of life 'in Jesus Christ' (cf. Romans 6:1-11).

These crucial words about a follower of Christ appear in all three synoptic gospels:
If anyone wants to be a follower of mine, let him renounce himself and take up his cross and follow me.
Matthew 16:24; *Mark 8:34*; cf. *Luke 9:23*

Disciple: A teacher (elder) collects students or pupils (disciples); in the New Testament those who follow Jesus over a long period are called disciples (as distinct from the Twelve Apostles; → II).

Synoptists: Matthew, Mark and Luke are called synoptists. Their gospels have much in common; set out side by side, in three columns, they give an overall view (Gr.: synopsis → 20.4).

Conversion: We use this word of a non-Christian who becomes a Christian (or of a non-Catholic who becomes a Catholic). 'Change of heart' is an alternative expression. It means a deep, interior turning of oneself towards God, and is desirable also for those who are already nominal followers of Christ.

1.3 Life in the community of the faithful

→ 21.1 Church as community; 21.3 community of holiness

Christians are dependent on one another — in their faith too. The disciples of Jesus form a *community* of belief in Jesus and they *trust* in his message about a God who loves mankind. This faith has an origin and a history, not just in the past; this history is always ongoing. The *Church* as community of the faithful bears witness to this. She is commissioned to keep alive the remembrance of her origins and the goal of her future history, to hand on the faith, to pass on salvation and to go forward in trust towards this goal.

The individual Christian lives in this community and in its *traditions*. He cannot live for himself alone. He has heard the message from others who have been its witnesses and he too must work to spread it further. In keeping with this message he sees his fellow-men as *brothers* and is prepared to serve them with love. He thanks God for this privilege and he prays for his brothers. In the community, with his fellow-believers, he celebrates the memory and, at the same time, the presence of God's love in the *Eucharist*.

In the third Eucharistic prayer the Church prays:
**Strengthen in faith and love your pilgrim Church on earth;
your servant our Pope, our bishop
and all the bishops,
with the clergy and the entire people your Son has gained for
you.**

Eucharistic Prayer or Canon: The central prayer of praise and thanksgiving in the Eucharist. It begins with the Preface, is said aloud by the priest and concluded by the congregation's acclamation: 'Amen' (→ 27.2).

1.4 Reading the Bible

→ 20.3 the Church's book; 20.4 unity in diversity; 34.9 Christian unity

Christianity is not a religion that relies for its supreme authority on a book. Christianity relies on a person. For Christians *Jesus* of Nazareth is the trustworthy witness of *God's love*. However, all Christians do turn to a book, the Bible, as the document for their faith. The Bible is the witness to the long history of their faith stretching right back to the beginnings of God's chosen people, the Israelites. The *sacred writings of Israel* — the writings of the Old Testament as we call them — are also a standard work for Christians.

Next to these early writings Christians have placed the document containing the beliefs of the disciples of Jesus: the *sacred writings of the new covenant*. These testimonies to faith — the Old and New Testaments — are common to all Christians, even if, in the course of history, some have gone their separate ways. The *Bible* unites them all; they are convinced that God reveals himself to man, speaking to him in a language that he can understand. As *Christians* they are united in the belief that God has spoken finally, and in a way never to be surpassed, through his Son Jesus Christ.

Many people find helpful these words of the psalmist in the Old Testament:
Your word is a lamp for my steps
and a light for my path.
By your word give me life.   *Psalm 118 (119):105, 107*

Inspiration: → 20.3; **Gospel:** → 4.1; **Interpretation of the Bible:** → 10.3

1.5   Seeing the world through the eyes of Jesus
→ I Our Father; 37.3 taking the world seriously

In the gospels we learn how Jesus thought and spoke about God and man. In them the close connection that he saw between God and the world is made very clear.

We may be surprised how frequently Jesus referred to *everyday things* when he was proclaiming the coming of the *kingdom of God*. He spoke of the beauty of the lilies of the field (Matthew 6:28), of the sparrows falling to the ground (Matthew 10:29); he compared the coming of God's kingdom to a woman kneading dough (Matthew 13:33) or the tiny mustard seed growing into a large shrub (Matthew 13:32)

For someone who speaks in this way there is no separation between God's world and our human world. Jesus sees them both as closely connected and he cannot speak of one without the other. He looked on the world around him with eyes full of love. For him details become clear *signs* of God's kingdom. When he wanted to speak of *God* and his *love*, he spoke of what was familiar to those listening to him. He took note of his surroundings and was seriously concerned for everyone who crossed his path: in each person he saw God's likeness.

The following hymn expresses something of this for us:
Oh, the love of my Lord is the essence
of all that I love here on earth.
All the beauty I see
he has given to me
and his giving is gentle as silence.   *Estelle White*

Part I : Our Father

Our Father, who art in heaven,
hallowed be thy name.
Thy kingdom come.
Thy will be done on earth,
as it is in heaven.
Give us this day our daily bread
and forgive us our trespasses,
as we forgive those who trespass against us.
And lead us not into temptation.
but deliver us from evil.

(Matthew 6:9–13)

For thine is the kingdom, the power and the glory
for ever and ever. Amen.

Introduction

The Our Father is the prayer that, according to tradition, Jesus himself taught his apostles. Therefore, it is a very special prayer for Christians and is, moreover, the pattern of all prayer.

In the *Our Father* Jesus tells us of the relationship between God, man and the world. God is the loving *Father* of mankind — despite his great *glory*. His *will* is more beneficent than anything man could ever conceive or plan. His kingship brings happiness and salvation. He gives us our daily bread and forgives our sins. We are invited to rely on this God. It is his will to set us free from all that threatens us. Everyone would gladly respond to such an invitation — and yet there is the temptation to turn one's back on God, take risks and seek happiness elsewhere. God counts on his disciples to pray that they may not be led into temptation.

By treating of the Our Father in Part I, this book is following an ancient tradition. By deepening our insight into the Our Father, we come to understand the way Jesus thinks and acts. We penetrate into the *Spirit of Jesus* and this Spirit teaches us how to live as disciples of Jesus and to talk to God as to a loving Father.

The Our Father is found in two places in the New Testament: in a shorter form in Luke (11:2-4) and in a longer form in Matthew (6:9-13). Early in the Christian era the Church adopted Matthew's version for general use.

Some Christians added the concluding doxology 'For thine is the kingdom . . .' to the Our Father. This ancient Christian conclusion is found in the early 'Teaching of the Twelve Apostles' and also in some Greek Bible manuscripts. Because Martin Luther used this version in his translation of the Bible, it has always been used by non-Catholics. In some countries, including Britain, it is now used by Catholics at Mass, after the prayer that follows the *Our Father*. It is also sometimes used at ecumenical services or in informal group prayer.

Teaching of the Twelve Apostles (often called the *Didache*): The oldest Christian document after the New Testament (beginning of the second century A.D.); it contains rules for life in the early Church, arrangements for church services, Eucharistic prayers.

Doxology (from Gr. doxa = honour, glory): Solemn prayer in praise of God (e.g. Our Father, Glory be to the Father, the Gloria, conclusion of Eucharistic prayers at Mass) in which the three Divine Persons are usually mentioned by name.

2 Our Father who art in heaven

→ 11 Father/the Almighty

God is worshipped in many ways. People invoke him, giving him special *names:* Almighty, Most High, King, Lord. The people of Israel were confident that they really knew God's name and based their confidence on God's revelation of his name to them: 'I am Yahweh'; 'I shall be with you'.

Is the great unknown One, who reigns far away in 'heaven', really close to us? Can we trust him or should we fear him? Who is to tell us what God is like?

People in the Bible, holy men and women of all times, tell us of their experiences of God; but above all it is Jesus who has made him known to us (John 1:18). Jesus calls God '*Abba*', which means 'loving Father'. Jesus trusted this loving Father and he prayed to him. He told men about him and revealed to them his loving kindness. Jesus also encouraged his disciples to speak to God as to their loving Father.

Israel: Jacob (Isaac's second son) received from God the name Israel (= God's warrior; cf. Genesis 32:29); his descendants, the 'sons of Israel', God's chosen people, are called the 'people of Israel' after him. Israel is also the name of the state established in 1948 by the Jewish people.

Children of God: This expression summarises belief in redemption through Jesus Christ. By his incarnation, life, death and resurrection Jesus Christ became man's brother and at the same time he made all men his brothers and sisters so that they might call God their Father (→ 19.3).

2.1 God is close to us

→ 3.3 men worship God; 25.2 the known/unknown God

There are people who say that they have experienced God's nearness. They are certain — they say — that God is present in their everyday lives. Down the centuries experiences of this kind have been handed on to us by Christians known and unknown. But it is also true that people who do not call themselves Christians have had these *experiences of God*.

Again and again Christians have put their trust in God, have abandoned themselves to him and have experienced that they can rely on him. Therefore they maintain that God wants to be as intimate with man as is a friend. Moses is one such witness. In the Old Testament we are told that he is called by *Yahweh* (Exodus 3) and he is quite sure that *God is present*. God is close to those who call upon him — for example, to his people in slavery.

If this is God's attitude to man, it is indeed *Good News* for those who feel lonely or perhaps abandoned by everybody. But if anyone asks: 'Where is God now?', the answer given in the Bible is that we experience that God is close to us in the measure in which we trust him, and not by waiting to see if he is going to reveal himself.

Yahweh is not only a name, but also a promise:
I am Yahweh, I am who Am.
Say to my people: I Am has sent me to you — this is my
name for ever. cf. *Exodus 3:14–15*

Yahweh: According to Exodus 3:14, the name which 'the God of their fathers' reveals to Moses is 'I am who I am'. An incorrect reading of the text renders the Hebrew word as 'Jehovah'.
Moses: With the other elders (= patriarchs) of Israel, Moses is one of the most important people in the Old Testament; he was chosen by God to lead his people out of their slavery in Egypt (*c.* 1200 B.C.)

2.2 God in heaven — Our Father
→ 11 Father/the Almighty

Jesus encouraged his disciples to call on God in *heaven* as their loving Father just as he himself addressed God. The disciples considered this so important that they retained the word '*Abba*' in its Aramaic form. To call God 'Father' means to hope that he is the very foundation of our existence. Father means life, security and therefore also *future*. A God who is our Father embraces and sustains everything; we are wholly indebted to him for everything.

A loving father cares for each one of his children; the *child* knows that his father loves him even when he seems strict. Tenderness is not the only way of showing affection. Such a father wins his child's confidence. The child recognises his father's wisdom and he admires him; he is never afraid of him. His love for his father is quite natural.

There are people for whom this image of a father presents problems; perhaps they may have found their own father overpowering and exacting, or feeble and helpless, and they do not associate affection and *trust* with this word. Yet the Father of whom Jesus speaks is the 'Father in heaven'. By heaven is meant perfection, the *fulfilment* of all our expectations, the object of all our desires, fellowship with God and with one another. The 'Father in heaven' is the one who fulfils all man's longings.

We must address this Father familiarly as children in a family circle speak to the Father they love.

A contemporary Christian has expressed his trust as follows:
We are sheltered by You as a bird in its nest,
We live in You as a fish lives in the sea,
We dwell with You as a child in his own home.
Wilhelm Willms

Aramaic: A language akin to *Hebrew* (the language of the Old Testament); it was spoken in Palestine during the lifetime of Jesus.

Abba: Familiar form of address for one's father (cf. Papa, Dad, etc.); used within the family even by grown-up children. The Aramaic form is retained in Greek texts not only in Paul's Greek Letters to the Galatians (4:6) and the Romans (8:15), but also in the prayer of Jesus in the garden of Olives (Mark 14:36).

Heaven: A biblical image for God's 'dwelling' 'above' the firmament. Above all, the descriptive word for God's 'world of happiness' opened up for human beings by Jesus Christ. Collective word for final salvation promised by God to man: the sum total of all that is good and fulfilling, the object of Christian hope. (It does not mean the 'heavens' or outer space above us explored by the astronauts.)

2.3 God is a Father to everyone

→ 12.3 God's creature; 5.3 misfortune

Everyone likes to have his own possessions and says: my bicycle, my bed, my coat. He could also say: my family, my parents, my friend, my lover; this means: we belong to one another; you are important to me. Can each one also say '*my God*'?

Those about whom the Bible writes believe that God loves each one as though he were the only person in the world. Each one is *loved* by God whole-heartedly, without limit or reservation; in spite of the countless number of human beings God loves each one wholly and completely. So everyone can say to him: 'my God', '*my Father*'.

When we call God 'Father' we do not mean that his characteristics are solely 'masculine' ones. The prophet Isaiah says: 'Like a son comforted by his mother will I comfort you' (Isaiah 66:13), and Hosea says of God: 'I was like a parent who holds an infant close to his/her cheek' (cf. Hosea 11:4). The examples show that God also loves as a mother; he loves each one wholly and completely.

But if God is a Father to everyone, all are his children and among themselves they are sisters and brothers. That is why Jesus teaches his *disciples* to pray with one another: 'Our Father who art in heaven'. In the *Spirit of Jesus* they understand that they must not begrudge one another the Father's love. No one is loved less than another; therefore they talk to one another about him, support one another on their way to him and rejoice mutually in his love.

The second Letter to the Corinthians appeals to the fact that what God promised in the Old Covenant has happened through Christ:
I will welcome you and be your father, and you shall be my sons and daughters.   *2 Corinthians 6:17–18*

Isaiah: The first of the so-called 'major' prophets, writer of the book which bears his name; he lived in the eighth century B.C. — Parts of the book of Isaiah are dated much later (→ 19.2).
Hosea: One of the twelve 'minor' prophets; eighth century B.C. (→ 19.2). The distinction between major and minor prophets is based on the length (or brevity) of their writings.

3 Hallowed be thy name

The statement that God's name should be hallowed sounds strange to most of us. What does it mean?

Two descriptions often used in Jewish prayers are easier to understand. Repeatedly these prayers say that people should magnify God's name; they should 'glorify' it. To hallow God's name means to affirm his grandeur and his *glory*.

The word 'hallow' is explained in a prayer said by Jesus and given in John's gospel: 'Father, glorify your name!' (John 12:28). Here human beings do not hallow *God's name* but it is God himself who shows that he is the all-holy One.

We might reword the desire here expressed as: Father, make my life and that of the world attuned to you, may we recognise you as God; may we realise that your name is more important than all the big names we run after; may we see that you are the great God and that only in you shall we find *peace*.

To hallow: what belongs to God (= what is put aside for him alone) is holy. To hallow God's name (= to consider it holy) means to give God what belongs to him alone. God sanctifies his name (= proves it holy) when his actions move us to an acknowledgement that he is God.

3.1 God's name
→ 2.1 God is close to us; 35.1 God first loved us

A man's name belongs to him; he sees it as a part of himself. When one knows a person's name one can address him. If he has particular qualities — outstanding ones or ones that appeal to us — he is often given a pet name or a nickname which distinguishes him in a special way.

This can be applied to the many names people in the Bible gave their God. These names tell us something of the experience people had of this God. When they experienced his goodness they prayed to him as the *good God*. When they recognised his power they called him *Lord*. Because by the name we understand God himself, we have a duty to glorify the name of God and make it known.

It is a long-standing Christian custom to begin our times of prayer in God's name. We call on his name when we have to accomplish a difficult task. People place their plans and their actions under his protection.

But this constant use of God's name is not without its dangers. The *name of God* is misused not only by those who insult or blaspheme him but also by those who intend to vindicate him. No word in human speech is as much abused as the word 'God'. Here the biblical warning not to take God's name in vain, or misuse it, is indeed appropriate. Even today orthodox Jews, out of respect, avoid pronouncing God's name.

In the Missal there are prayers for daily use. One of them begins:
Father,
guide and protector of your people,
grant us an unfailing respect for your name,
and keep us always in your love.
Masses for weekdays, Opening Prayer No. XII

Second commandment: 'You shall not take the name of your God in vain' (→ 35.4 ten commandments).
Blasphemy: Defiant mockery or contempt of God by word, deed or attitude.

3.2 God is the all-holy One

→ 2.1 God is close to us; 25.2 the known/unknown God; 11.2 the great God

We can talk about God and try to describe him in various ways, but no words are adequate. A believer knows that God is always more than people think and always greater than they can imagine. No concept, no image, suffices; the sum total of all concepts and images falls short. Theologians say 'God is the wholly Other'. The Bible means the same thing when God is called the all-holy One: holy his name, to be feared (Psalm 111(112):9).

We are accustomed to apply the word 'holy' to men and women who have striven to live wholly for God. Yet no human efforts are sufficient to make a person *holy*. Only because God takes a person up into his own holiness does he belong to God and become holy. No one, on the other hand, becomes holy without willing it. This is the meaning of this sentence of the Old Testament: 'It is I Yahweh, who am your God. . . . You must therefore be holy because I am holy' (cf. Leviticus 11:44–45).

In every *Eucharistic celebration* the whole *congregation* is united in praise of God's *holiness*, thus showing how necessary for its life is the recognition of God as the all-holy One.

In the Eucharistic Prayer God's holiness is proclaimed in the *Sanctus* which is derived from the words of the prophet Isaiah (6:3):
Holy, holy, holy Lord, God of power and might,
heaven and earth are full of your glory.

Celebration of the Eucharist (= thanksgiving): The Mass. The Church remembers with gratitude the life, death and resurrection of Jesus and celebrates the foundation of her faith (→ 27 centre of the Church's life).

3.3 Men worship the all-holy God
→ 9.1 praise and glorify

When we hear the word *prayer* we think first of petition, of a cry for help from a person who in his need calls on God for salvation. If we make our petition to God because we acknowledge him to be God, then there is an element of worship underlying our petition. However, the only one who can really make requests is the one who knows and recognises God's saving power. Praise of God should therefore take precedence over all other forms of prayer.

Those who have had *experience* of God are convinced that no one could ever know anything about God unless God had revealed himself to man. What we are told of this is proof of the importance of such an encounter. God's approach to man is so amazing that in this *encounter* man is fundamentally transformed.

We are told that Moses veiled his face when God appeared to him in the burning bush (Exodus 3:6). When, on Mount Sinai,

Moses asked God if he might see his face, God placed him in a cleft of the rock and Moses was allowed to see only his 'back' as God passed by (Exodus 33:22–23). When Isaiah was *called* by God and permitted to see the reflection of his glory, he is said to have cried out: 'Woe is me, I am lost' (cf. Isaiah 6:5).

Although the Old Testament attempts, by comparisons such as these, to express something of God's greatness and *holiness*, he still remains unfathomable. But the New Testament bears witness to the incomprehensible God through his Son Jesus *Christ*. He is for us the image of God (2 Corinthians 4:4). In him we come to know the nature of God's holiness and greatness, a holiness and greatness which do not exclude self-abasement and *poverty* (Philippians 2:7).

In the third Eucharistic prayer at Mass the Church prays:
Father, you are holy indeed,
and all creation rightly gives you praise.
All life, all holiness comes from you
through your Son, Jesus Christ our Lord,
by the working of the Holy Spirit.

---

4 Thy kingdom come

→ 5.1 to ask God's will; 23.3 sign of hope

The kingdom of God is close at hand: this is the main theme of Jesus' message. In Mark's gospel (1:15) the proclamation of this kingdom is Jesus' life's work; the content of the '*gospel*' is what he brings from God. *God's kingly rule* was, at the time of Jesus, the essence of all *hope*. God was to set up his kingdom and thus finally establish justice and *peace* for everyone.

This long-awaited *justice* is more than political greatness. It means a new world, free from oppression, suffering and death — a world therefore where the devil no longer holds sway.

Is this kingdom of God a reality only in the next life, a future reality? Or has it something to do with us and our world? What is meant when Jesus says it is close at hand? Is it *coming* even now? Can we see it coming — in Jesus Christ and in those who believe in him?

Kingdom of God: The real meaning of the Greek word often translated by 'kingdom' is 'kingly rule', i.e. the situation in which God is really the ruling element in our lives. In many places, especially in Matthew, the term 'kingdom of heaven' is used.

4.1 Jesus proclaimed the kingdom of God

→ 15.1 who so lives; 1.2 to follow; 27.1 the Church preaches

Even the *prophets* spoke of the coming of God's kingdom. They said that his kingdom would dawn and change the world for the better. *Jesus* makes the proclamation of the *kingdom of God* the very heart of his message. He lets the people around him experience that, with him, a time of joy and happiness has dawned.

The conclusion to be drawn from the words and actions of Jesus is that the kingdom of God is something wonderful, something which the heart of man would never dare to hope for — a victory over suffering and loneliness, over sin and death. The kingdom of God means great *peace* for man and for nature in God's sight, a community of *love*, a home with the Father, a kingdom of *freedom*, *reconciliation* and *justice* for the children of God, where there is pure joy and all tears are wiped away. For Jesus this kingdom of God is a reality; it is present, beginning now. Although human beings cannot establish God's kingdom, it does not dawn without their co-operation. It comes through Jesus; it comes through those who *follow him*, people who stake their all for it, so that, through their actions and their sufferings, it may dawn. But the kingdom of God will be brought to its fulfilment by God himself.

So the message of God's kingdom is a *mystery*. It will be revealed only to those who commit themselves to this message; it is to them that it will be entrusted (Mark 4:11). Only those who follow Jesus learn to understand what he is saying, to grasp what is meant by the dawning of God's kingdom.

Mark the evangelist summarises in a single statement this message of Jesus:

Jesus went into Galilee. There he proclaimed the Good News from God. 'The time has come', he said, 'and the kingdom of God is close at hand. Repent, and believe the Good News.' *Mark 1:14–15*

Gospel (Gr. evangelium = good news): News which is a source of rejoicing — e.g. news of a victory after a battle; in the New Testament the proclamation of the time of salvation finally dawning in Jesus Christ. Word also used as 'title of a book' for the four collections of the preaching about the life, words and deeds of Jesus: Gospel according to Matthew, according to Mark, according to Luke, according to John (= *evangelists* → 20.4). The evangelists are, as it were, the editors and they write for specific groups in the early Church, answering various theological questions. Time of composition of the four gospels: between 70 and 100 A.D.

Mystery (from Gr.): 'Mystery of salvation' — central statement of the Christian message; cannot be explained by reason; learnt only by prayer, by reflection, by the intuitive experience of faith and above all by courageous surrender (→ 25.2 mystery); something inexpressibly precious, a free gift from God.

4.2 Jesus speaks of the kingdom of God in parables

→ 15.1 who so lives; 1.5 through the eyes of Jesus

We can speak in various ways of things, events and people. Sometimes a careful, accurate description is necessary; at other times the meaning is quite clear. A matter that is profound and complex may be more easily understood by means of a story. If it is a question of moods and feelings a short poem is often more effective than many words. An artist can 'say' more by means of a *picture* than another person by a series of photographs or a scientific treatise. A story gives more food for thought than a concept. A concept which tends to be clear and definite may restrain our minds in thinking about God (who cannot be defined), whereas a story, a poem, a picture may suffice to unfold facets of God which a cold definition could not give.

When Jesus spoke of the *Kingdom of God*, he told *parables*; he did not explain by concepts but involved his listeners in a story from everyday life. The kingdom of God comes as unobtrusively and naturally as the growth of a seed. The kingdom of God has to be searched for as indefatigably and as thoroughly as a lost treasure. Jesus told parables above all for his opponents so that he might make them aware of their attitude and win them over to God, or so that he might refute them.

He clarified for his listeners the nature of the kingdom of God which begins insignificantly and imperceptibly like a mustard seed (Luke 13:18-19); when the seed grows it yields a rich harvest (the sower: Mark 4:1-8); it is a gift from God (labourers in the vineyard: Matthew 20:1-16), a precious find (treasure in the field: Matthew 13:44); it comes despite obstacles ('wicked' husbandmen: Mark 12:1-12); it demands *determination* and *watchfulness* (ten bridesmaids: Matthew 25:1-13); it is a great banquet radiating joy (wedding feast: 22:1-14).

There are numerous parables. Repeatedly Jesus tries to open the hearts of his listeners to *God's beneficent kingship* by fresh comparisons and metaphors. He wants 'anyone who has ears' really to hear (Matthew 13:9) and he wants his listeners to reach out towards this kingdom.

The shortest parable is in Matthew's gospel:
The kingdom of heaven is like the yeast a woman took and mixed in with three measures of flour till it was leavened throughout. *Matthew 13:33*

4.3 The mighty deeds of Jesus bring the kingdom of God near

→ 15.1 who so lives; 39 do likewise

Jesus did not only speak of the kingdom of God, he also made it present by his actions. What the prophets announced as a time of *grace* became a reality in Jesus.

When John the Baptist sent the disciples to ask if Jesus was the one they were waiting for, Jesus answered with words from the book of Isaiah: 'Go back and tell John what you have seen and heard: the blind see again, the lame walk, lepers are cleansed, and the deaf hear, the dead are raised to life, the Good News is proclaimed to the poor' (Luke 7:22; cf. Isaiah 26:19; 35:5–6; 61:1).

Many people who met Jesus experienced something of his mighty deeds. His nearness brought healing and his words the gift of *forgiveness*. *Trust* in him made people free. Full of wonder and amazement the people repeatedly said: 'We have never seen anything like this' (Mark 2:12). And the demons cried out: 'I know who you are: the Holy One of God' (Mark 1:24).

When we speak of these mighty deeds of Jesus we are speaking of *miracles*. In the New Testament the word is used sparingly; the expression 'his mighty deeds' is preferred. Jesus did not work miracles when people demanded them of him. His mighty deeds were not intended to fascinate the crowds; they were designed to point to the coming in him of the kingdom of God and to strengthen man's faith. That is why John calls them *'signs'*.

Jesus' mighty deeds point to the kingdom of God. Therefore Jesus says:
If it is through the finger of God that I cast out devils, then know that the kingdom of God has overtaken you.
Luke 11:20

John the Baptist: He preached penance on the banks of the Jordan in Jesus' time; according to the information given in the gospels he sends his disciples to Jesus; he is the 'last prophet' of the Old Covenant (Luke 7:28); Herod ordered him to be beheaded (cf. Luke 3:1–22; 7:18–35; John 1:19–34).
Miracles: Events in the Bible leading the believer to God; events bringing healing and grace. God's wonderful deeds can make people attentive and watchful so that they are moved to believe. What is important about miracles is not that they are contrary to experience and to all the laws of nature, but that they serve to lead man to God and to healing and salvation (→ 12.4 God can be found in our world).

4.4 God's glory is revealed

→ 24.2 the last days; 23.2 faith gives us courage

As long as we live we shall never find and give to others sufficient *love*, joy, freedom and truth. And yet hope urges us on unflinchingly towards a more humane world, a more perfect life in the community of the Church, a better *future*. In this way Christians see the expectation — conscious or unconscious — of the human race for the kingdom of God, for the revelation of God's glory, and it makes every commitment worthwhile.

In many ways a believer sees *signs* of God's glory. He discovers them in the leading of the *Israelites*, in the words of the prophets, in God's *creation*, in the path of history, past and present. But in a unique way the believer sees God in *Jesus Christ* — in his life, death and *resurrection*. And he sees God at work among the faithful in the Church. Where people live with Jesus Christ, something of God's glory shines through even now.

The Bible speaks of the full *glory* — still to come — in the image of the everlasting city of Jerusalem where God dwells among men. Christians believe that when God finally lives among us, we shall be free from all unhappiness and all evil. When we are close to him, all will be well. When God finally appears, all who belong to him will see and recognise what they have believed: he is Lord and Father; his kingship gives man life, perfect, everlasting *life*.

In the Revelation of John, the last book of the New Testament, we read of the new heaven and the new earth:
He will make his home among them; they shall be his people, and he will be their God. . . . He will wipe away all tears from their eyes; there will be no more death and no more mourning or sadness. The world of the past has gone. The One sitting on the throne spoke: 'Now I am making the whole of creation new.' *Revelation 21:3–5*

Glory: → 17.2

5 Thy will be done on earth as it is in heaven

→ 1.1 to model one's life on Jesus; 15.1 who so lives

There are people who try to act according to *God's will*. They acknowledge that for them this is the only kind of life worth living.

Others say: I don't want to know about it; in the name of this maxim far too much has already happened that was certainly not God's will. Or they say: 'God's will' — this sounds like subjection. I want to manage my own life. Many who hear the words 'God's will' immediately think of self-denial and sacrifice and turn away; they are not interested. One might also ask: Is God's will really done by human beings? Isn't it accomplished without them? Can they make some contribution, or does God do what he wants? People can also be resigned: who knows what God wants of us!

Christians ask this question of Jesus. For they believe that he has lived out the will of God. God's will is his line of conduct for the *kingdom*. The *disciples* of Jesus are told to ask in the Our Father that God's will may be done and his kingdom come.

5.1 Asking what is God's will

→ 11 Father/the Almighty; 9.4 kinds of prayer; 39.10 praying to God

God's will and *God's kingdom* are closely connected in the Our Father. What is meant by the 'kingdom of God' becomes clear when God's will is done. When we do what God wills, the good that God holds in readiness becomes a reality. Christians pray: Let us see the *salvation* and happiness which you wish to bring us in your kingdom.

In Jesus and in his words and deeds this kingdom has already begun: to the poor he has brought the Good News, to the sick healing, to sinners pardon (Luke 4:18). His own life was completely determined by the will of God: 'My food is to do the will of the One who sent me' (John 4:34) is John's description of the attitude of Jesus.

Thus *Christians* can pray: Thy will be done on earth as in heaven, in small things as in important things, by us as it is done by Jesus, expressing *trust* in God's *love* which he has given to man once and for all.

This petition in the Our Father embraces every Christian prayer. For whatever a Christian may ask of God, it is on condition that his will be done.

Prayers and hymns express this Christian trust in God's will:

Christ be my way, my path to find the Father,
my guide when there's no trusting sound or sight;
Christ fill my mind to cleanse the understanding,
to be my truth, a beacon blazing bright;
Christ all I hope for, strengthening, upholding,
my breath of life, my pride and my delight.
> **Truth on my tongue,**
> **his way to guide my walking,**
> **and I shall live,**
> **not I, but Christ in me!**   *Luke Connaughton*

5.2 Doing God's will
→ 35.3 loving God; 35.4 ten commandments; 39 do likewise

In a particular situation often it is not easy to say what the *will of God* is. What are we to do then? Prophets and *saints*, holy people in every age, have given us advice and guidance as to how an individual can find out and practise God's will. There are collections of directives and counsels, of *commandments* and *laws*, above all in the Bible. The best-known are the 'ten commandments' which, according to biblical tradition, were given by God to Moses on Mount Sinai (Exodus 20:2–17).

Jesus referred to these statements from the Old Testament, but he also gave a fresh interpretation of how the commandments a to be understood. The Sermon on the Mount testifies to this; the interpretation he gave was so unfamiliar that the scribes of his time were antagonised by it.

When reading the *Sermon on the Mount* in Matthew's gospel (5:1–7:29) we might certainly ask whether Jesus intended to lay down, once and for all, in list form, directives as to what God wants — what he wants of me here and now. The sermon on the mount begins with a 'list' of instructions or directives, of pointers for guidance in *Christian living*; yet the summary is of a special kind; salvation is proclaimed for people from very different walks of life: people who have no recourse to violence, who are merciful, who wish to do good to others unreservedly, who devote themselves to the cause of *peace*, who — even when persecuted and scoffed at — remain faithful to God. To all of them the *kingdom of God* is promised. Jesus approves, too, the lives of those who are poor, helpless and unsuccessful, those who suffer from the power or lack of consideration of others but still do not lose hope in God and their fellow-men.

The Beatitudes are a summary of the fundamental attitude of a Christian.
Jesus teaches his disciples:
How happy are the poor in spirit:
theirs is the kingdom of heaven.
Happy the gentle:
they shall have the earth for their heritage.
Happy those who mourn:
they shall be comforted.
Happy those who hunger and thirst for what is right:
they shall be satisfied.
Happy the merciful:
they shall have mercy shown them.
Happy the pure in heart:
they shall see God.
Happy the peacemakers:
they shall be called sons of God.
Happy those who are persecuted in the cause of right:
theirs is the kingdom of heaven.
Happy are you when people abuse you and persecute you
and speak all kinds of calumny against you on my account.

> **Rejoice and be glad, for your reward will be great in heaven; this is how they persecuted the prophets before you.**
>
> *Matthew 5:3–12*

Sermon on the Mount: Matthew 5–7. Collection of sayings of Jesus. Name originates from the introductory sentence (cf. Matthew 5:1): Jesus went up the mountain . . . and taught them (= like Moses, he goes up on the mountain: cf. Exodus 19; he is the new Moses who gives God's instructions). A comparable passage is to be found in Luke (6:17–49) and is called in many editions of the Bible 'the *sermon on the plain*' (cf. Luke 6:17).

Commandments and laws: Christians do not understand commandments and laws rooted in the message of Jesus and handed down by the Church as strange or as arbitrary. They are rooted in the nature of God and the relationship of the Creator to his creatures. Without them our development as God's creatures would be stunted (→ 35.4 ten commandments; 34.3 Church precepts; 36.2 freedom of the children of God).

5.3 Misfortune and the will of God

→ 10.4 I believe; 12.5 world order and its problems

In the world there is joy but there is also sorrow and distress. When people experience what is good they are inclined to take it for granted. But when they are overtaken by sadness or some *misfortune*, they tend to reproach God and to ask: How can he allow it? Because there is so much evil and such dreadful misery, many find it hard to believe that God is with them. Nevertheless Jews and Christians live *confident* that God holds the world in his hands and that, despite troubles and misfortunes, it is guided by him. They are convinced that God does not will suffering and evil.

To continue to be confident in the face of contradictory experiences is difficult. Those of whom the Bible tells us had the same anxious questions as ourselves: Why does God allow it? Why does God remain silent? Why does he not pevent people from suffering? The writer of the book of Job broods over the reason why even a person who does *God's will* has to suffer. Why doesn't God at least stand by those who remain loyal to him?

In such situations Christians contemplate Jesus. From God he brings us happiness, *life* and *salvation* and yet he is crucified because he does so; he devotes his life unflinchingly and unreservedly to men; he passes on to them the message from a *God* who loves them and yet he endures hatred and death. So for Christians it means that this is our fate — and God's fate. He accompanies those who suffer, he goes the same way through life, through the darkness that we suffer.

Christians try to model their lives according to these principles. They attempt to come to grips with unhappiness in the world. They believe that God wants life, not death. God does not let us down, despite all appearances to the contrary. He is guiding us even when we cannot tell in what direction. He leads us even when we fail to understand.

Catholic and Orthodox Christians show special honour, among all the saints, to Mary as the one who was wholly open to God's will. Even in the depths of suffering, at her Son's death, she did not not hesitate to say 'yes' to God's will. It is in this spirit that she is often depicted at the foot of the cross, or with her dead Son on her knees — a consoling picture for many Christians.

> Christians can pray with the psalmist in the Old Testament:
> **If I should walk in the valley of darkness**
> **no evil would I fear.**
> **You are there with your crook and your staff;**
> **with these you give me comfort.** *Psalm 22(23):4*

Book of Job: Old Testament book belonging to the so-called wisdom writings. Account of a man who is tested by suffering, and struggles with God. Eventually he submits, recognises the greatness of God and thus experiences salvation.
Pietà: → 15.2

6 Give us this day our daily bread

→ 39.7 sharing; 39.8 living differently

Jesus wants us to make God's concerns our own. His name, his kingdom and his will are among the first petitions in the Our Father.

But Jesus also tells his disciples that God makes our concerns his own.

We are entitled to ask him for what we need in our lives. *Bread* preserves us from hunger and death.

This sounds reassuring. We think of rich harvests, of barns full to overflowing, of banking accounts and industrial prosperity, of provision for lean times. But these things prompt another question: What about this policy of providing for the future? May a Christian be preoccupied with a sense of security? What about the two-thirds of the human race suffering from hunger? Praying for our daily bread is genuine only if it is an expression of practical *responsibility* for all who are hungry: give us and them our daily bread today. Let us not be anxious about tomorrow. Each day has trouble enough of its own (Matthew 6:34).

6.1 Do not be anxious

→ 39.8 living differently; 39.4 work — celebrate; 2.2 our Father

The request for our daily bread is usually understood in this way: give us and those who have nothing to eat everything we need for our lives each day, throughout our whole lives.

We can certainly pray for this — but it is not what the Our Father is saying. The Lord's *disciples* follow their Master, travelling light, with bread for today and even for tomorrow. But piling up stocks, guaranteeing one's own security is questionable.

On their *road* to the promised land the people of the old covenant experienced that God was close to them and ready to help. He was present during their march through the desert. The Bible tells us that God gave them their daily food. But they were allowed to collect bread only for one day at a time, they were not allowed to hoard (Exodus 16:16–32). In this way they learnt that they were indebted to God alone for their daily sustenance and that therefore they should live *trusting* in him.

A disciple of Jesus is confident too that the one he calls Father, the one he trusts, for whose kingdom he longs, will give him bread at the right time — *bread* for him to survive, bread as a *sign* of God's ever-present *love*.

Therefore Christians should face with courage the temporary nature of their own lives. They ought, above all, to work towards a sense of security for others. For themselves they should pray: do not allow us to become greedy; do not let our hearts become anxiously attached to anything which would prevent our doing your will, which would deprive us of the daily experience of your goodness. Give us the bread we need today. Tomorrow we can renew our *request*. But continue to make us feel uneasy about the many who have nothing to eat today.

In the Sermon on the Mount Jesus gives the norm for a Christian's worries:
Do not worry; do not say, 'What are we to eat? What are we to drink? How are we to be clothed?' It is the pagans who set their hearts on all these things. Your heavenly Father knows you need them all. Set your hearts on his kingdom first, and on his righteousness, and all these other things will be given you as well. So do not worry about tomorrow; tomorrow will take care of itself. Each day has trouble enough of its own. *Matthew 6:31–34*

6.2 Bread for others too

→ 39.7 sharing; 38.5 the person who crosses my path; 34.5 good works

There is a German hymn which contains the words: 'Let God do as he pleases'. This is often interpreted as 'God does this anyway'. All we need to do is to look after our own affairs. Perhaps we might help our relatives and our neighbours if they are in need; let us leave God to see to everything else.

The Our Father recognises no such distinction: there is no question of 'my bread' and 'bread for others', but simply 'our *daily bread*'. A disciple of Jesus will share with the hungry the bread that God gives him each day — this is taken for granted. The person who has more than he needs and is unaware of those who lack the barest necessities has not understood that God intends to care for others through us. Jesus, then, teaches his *disciples* that they are not to defend their own possessions selfishly. Free from anxiety, they can *share* because they know that to him who gives it shall be given in return. The Christian 'who lets God do as he pleases' trusts him completely and he is therefore free to use his energies wholly *for others*. Exemplary Christians have done this in striking ways, and not only in the past.

In the Letter of James there is a challenge to care in a practical way for those in need:

If one of the brothers or one of the sisters is in need of clothes and has not enough food to live on, and one of you says to them, 'I wish you well; keep yourself warm and eat plenty', without giving them these bare necessities of life, then what good is that? *James 2:15–16*

---

7 And forgive us our trespasses, as we forgive those who trespass against us

→ 30 guilt

Normally the *kingdom of God* escapes our notice in this world. There are several reasons for this: we easily overlook the *signs* of this kingdom because our attention is concentrated on other things. Furthermore, we ourselves hinder the possibility of God's will being done, of his kingdom becoming visible and of his love permeating everything. We thus become God's debtors because we obstruct good plans which he wills to bring to completion only with our co-operation. And we also become indebted to our fellow-men in that they have to suffer from the evil we have caused.

A person who is guilty can stake no claims. All he can do is to ask for *forgiveness* and then make real efforts to be freed from his *sins*; he can try to make amends for the wrong he has done. But which of us likes asking forgiveness? Who is prepared to admit that he has done wrong? Is anyone ready to pardon? Why is it that we find it so hard to forgive others sincerely from our hearts?

7.1 No one is without sin

→ 22.2 power of sin; 30.2 who is a sinner?

'You are guilty' is a daily reproach. We are frequently at fault and through carelessness, cowardice or malice we have brought upon ourselves *guilt* of many kinds.

Even when we have goodwill and do not plan wrong-doing, evil still creeps in; we lose control and do harm. Much evil can arise from our lack of vigilance — which is our own fault — and we have to answer for it. Such guilt — great or small — accumulates and becomes a burden. No one is an exception. A great deal has to be brought back into line and there is much too that the victim can forgive.

But what about the sense of guilt which remains — leaving lasting traces in the life of another person? What about the guilt towards the dead and towards people with whom we have lost contact, or the guilt that weighs too heavily to be pardoned by human words? Is this guilt not guilt before God? And what about the failings by which men oppose God himself, deny him, act in his presence against their better judgement?

A person who has incurred guilt cannot rid himself of it, he can only *beg* someone else to help him out. Who is to make good what we human beings can never make good? Who is to forgive a guilty person and set him once more on the right path?

Jesus teaches his *disciples* to beg God to *forgive* their sins. A Christian lives in the belief that God is a God who forgives. Such *belief* brings joy, but it also implies obligations

---

In his first Letter John emphasises that none of us is without sin:
**If we say we have no sin in us,
we are deceiving ourselves
and refusing to admit the truth.**   *1 John 1:8*

Sin and guilt: These are two related theological concepts, fundamentally concerning our relationships with God. *Sin* means a deed consciously willed, through which harm is done to another: e.g. a confidence not honoured, a promise not kept, inconsiderate exploitation of another, thinking only of oneself, wanting to dominate, etc. When a person of sensitive conscience becomes aware of such action in his life, he realises that his relationship with God is affected: he is no longer at ease with God, in a state of relationship with God: this condition is known as *guilt*. In everyday speech the ideas of *guilt* and *sin* are not strictly separated.

7.2   Jesus reveals to us a God who forgives
→ 22.1 being reconciled; 30.4 various kinds of forgiveness

Forgiving sin is not an activity on God's part that can be called forth by a specific attitude on man's part; forgiveness is something that appertains to God's goodness, as Jesus has explained for us (John 1:18). *Forgiveness* is of the essence of God (cf. Psalm 102:8).

The depth of God's love for man becomes visible in Jesus. He shows how passionately God in his *friendship with man* freely forgives him his sins: Jesus sought out the tax-collector Zaccheus, who had been ostracised by pious folk, sat down at table with him and thus gave him confidence: God wants to *stay at your house* today (Luke 19:1-10). By appealing to their own consciences Jesus made those who accused the adulteress slink away; he spoke to outcasts and encouraged them to make a fresh beginning (John 8:1-11). In the parable of the loving father and his prodigal son he showed how God welcomes with open arms a guilty son and makes him his heir again, even if he has forfeited his claim to being received home once more (Luke 15:11-32).

Christians believe that God forgives without our having to 'do' anything. We need only to open our hands to receive his forgiveness. We experience forgiveness and God's love when we entrust our sins to him and *ask his forgiveness*. Jesus affirms this in the parable of the Pharisee and the tax-collector (Luke 18:10-14). A disciple of Jesus may pray: Forgive my sins. Make good what I am incapable of making good. Bring *grace* where through me evil has occurred. Remove from my path all that separates me from you and my brethren.

We can ask God's forgiveness in the words of a verse from
the hymn 'O sacred head sore wounded':
I pray thee, Jesus, own me,
me, shepherd good, for thine;
who to thy fold hast won me,
and fed with truth divine.
Me guilty, me refuse not;
incline thy face to me.   Translated by *Robert Bridges*

Sin and guilt: → 7.1
Remorse or contrition: The acknowledgement of one's own sin and a resolute
'No' to it before God (→ 30.2)

7.3   The person whom God forgives can forgive others

→ 37.7 gift of oneself; 30.4 various kinds of forgiveness; 30.1 sin and
penance

The person who has experienced God's goodness realises he has,
in his turn, an obligation to be generous. A person who has been
forgiven cannot fail to *forgive*. This is certainly how Jesus sees his
followers acting.

The reality, often enough, is different. In Matthew's gospel the
story is told of a man who owes his master a large sum of money.
Because he cannot pay he and his whole family are to be sold into
slavery; on his knees he asks for time to pay. The master is *sorry
for him* and remits the whole debt. As the man leaves his master,
he meets another servant who owes him a mere pittance. And
what happens? He demands all the money owed. When the other
asks him to be patient, he has him mercilessly thrown into prison
(Matthew 18:23-35).

This is a reflection of our own behaviour. How hard we find it
to *forgive* if someone has done us an injustice! We demand our
rights. Even we Christians act in this way: we who believe that we
have life only because God does not keep an account of our *faults*.
God's forgiveness is the Good News of the gospel; his goodness is
boundless. He does not calculate as we do when we forgive one
another. On the contrary; because God forgives unreservedly, we

are called upon always to forgive. Every time we celebrate Mass it is taken for granted that as disciples of Jesus we have already been reconciled with our brothers (Matthew 5:23-24).

The question as to how often a Christian should be ready to forgive is clearly answered in the gospel:
Then Peter went up to Jesus and said, 'Lord, how often must I forgive my brother if he wrongs me? As often as seven times?' Jesus answered, 'Not seven, I tell you, but seventy-seven times.' *Matthew 18:21-22*

---

8   And lead us not into temptation, but deliver us from evil

→ 22.2 power of sin: 12.5 world order and its problems

God leads mankind. He holds in his hands everything that happens. This was what the children of Israel believed and trusted in throughout their eventful history; this is what Jews and Christians down the centuries believe.

This *belief* does not go undisputed. If God is leading us, what about the dark side of our lives? If God leads each one, what about man's free *choices*? If God is our leader in every situation, is he leader too when man is brought to the brink of despair, when he is plunged into wars and catastrophes?

These are questions arising from the life-experiences of the human race — questions which beset even the *disciples* of Jesus; perhaps they are threatened more than others who leave God out of the reckoning.

The experiences that press us to ask such questions are a threat to our faith. Therefore Jesus calls on his disciples not to seek an answer to them without God's help. From the *evil* which overpowers the world only God can *set man free* — through Jesus, through those who follow him.

Temptation: Usual meaning: attraction to sin. In the Bible the word generally has very serious overtones: danger to faith, risk of a serious lapse affecting one's whole life.

8.1 God's gamble

→ 5.1 God's will; 11.1 power and fidelity; 36.2 freedom

As Christians we believe that God holds our lives and the destiny of the world in his hands. And at the same time we believe that God does not deprive man of the power to make *decisions or choices*, he wills man to be *free*, he opens for him the way to freedom. The ability to make free decisions means that we are *responsible*; this is a source of happiness but also of suffering. We cannot understand how *God's will* and our freedom are compatible. Does God really allow his plans to be thwarted by man's decisions?

However this may be, it is abundantly clear in the whole of Scripture that God always courts man's love. He takes upon himself the risk which our freedom entails. In so doing he takes into account that man may deny him, that he may say: 'Not thy will but mine be done'. Does God then allow man's will to be done with all the consequences that this involves?

This terrible possibility that man can do evil without God intervening shows a believer that not only does God admire human freedom, but also that he expects much of a human being. The freedom given to man is also a danger for him, a *temptation*. He can lose sight of true standards and make his own yardstick for all he does; he can lose sight of the one who has given him his freedom. God's gamble then becomes man's gamble.

Man's situation is vividly described in the hymn written by Cardinal Newman when he was unable to see his way clearly:

**I was not ever thus, nor prayed that thou
shouldst lead me on;
I loved to choose and see my path; but now
lead thou me on.
I loved the garish day and, spite of fears,
pride ruled my will; remember not past years.**

John Henry Newman

8.2 Let us not yield to temptation

→ 30.2 who is a sinner?; 30.6 guilt/self-knowledge; 12.2 power and violence

When a Christian begins to understand the dignity of his *calling* and realises how little he responds to *God's love*, he may become anxious. The New Testament is familiar with these feelings of anxiety. The Letter to the Philippians speaks of working out our salvation in 'fear and trembling' (Philippians 2:12). Matthew writes that Jesus warns his disciples in the hour of temptation in the garden of Olives: 'You should be awake, and praying not to be put to the test' (Matthew 26:41). And Paul warns the Corinthians against *self-assurance*: 'The man who thinks he is safe must be careful that he does not fall' (1 Corinthians 10:12). But he goes on to console them in their faith: 'You can trust God not to let you be tried beyond your strength' (1 Corinthians 10:13).

If a Christian prays: Lead us not into *temptation*, and if he trusts that God will not allow his followers to fall, he must take the consequences. What is said of *forgiveness* is applicable here too: we must do for others what we ask for from God; we must ask insistently what we are to do. If God is to strengthen us, we too must strengthen one another, remain close to one another and help one another. Above all we must strive to avoid leading anyone into temptation. This means that we must so live and so speak that our neighbour will not be unfaithful to his calling; we must not make it unnecessarily difficult for him to be a good Christian. We need to remember that in all dangers a *Christian* can have recourse to God and *pray*: Do not let me ever be separated from you.

The following psalm verses may help us in time of temptation:
He who dwells in the shelter of the Most High
and abides in the shade of the Almighty
says to the Lord: 'My refuge,
my stronghold, my God in whom I trust!'
It is he who will free you from the snare
of the fowler who seeks to destroy you;
he will conceal you with his pinions
and under his wings you will find refuge.   *Psalm 90(91):1–4*

8.3 Deliver us from evil

→ 12.2 power and violence; 22.2 power of sin

Anyone who has understood a little of the world and human beings senses that men and the world are in confusion. He knows too that this is true of himself. There is abundant promise of a beautiful world, but in many places destructive powers are at work. It is bad enough that car accidents, plane crashes and earthquakes cause havoc, but men themselves do harm to one another: envy, murder, torture, exploitation, terror, violence, abuse of power, theft, lies, unfaithfulness. These are but a few examples taken from a comprehensive list of evils. In one form or another we are both victims and culprits. Evil can weave such a network that there is scarcely any possibility of escape.

When we pray: *Deliver us* from *evil*, we can think of minor and major catastrophes threatening human life. They are disturbing — small wonder that people are shattered by them! Yet when saying this petition of the *Our Father* we should reflect rather on the evil to which we are prone, in which we are involved and involve others. These may be small failings in our everyday life, in which everyone of us shares in one way or another, or they may be part of that real evil which goes to the heart of all goodness, gathers momentum and is bent on the destruction of life. Everything by which people upset and destroy themselves and one another; all that spells ruin, all those things by which people bring death upon themselves — this is what is meant by evil. Traditionally, our faith says: this is the *evil one*, and so our prayer is not only: Preserve us from our personal pitfalls, but: Free us from evil, deliver us from the *power of evil*, snatch us from the evil one.

In the closing chapter of Peter's first Letter, Christians are warned:
Be calm but vigilant, because your enemy the devil is prowling round like a roaring lion, looking for someone to eat. Stand up to him, strong in faith. *1 Peter 5:8–9*

Evil (either 'evil' or the 'evil one'): The Greek text of the Our Father allows both translations: the 'evil one' or simply 'evil' (→ 12.2 power and violence). Other places in the Bible and in Christian tradition take the experiences of evil so seriously that they speak of it as a personal power: 'the evil one (devil) prowls around'.

Devil (from Gr. diabolos = one who confuses. Hence, diabolical = devilish): Biblical name for the evil one, for a creature who rebels against God, causes evil, for the 'prince of this world' (John 14:30), who is still at work despite the fact that his power has been crushed by Christ (Hebrews 2:14).

9 For thine is the kingdom, the power and the glory now and for ever

→ I Our Father

This expression of praise is omitted by Catholics, at least in some countries. Although it does not appear in the gospels it was added to the text of the Our Father in the course of the second century and is in keeping with the spirit of the Lord's Prayer. For in the Our Father man's *happiness* and God's honour, far from being opposed to one another, are closely connected. *Glory* and *praise* arise out of our requests: the God who is good is also powerful; his *love* and *fidelity* are the object of the trust of the one who is praying. A person who seldom says a prayer of praise may be reminded by this conclusion to the Our Father that the whole of *creation* should praise God.

9.1 Praise and glorify

→ 3.3 men worship God; 11.2 the great God

Whoever bases his life on God's love for man accepts whatever each day brings. For he believes that nothing that happens is mere chance. Such an attitude is more than the silent fulfilment of one's duty. It is a 'Yes' to life with all its ups and downs and its daily monotony. It is a readiness to venture forward in faith.

The person who recognises that God is responsible for everything and holds all in his hands can hardly refrain from saying so.

Perhaps he may even sing his thanksgiving and joy: 'We *worship* you, we *praise* you, we adore you'.

The faithful of the Old and New Testaments, as indeed many who pray today, both Jews and Christians, do not merely make requests; for them, praise is as important, perhaps more important. Many of the *psalms* are songs of praise in honour of our God who is both great and good. In the New Testament, above all in the Letters, are several *doxologies* and *hymns* used by the early Church. The best-known hymn of praise is the Magnificat (Luke 1:46–55). Songs of praise have also been handed down to us by the Saints; one of the most famous is the 'Canticle of the Sun' of St Francis. But it is above all in celebrating the Eucharist that we expressly proclaim our praise of God. When we praise God and glorify his *name* we do not merely say something about God, we also say something about ourselves: it is good that I belong to God.

In the Liturgy of the Word the Church uses the great hymn of praise:
Lord God, heavenly King,
almighty God and Father,
we worship you, we give you thanks,
we praise you for your glory.   From the *Gloria*

Hymn (Gr. = song): Song in praise of God's mighty deeds.
Psalter or **Psalms** (Gr. = singing): Collection of 150 hymns/songs and prayers of the Israelites (= book of Psalms). *Psalmist* = collective title for the poets who wrote the psalms; how many contributed to the 150 psalms we do not know; there are also some psalms not found in the psalter or in the Old Testament.

9.2   Jesus teaches us how to pray

→ 1.5 through the eyes of Jesus; 2.2 our Father

The *gospels* often speak of the prayer of Jesus: at the feeding of the five thousand (Matthew 14:19); at the transfiguration (Luke 9:28); at the healing of the deaf mute (Mark 7:34); at the raising of Lazarus (John 11:41); at the Last Supper (Matthew 26:26; John 17:1–26); in the agony in the garden (Matthew 26:36–44); and when he was dying on the *cross* (Luke 23:34–46; Matthew 27:46; Mark 15:34).

Jesus often took part too in public prayer in the *synagogues*; he went 'as usual' on the *Sabbath* (Luke 4:16), or he visited the 'house of prayer' of the temple (Matthew 21:13). But the attitude of Jesus shows us that, like the prophets, he kept aloof from the ostentation in the practice of prayer which had become widespread among his people. He often sought solitude on a mountain or in a desert place in order to pray alone (e.g. Matthew 14:23).

What Jesus himself did, he commissioned his *disciples* to do: pray, entreat, beg in my name for what you need (Matthew 5:44; John 14:13). He pointed out the necessity of praying and of persevering in *prayer* (Luke 18:1). But above all we conclude from the gospels that the fundamental attitude in prayer is *trust* and the knowledge of our own neediness.

Prayer might be described as speaking, in faith, about our life; an awareness of God's presence, taking it seriously, recognising his greatness and trusting him. We could also say that prayer is listening to God's word and giving him an answer; bringing before God man's joys and needs, being a representative for others. Perhaps we can also say very briefly: prayer is living consciously with God.

When the disciples, influenced by Jesus' own prayer and his unique relationship with God, asked him: Teach us to pray!, they were saying that of themselves they did not know how to pray nor what they should ask for (cf. Romans 8:26–27). Jesus gave them — and us — in the Our Father a model for *Christian prayer* that is valid in all ages.

The Jewish writer Simone Weil (1909–43) expresses the attitude of faith:
Why should I worry? It is not my business to think of myself. My business is to think about God. It is God's concern to think about me.

Synagogue: Since the first destruction of the Temple in Jerusalem (587 B.C.) the gathering place for a Jewish community (building used for worship and for purposes of instruction).
Sabbath (Hebr. = rest day): The seventh day of the Jewish week (from Friday

evening till Saturday evening) with strict rules for resting from work, important above all for the protection of servants; a reminder of the deliverance out of slavery in Egypt (cf. Deuteronomy 5:13-15); religious service in the family and in the synagogue. The Jewish Sabbath rest and many Jewish Sabbath customs were transferred by Christians to Sunday (day of the resurrection).

9.3 Pray without ceasing

→ 27 centre of the Church's life; 5.2 God's will

In his Letter to the Thessalonians Paul urges the Christian *church* there to 'pray constantly' (1 Thessalonians 5:17). Can one do this? How? Some people say at the beginning of the day: 'All to the glory of God'. This means: All that I do and suffer today, my whole day's work, is to be my *prayer*. A person who strives to make his daily life a prayer will try to do everything in such a way that it is attuned to *God's will*.

Others see that whatever happens to them during the day becomes a reminder of God. If something is successful they thank him. If they are surprised at something, they praise him silently. If they have been at fault, they ask God's pardon (act of contrition). Before beginning something important, they ask God's help. At times this prayer can be brief, like a cry or call for help. Such prayers are known as *ejaculations*.

The Church enjoins on the faithful to pray at definite times in the course of the day. In the morning a Christian should take time to begin the day in God's presence (*morning prayer*). He should end it by reflection and thanksgiving and a prayer for the night (*night prayer*). At table Christians thank God for his gifts (*grace before and after meals*). In some places the *Angelus* is rung and people can hear it even in a noisy street. It calls on the faithful morning, midday and evening to remember God in the midst of their *work* and to reflect on what he has done and does for them through Jesus Christ.

The early Church had specific *times of prayer*: in the evening or when day dawned. Later, Christians prayed at the third, sixth and ninth hours of the day in memory of the coming of the Holy Spirit (Acts 2:15), the crucifixion (Mark 15:25) and the death of Jesus (Mark 15:34). Thus a structure of times of prayer was built into the Church's life: the prayer of the Breviary, also known as the

'Liturgy of the Hours'. Many Christians called to special service in the Church (priests, members of religious orders) continue to observe these times of prayer or at least try to do so. They pray as representatives of all *Christians* whose work makes this impossible.

Anyone who wishes to take up the challenge to 'pray constantly' in his daily life may perhaps be helped by the so-called *Jesus prayer* used by monks and the faithful in the Eastern Church. Breathing in, they say: 'Lord Jesus Christ, Son of the living God', and breathing out, they say: 'be gracious to me and have mercy on me'. At first beads were used for counting, but as time went on, a rhythm was established with breathing and heartbeats. This form of ceaseless prayer is not according to everyone's taste, nor is it acquired in a day. But not a few have found it a helpful method of prayer.

In his Letter, James exhorts Christians:
If anyone of you is in trouble, he should pray;
if anyone is feeling happy, he should sing a psalm.

James 5:13

Liturgy (Gr. = people's service): Collective term for the various official Church services, each with their special texts; celebration of the Eucharist and the Office or Hours. The liturgy is often chanted or sung in choir, usually by religious, but also by choirs of lay people.

Breviary or Hours: Regular prayer consisting chiefly of hymns, psalms and readings to which priests and religious are obliged and to which the faithful are invited: Morning Prayer (or Lauds) at the beginning of the day, Midday Prayer in the course of the day and Evening Prayer (or Vespers) in the evening. The Church's Night Prayer is Compline. In earlier times the day was counted as beginning at 6 a.m. (Lauds) and ending at 6 p.m. (Vespers); the third hour was therefore 9 a.m., the sixth 12 noon and the ninth 3 p.m. (cf. Luke 23:44; Acts 2:15 and elsewhere).

Angelus: Call to prayer morning, midday and evening; the prayer recommended by the Church begins with the words: 'The angel of the Lord declared to Mary . . .'. The custom of ringing a bell in monastery churches in the Middle Ages at these times spread to other churches.

Rosary: → 16.3

Novena (from Lat. = nine): Nine days of prayer according to the prototype of the *nine days' prayer preceding Pentecost* (between the Ascension and Pentecost or Whitsunday). During these nine days the apostles 'joined in continuous prayer'.

Ejaculations: A prayer, phrase or sentence, suited to a particular occasion or situation ('Lord, have mercy' — 'All to the glory of God' — 'In the name of the Lord').

Grace before and after meals has long been customary in Christian circles. In addition to the usual familiar formulas, it is good to thank God for the people who have prepared a meal as well as thanking him for the food itself.

9.4   Kinds of prayer

→ 27.3 the Lord's surrender; 27.5 each week Easter; 39.10 praying to God

If one searches in Scripture to find out what prayer is, the answer is always that calling upon God is not separated from the rest of one's life. Praying is the answer in faith to all that takes place in the midst of one's everyday life. Therefore praise and lament, searching and questioning, requesting and imploring often merge into each other. Yet we can also distinguish between various forms of prayer.

In *praise* man expresses his joy in the greatness of God; in *thanksgiving* he expresses his gratitude to him for the good things he receives from him. *Petition* is the most common form of prayer: man asks for what he needs. In *intercessory* or *bidding prayers* others are brought into one's prayer. In *penitential prayer* and those expressing *sorrow for sin* the faithful ask for God's mercy for themselves and others.

Each one can pray alone in his 'private room' as Jesus recommends in the *Sermon on the Mount* (Matthew 6:6), but for Christians community prayer, *public prayer*, is important too. Those who pray together are like a large choir singing in harmony. The *liturgy* is the official prayer of the Church; that is why we are continually exhorted: let us pray. The Our Father too is an official prayer; it is the 'community' prayer of the *disciples of Jesus*.

There is prayer in set words: formulas are a help for the one praying. But there is also prayer without set words. The two forms are complementary. It is also possible to pray as one reflects on a sentence from the Bible, or a poem, a picture or an experience. Attentive reading of *Holy Scripture*, or of another book with special significance for the individual, can also be prayer. The contemplation of a crucifix, or time spent quietly in a church, is prayer. The *contemplation* of a person, a flower, a landscape can become a prayer. Prayer of this kind, without words, is called contemplation or meditation. Sometimes the one praying has the impression that he is speaking and that God is listening to him; sometimes it is as if he were speaking into an immense dark silence. Perhaps the person will then be silent and listen to what God wants to make known to him. For in the last analysis prayer is not speaking but *being silent* in order to listen. God speaks first — but he 'speaks' in his way; in prayer man answers. This answer does not have to be given in words but it does have to embrace the whole of our life. A person cannot pray well if he is not in earnest about his everyday life, his *work*, his *responsibilities*, and the people with whom he lives.

> We can pray in various ways: what St Augustine, a Father of the Church, says, is appropriate:
> **Man does not pray in order to adapt God to his views, but in order to adapt himself to God's views.**

Church service: Public praying and singing in God's honour (usually in a fixed form).

Piety: Attitude of trust in, and surrender to God; prayer is the elementary expression of this.

Meditation: Reflective contemplation or recollection (exists also in non-Christian circles).

Mysticism (from Gr. = closing the eyes and lips): Direct experience of God (→ 36.1)

Procession (Lat. = moving forwards): Solemn walk in a religious context, usually accompanied by prayer and hymn-singing. Christian significance connected with image of the 'pilgrim' Church en route towards her goal.

Pilgrimage: Walk (or journey) to a 'holy place' (e.g. Rome, Assisi, Lourdes, Fatima, Walsingham); also exists in non-Christian religions (e.g. Mecca, Jerusalem); this experience of the community of the Church can serve to strengthen one's faith.

Objects of piety: Holy pictures, candles, rosaries, crosses, statues of the saints, cribs, etc.

Part II: The Creed

I believe in God,
the Father almighty,
creator of heaven and earth,
and in Jesus Christ,
his only Son, our Lord,
who was conceived by the Holy Spirit,
born of the Virgin Mary,
suffered under Pontius Pilate,
was crucified, died and was buried.
He descended into hell.
The third day he rose again from the dead.
He ascended into heaven,
sitteth at the right hand of God
the almighty Father.
From thence he shall come
to judge the living and the dead.
I believe in the Holy Spirit,
the holy Catholic Church,
the communion of saints,
the forgiveness of sins,
the resurrection of the body
and life everlasting.
Amen.

Introduction

From the beginning Christians have tried to summarise their faith in short statements. For example, they used to say '*Jesus* is the *Christ*'. They meant, 'We believe that Jesus, promised by God and filled with the Holy Spirit, is the Messiah and *Saviour* of mankind'. A similar sentence was 'Jesus is *Lord*' — Lord in a way that no one else is Lord, none of the gods revered by the nations, nor the Roman emperor. During the first centuries, in times of persecution, Christians went to their death as *martyrs* for this *profession of faith*.

More recently, too, Christians have attempted to express their faith briefly and yet comprehensively. Down to the present day, in the Catholic church and in many other Christian churches, the 'Apostles' Creed' has remained the most usual profession of faith.

It is the *Apostles' Creed* in the sense that it is a valid summary of the Christian message handed down from the apostles. Originally, the three sections of this creed were the answers to three questions addressed to the *catechumen* at baptism: Do you believe in God, the almighty Father? Do you believe in Jesus Christ, our Saviour? Do you believe in the Holy Spirit and in his work? These same three questions are still asked when Christians renew their *baptismal promises* at the Easter Vigil.

Since the third century it has become customary for the catechumen or his godparent to recite this profession of faith as one continuous text. Before the assembled *parish congregation* he professes his trust in God — Father, Son and Holy Spirit.

The creed, then, is first of all an expression of *trust* and of a very real relationship of man with God: 'I believe in you and I entrust myself to you'. At the same time it is a hymn of praise in honour of all God's deeds; this is why the creed is often sung. Even from early times the faithful assembled together understood it as a valid summary of the fundamental truths of their faith.

Today many Christians try to express their *faith* in new ways; this is important and there is ample justification for it. However, it is not easy to formulate the earlier Christian creed in different words without changing its content. On the other hand one should not cling to words without being aware how the meaning of certain concepts has changed. It is good therefore to *formulate afresh* but also good continually to return to the earlier text. In this way the sum total of what Christians have believed down the ages is expressed once more; at the same time it is made quite clear that Christians of today are not isolated in their faith; they believe within the *community* of the whole *Church*, and they are united with Christians of all times.

Apostles (Gr. apostolos = envoy): The twelve disciples chosen by Jesus to preach his message; Peter is generally named as the first (cf. Matthew 10:1-4; Mark 3:13-19; Luke 6:13-16); after Judas had betrayed Jesus, Matthias was chosen (Acts 1:26). Paul insists (Galatians 1) that he was called by Jesus as 'apostle to the pagans'. In the New Testament other believers were sometimes also called 'apostles'.
Nicene Creed: An expanded version of the Apostles' Creed coming from the General Councils of Nicaea (325) and Constantinople (381); recited on Sundays and solemn feast days at Mass.
Credo (Lat. = I believe): Because the creed in Latin begins with this word, the creed itself is often known as the 'Credo' (especially in the musical settings of sung Mass).
Catechumen (from Gr.): In the early Church baptism was often preceded by preparation over a considerable period of time; this is the case today for adult baptism, especially in missionary countries. The person preparing for baptism is called a catechumen. A restored Rite of Christian Initiation of Adults has been promulgated.

10   I believe in God

→ 25 Amen

In everyday speech 'I believe' means: I suppose; I do not know exactly. 'I believe you' says more: I trust in you, I rely on what you say. But when someone says 'I believe in you', he means: I trust you to such an extent that I would risk my life for what you say. This is almost what we mean by *'belief in God'*.

Although we cannot take it for granted that people believe in God, we can assume that they pose the question: they ask not only why this or that person behaves as he does; they also inquire into the *meaning of their lives*, into the beginning and end of the world. And everywhere there are people who search for God and find in him the answer to their *questions*.

At all times people seeking, in faith, for purpose in their lives, have asked about God. Many *religions* are proof that God has not left their questioning without an answer. Christians, too, believe this. But what is special about becoming a Christian and saying 'I believe'? In what way does the faith of *Christians* differ from that of other people?

10.1 People ask questions

→ 2.1 God is close; 1.1 modelling one's life on Jesus

It is inherent in the nature of man to ask questions. He cannot help it even when it becomes burdensome to him. Ability to ask questions is in keeping with man's human greatness. With the help of *science* many questions and problems can be resolved. Technological advances and many improvements in human life are made possible because science provides the answers.

But there are numerous questions asked by man which remain without a definitive answer: What is the *meaning* of our life? Where does the world come from? On what foundations can I build my life? What will happen to me at death? What can I hope for? To such *questions* the results of scientific efforts do not provide full answers that are entirely satisfying. In these situations many turn to the different religions and place their crucial questions before God. In *faith* they hope for an answer.

> St Augustine, Bishop and Doctor of the Church (fifth century), writes in his *Confessions*:
> **You have created us for yourself, O God, and our hearts are restless until they rest in you.**

Polytheism: Recognising and honouring several gods.
Monotheism: Recognising and honouring only one God (Judaism, Islam, Christianity).
Atheism: Outlook on life which assumes that God does not exist.
'New religions': New religious movements, adopted especially by young people who seek a meaning to their lives and fail to find what they are seeking in the great religious institutions (Catholic or Protestant); chiefly a mixture of Christian and non-Christian elements; much about them is questionable and dangerous. These religions are a serious challenge to the credibility of Christians (→ 19.3 Sect: Children of God).

Doctor of the Church: Title of honour given to certain outstanding writers in the Church because of the orthodoxy of their teaching and because of their personal holiness.

10.2 People from all nations search for God

→ 2.3 God is a Father to all; 12.4 God can be found in our world

However varied their culture, in different ways people of all nationalities call on *God*. In addition to the many traditional religions there are five great *world religions*: their numerous adherents are spread throughout the world. They are: Christianity, Judaism, Islam, Hinduism and Buddhism.

These religions are not completely unrelated to one another. Much of what Jews and Christians believe is found in other religions. In these, *Christians* see an indication of the fact that God makes himself known in various ways. Muslims, Jews and Christians acknowledge one God. Christians and Jews have in common the part of the Bible which Christians call the Old Testament. The newly-assembled people of God, the *Church*, is — as Paul says — like a new branch sprung from the ancient olive-tree of Israel (Romans 11:17). It is characteristic of all religions to point out ways to *freedom* and to give directives for life. Not only the great world religions but also the traditional religions of tribes and peoples give proof of questioning and seeking on man's part. The Second Vatican Council says of them: 'Nor is God himself far distant from those who in shadows and images *seek* the unknown *God*' (*The Church*, para. 16).

> In many psalms of the Old Testament people are called on to praise God; the shortest psalm is the following:
> **O praise the Lord, all you nations,**
> **acclaim him all you peoples!**
> **Strong is his love for us;**
> **he is faithful for ever.** *Psalm 116(117):1–2*

First commandment: I am the Lord your God. You shall have no other gods besides me (→ 35.4 ten commandments)
Judaism: Religion of the Jews, a national and religious community, descendants

of the people of Israel (cf. the state of Israel with Jerusalem as capital). Basis: 'sacred writings of Israel' (= Old Testament for Christians); these writings show clearly that the Israelites believed themselves to be 'chosen by Yahweh'. The words 'Judaism' and 'Jews' are derived from the name of the tribe of Judah.

Pagans: A collective term in everyday speech for 'unbelievers' and non-Christians. Nowadays out of respect for other religious persuasions, this term is often avoided because the word 'pagan' has derogatory undertones. In the Bible 'the people' (sing.) equals the Israelites and is often contrasted with 'the peoples' (plur.), often translated by 'pagans'.

Islam: Founded by Mohammed in the seventh century A.D.; he preached monotheism in contrast to the traditional religions of Arabia: related in many ways to Judaism and Christianity. Prevalent today among the Arab peoples, in parts of Africa, in the Near and Middle East and in parts of Asia. Muslim communities now exist elsewhere, including many British cities.

Koran: The holy Book of Islam; a collection of psalm-like texts, prayers and directives (divided into 114 *Surahs*). According to Muslim belief the Koran stems directly from God and was written down by Mohammed, God's prophet.

Hinduism: Prevalent above all in India; does not refer back to a particular founder; is described as a collection of various kinds of religious views. Hindus are united not by a common profession of faith but by membership of a recognised common culture of different castes (groups).

Buddhism: Goes back to the teaching of Buddha (= the enlightened one; sixth century B.C.); prevalent today above all in Sri Lanka, Thailand, Vietnam and Japan. Buddhist thought and life-styles have recently found adherents in Europe and America.

Religion: → 39.6

10.3 God reveals himself

→ 4.4 God's glory is revealed; 12.4 God can be found in our world; 13.2 Son of God

Christians — like the Jews — are firmly convinced in their belief that God is not silent; he is with man, he speaks, shows himself and reveals himself. In the midst of our everyday world he is at work and enables us to know him. This is a source of joy for the community of the *faithful*, a joy that is lasting, and they recall how their ancestors knew God.

Such events are passed on, not merely to give information about the past, but to hand on to others the way in which *God* has revealed himself in the *life-history* of his people, how they have known him as their leader, how, through this experience, he has formed a group of people into a community of believers, how, in faith, they have become certain of God's clear revelation of himself in the history of his people.

In continuing to show himself in the history of mankind, God is acting with human beings, in human history, he is speaking to human beings in human words, in the 'here and now' — this is our experience of God revealing himself. These words mediate *God's word* to us: God's word in human words — this is how *faith* views it. God brings about *salvation history* in human history.

Christians believe that history came to a climax in *Jesus Christ*: he is God's final and unique 'word'; in him men see the *glory* of God (John 1:14). But Christians also believe that the history of God with men continues, that God, with mankind, still makes history and reveals himself in seemingly trifling events. And because they believe that Jesus Christ is God's final word, Christians turn to him for an understanding and interpretation of their history.

The opening words of the Letter to the Hebrews speak with enthusiasm of revelation:

At various times in the past and in various different ways, God spoke to our ancestors through the prophets; but in our own time, the last days, he has spoken to us through his Son.
Hebrews 1:1-2

Revelation: The Bible relates in various ways how God speaks/acts/lets himself be recognised, calls/leads men, announces his will; it tells how men know him/hear him/do not wish to hear him/respond to him. All this the Church calls 'revelation': God 'speaking' to man (in creation, through events and experiences; through those called by God, e.g. the prophets, apostles, above all through Jesus Christ). The Church is commissioned to preserve, hand on and explain what God has revealed (→ 20.2). In teaching that there is no further revelation, that it is closed, she teaches that God has revealed everything necessary for man's salvation.

Preaching/teaching: A keyword with reference to the gospel: Good News is preached or taught as news that brings salvation and is joyful news for all concerned. Proclamation of the gospel is addressed to the one who listens, challenging him to a commitment: 'this concerns you'; 'this is important for you'.

Bible (from Gr. biblos = book): Collection of writings recognised in the Christian Church as documents of revelation, also called *Holy Scripture*. Chief parts: *Old Testament* (O.T.) and *New Testament* (N.T.). 'Testament' is the Latin translation of the Greek word for 'covenant' or 'bond'. The writings belonging to a covenant were later themselves known as Testament. The origin of the Old Testament extends over a period of time lasting more than 1,000 years, the New Testament over about only fifty years.

Explanation/interpretation of the Bible: Like any other text, the Bible needs some explanation and interpretation. For this there is a specific procedure (→ 34.2 exegesis). But because the Bible is also the Church's special book, because the Church is aware that she is guided by the Holy Spirit (→ 20.3) and because the Church was in existence before the Bible was completed by the writing of the New Testament, the Catholic Church claims for herself authoritatively the application of possible interpretations (→ 20.2).

10.4   I believe
→ 28.1 new life; 25 Amen

In daily life many never think explicitly of the basis of *trust* which underlies and supports their lives. It is, however, important to be clear on this matter. If a person trusts in something which is no support to him, he is left in the lurch.

When a Christian says: I trust in God; I abandon myself to him, he is speaking of his faith. The one who says 'I believe' is convinced that God is with him; 'He knows me; he loves me; he does not forget me'.

Faith is not merely a vague trust in God, it also has a content. '*What* do I believe about God?' A believer is answerable for what he believes. For Christian trust is based on what God has done with, and through, Jesus. Therefore Christian faith can be expressed in definite statements which reflect the content of this faith, as in the *creed*. In the last analysis 'I believe' means that I accept what God has revealed and am ready to base my life and actions on it. The whole of my life bears witness to what I believe, to what God means for me.

Anyone brought up in a believing family will in the course of time experience that not everyone shares his faith. He will live and work with people who hold few of his beliefs or who even quite firmly reject them. This will make him reflect on what he believes and why. A person who comes as an adult to the faith has experienced that faith is not to be taken for granted. He experiences that to be able to believe is a *gift*. And therefore this person must continually make efforts over his faith. Faith is equally a gift for a person baptised in infancy though he may not appreciate what has been given him. Equally, and for the same reason, such a person must make efforts over his faith. For faith is not something that one 'has' once and for all. Faith grows or becomes stunted; faith thrives or withers.

When the father of the epileptic boy asks Jesus: If you can do anything, help us, Jesus says:
If you can? Everything is possible for anyone who has faith. Immediately the father of the boy cried out, 'I do have faith. Help the little faith I have!' *Mark 9:22–24*

Doubt: Uncertainty and painful, searching questioning. Doubts in faith: confusion and restlessness as to whether God is really love and whether faith in him is prudent. Faith also means: endurance of one's doubts and the ability to pray about them (→ e.g. Job 5.3; 11.2).
Superstition: False faith; an attitude of reliance on something arbitrary, expecting salvation from it. *Things* are considered reliable, and as dominating people: magic powers are attributed to horoscopes, fortune-telling, charms, playing cards, etc.
Magic: Ascribing power to words, actions or things, and wanting, with their help, to exercise this power over God and man.
Doctrines of the faith: Definitions of the content of faith; they are expressed in the creeds used by the Church or in documents which make it clear that the controversial statements are binding on us.

10.5   Faith or knowledge?
→ 24.2 the last days; 23.2 faith gives courage

Faith is sometimes understood as the opposite of *knowledge*. This is limiting knowledge to what man can discover by the efforts of his *reason*, through research and experiment. Such findings are in fact very important for individuals and for mankind. They are, for example, the first essentials for the control of nature through science and technology.

Yet, even if this is so, important questions are left unanswered. What is joy, happiness, the meaning of life? Where does the world come from? Where is it going? In such questions we make progress only by believing the reliable *conclusions* of others.

Belief for a Christians means above all readiness to believe the experiences and message of Jesus and knowledge of him as the Christ and the Son of God; to believe what he has said concerning important questions and their relationship to God; to believe what his witnesses have *handed down* to us.

Reason is not excluded from knowledge thus acquired; on the contrary, it provides reasons for faith which can be expressed and given careful consideration. But faith itself is something in which one must be daring. Only a person who is prepared to take risks in his faith can also affirm: 'It's right; it makes sense'.

Faith then is no substitute for knowledge, but nor does knowledge make faith superfluous. They are two different, complementary ways of comprehending truth. Knowledge and faith have need of each other. Knowledge without faith is in danger of becoming meaningless and degrading for a human being; faith without knowledge becomes unreasonable and leads nowhere.

It is therefore part and parcel of reasonable faith to think out what one believes and to comprehend ever more fully what faith means for one's *life*. This is why we have *theology*, the special study concerned with faith. Not only theologians but also other Christians should use their understanding in matters of faith: 'Always have your answer ready for people who ask you the reason for the *hope* that you all have' (1 Peter 3:15). The basis for such knowledge is trust in God who is revealed in Jesus Christ.

Paul writes in his first Letter to the Corinthians about the incomplete nature of our knowledge and speaks of our hope for fulfilment which is to come at the end of time:
Now we are seeing a dim reflection in a mirror; but then we shall be seeing face to face. The knowledge that I have now is imperfect; but then I shall know as fully as I am known.
1 Corinthians 13:12

---

11 The Father Almighty

→ 2 our Father in heaven

Human beings have always reflected on the *origin of the world*. They imagined a master-builder, a 'first mover'; they spoke of a 'first principle', an eternal 'origin'.

But what has a supreme being — the origin of this wonderful order — to do with man? Is he man's opponent? Is he interested in him?

The Bible answers: the 'supreme being', the origin of this wonderful world, is a person who loves each individual; he is someone who can be loved and wants to be loved.

How is this compatible with the statement in the creed about the *omnipotence* of God? What has an almighty partner to do with a human being who is often so *helpless?*

11.1 God's power (omnipotence) and his fidelity

→ 2.2 our Father; 2.3 God, Father of all

'Almighty' is a word that is difficult to understand and its connotation is somewhat disturbing. A person who is conscious of his *limitations* and his own helplessness does not relish having near him someone who can do whatever he wills. Many Christians feel a certain unease at the thought of an almighty God.

And yet they believe that God's power and greatness are unlimited. God's *omnipotence*, however, is different from the power that men conjure up for themselves in their presumptuous dreams. God's power is not oppressive for man. It is revealed when God, as the mighty one, supports his people 'with a strong hand'. But it is also revealed in weakness when God is involved in the limitations of the world and of human beings.

The Bible has its own word for this concern on the part of God: it speaks of the *covenant* which God makes with man. In this case 'covenant' is not a relationship between two equal partners; it is the greater One who humbles himself; he makes his power a means of union, he comes down to the level of the lesser one, to be as equal to equal: this is the covenant.

In the *creed*, therefore, Christians acknowledge their faith in one God, the origin and Father of all, who, although he has power and omnipotence, goes out to man in *fidelity*. To this Father as the almighty One they entrust themselves; he supports them and he is with them.

Among the psalms most frequently used is the following:
The Lord is my shepherd;
there is nothing I shall want.
Fresh and green are the pastures
where he gives me repose.
Near restful waters he leads me,
to revive my drooping spirit.   *Psalm 22(23):1–3*

God's omnipotence: The Bible speaks of God's powerful deeds, shown in history and expressed in his fidelity and readiness to help people. God's power is not arbitrary, it does not oppress man. It is seen as a support for man, always available to him to make up for his inherent weakness. The true believer sees his weakness as enhanced by God's power.

God's fidelity: One who is faithful keeps his promises; he can be trusted. Faith in God's fidelity and power cannot be separated. God's power supports us because his power is not arbitrary.

Providence: This is how God's abiding relationship to his world is expressed; we can entrust ourselves to him; he it is who determines the beginning and end of man even if man is free. The word 'providence' is often misused to avoid professing belief in a personal God.

The all-wise or omniscient God: God's wisdom surpasses in an infinite degree all that man can plan and foresee; theologians sometimes use the expression 'omniscience'.

11.2   The great God

→ 25.2 the known/unknown God; 3.3 men worship God

Theologians at all times have been at pains to speak convincingly about God. But precisely the greatest among them knew that their thoughts were inadequate to treat of the greatness and *glory of God*.

The Bible tells the story of Job who, hounded and struck by misfortune, wrestles with God and challenges him to answer his question: Why does God torment me? Why must I suffer all this? But when God shows himself in the storm Job says: 'I knew you then only by hearsay; but now, having seen you with my own eyes, I retract all I said, and in dust and ashes I repent' (Job 42:5–6). Job's complaints are silenced before the majesty and *mystery of God*, and Job calls out, not in resignation, but in wonder, because he has been speaking of matters 'beyond his knowledge' (cf. Job 42:3).

People in whom faith in God is alive and active try to express their faith and they *praise* God in *prayers* and hymns. They thus bear testimony to the fact that they are ever increasingly struck by the greatness and glory of God. With one of the psalmists they can say: 'Come in; let us bow and bend low; let us kneel before the God who made us, for he is our God and we the people who belong to his pasture, the flock that is led by his hand' (Psalm 94(95):6–7).

The *faithful* trust that, at the end of time, God will enable them to know him fully, as he is, and *creation*, redeemed, will shout in jubilation to God in wonder, adoration and *thanksgiving*.

A Latin hymn, the *Te Deum*, has been handed down to us from the fourth century. It begins:
We praise you, O God; we acclaim you to be the Lord. Everlasting Father, all the world bows before you. All the angels sing your praise, the hosts of heaven and all the angelic powers.

Adoration: People can show honour and respect for various reasons; by adoration we mean the worship due to God alone (saints are honoured; we can pray to them, i.e. we can ask them to intercede for us with God; they are not adored).

Theology (from Gr. = talking/writing about God): Theologians are professionally concerned with the foundations and practice of our faith, its history and its practical consequences; theology is therefore the scholarly study concerned with the faith (→ 34.2).

God's eternity: 'Eternal' means more than having no beginning and no end; when the Church wants to say that God is outside all time and measurement of time, that he is greater than everything restricted by time, that he is therefore perfect, she speaks of God's eternity.

God's unchangeableness: When the Church wants to say that God is not fickle, that he remains true to himself and to his people, she speaks of his unchangeableness.

12 Creator of heaven and earth

→ 10.5 faith/knowledge; 23.1 finiteness

Today Christians know that the world was not made in six days, that it has a long *evolution* behind it; but this does not prevent them from acknowledging that God is Lord of the world; he sustains and maintains it.

They acknowledge God as *creator* of heaven and earth. The statement that man is God's *creature* is especially important for them: man is dependent on God and at the same time he is made in God's image.

We are *convinced* that the creator can be found in this world even if signs of his presence are often veiled. We know that God cannot be proved as something that can be 'produced and put on the table'; he is totally different from the world and human beings.

Yet the world presents many a problem for the believer: good does not always prevail; often it seems as though evil has the upper hand and asserts itself. There is much that even a believer cannot understand. What justifies Christians in their conviction that God sustains the world in spite of all disasters? that he is the *author of life*? and that the world is his *creation?*

Creation: Calling into being a thing, *or* the thing that is called into being; in religious language: making the world out of nothing, or the world as God's 'production'. Muslims, Jews and Christians understand creation not simply as the arrangement of a universe already existing; they believe in God as the author of everything.

12.1 The world comes from God

→ 5.3 misfortune; 3.1 God's name; 23.1 finiteness; 10.5 faith/knowledge

Today the *natural sciences* can tell us much about the origin and age of the earth, about the universe and its enigmas. We learn little of these in Scripture. Nor is it the task of a catechism to examine such matters, for faith is concerned with using the Bible for questions and answers as to who is the God of our world and our faith, to whom we are indebted for our life and for whom we live — where we are going.

Christians — and with them also people of other *religions* — believe that the world did not arise from blind *chance*, but that behind what we can state and examine are a wisdom and a *love* which we see as attributes of a personal God. So *faith* is not in opposition to scientific statements. It merely asks a different type of question. We can compare the world to a work of art. Someone who knows the material of which the work of art is made, its age, its size, its weight, who recognises and can name its form and colours, has still not completely understood the work of art. He knows nothing of the person who made it, nor is he acquainted with the artist's motives and intentions. The situation with regard to the sciences is similar. People can examine nature without seeing it as creation. Their questions are limited. Therefore they can give no complete answer to the *enigmas* the world presents.

The biblical *stories of creation* (Genesis 1-12) are not reports made by people who investigated the beginnings of the world. The people of those times thought very differently about physical, chemical and biological factors; they knew nothing of the laws of *evolution* with which we are familiar today. But they asked themselves, exactly as we do today, how one can live, faced as one is with the evil in the world. They looked for a *meaning* for their existence. They wanted to show why men are courageous enough to believe in God's *covenant* with his people, despite the fact that much of what man sees and experiences in life runs counter to the covenant. Among the Israelites, faith in God, the creator, faith in God's covenant with man, and faith in his saving deeds for human beings now and in the future are closely connected: 'Our help is in the name of the Lord, who made heaven and earth' (Psalm 123(124):8). This verse of a psalm is often used in the Church's *liturgy*.

When a Christian says: 'I believe in God, the creator of heaven and earth', he means I believe that everything in our world — however confusing it may appear — is sustained by God's wisdom and love. God has created the world out of nothing. Here and now God holds the world in his hand; he prevents it from falling back into nothingness. As *creator* not only did he establish the beginning but he 'presides' over the world and leads it to its final end. I can and do *entrust* myself to him.

12.1

> Many of the psalms express joy in God's creation; in Psalm
> 18(19) we read:
> **The heavens proclaim the glory of God**
> **and the firmament shows forth the work of his hands.**
>
> *Psalm 18(19):2*

World-picture: General view of man's knowledge of the world (e.g. biblical or modern world-picture) as distinct from *world-view* or *philosophy of life* (= complete view of the nature and meaning of the world, interpretation of the world and of its outward appearance).

Evolution (Lat. = development): According to modern knowledge of nature, living forms on the earth have not always been the same; there was, and is, continual change. From simple beginnings, in the course of millions of years — at times with essential differences — plants, animals and human beings have evolved to their present form. Scientific recognition of evolution is not contradictory to believing that God is the author and 'preserver' of the world and has a special relationship to man (→ 12.3 soul).

12.2   God is Lord over power and violence

→ 8.3 deliver us from evil; 12.5 world order and its enigmas

Whoever takes a realistic look at the world and man must affirm that we are not surrounded by what is good. *Evil* is so powerful in the world that, taken aback, one can often ask oneself in dismay how people are to come to terms with it. How can man believe in God as the good *creator* if the powers of evil are so terrible?

Many peoples have answered that there are two gods equally powerful, a good god and an evil one. Taught by their experience with the living God, Israel gave this answer: evil is indeed powerful, but even evil powers are only creatures; we call them *devils*, Satan, demons. Devout Israelites found an explanation for their existence; they described them as fallen *angels* who rebelled against God and upset order in the world. This, too, is the traditional teaching of the Church. Faith is confident that at the end of time it will be clear that God alone is Lord (Revelation 20:7-14). The question as to why God continues to let evil have power remains a *mystery* even for the believer.

Scripture is familiar not only with evil but also with good

powers which it calls angels. The Bible praises God's *great glory* by saying that angels surround his throne (Revelation 7:11–12); they praise and worship him. In many places Scripture speaks of *God's care* for mankind; God has appointed his messengers to protect man (Psalm 90(91):11).

The Bible never speaks of the evil powers without also speaking of the greater power of God. The believer knows that there is a struggle going on and it is not easy for him to maintain mastery over his life; but he trusts in the fact that he is precious to God and that therefore God will not abandon him.

The Protestant pastor Dietrich Bonhoeffer, imprisoned and in 1945 condemned to death by the Nazis, wrote a poem for that New Year ending:
While all the powers of good aid and attend us,
boldly we'll face the future, come what may.
At even and at morn God will befriend us,
and oh, most surely on each newborn day.
Dietrich Bonhoeffer

Angel (from Gr. angelos = messenger): In the Bible God's messengers have various duties; they are sent to deliver God's messages and, as his messengers, they are sent to protect human beings (*guardian angels*).

Cherubim (probably from Akkadian karabu = pray, bless): With the Seraphim they are said to form the heavenly court; they are portrayed on the ark of the covenant as winged beings, sign of the presence of God (cf. Hebrews 9:5). In the Revelation of John (4:6–8) and in the prophet Ezekiel (10:1–22) the Cherubim are mentioned as four mysterious beings.

Seraphim (from Hebr. = burn): In Isaiah's vision (Isaiah 6:1–13) they are named as heavenly beings who surround God's throne.

Thrones and Dominations: There is 'more between heaven and earth' than our knowledge is in a position to imagine; in Judaism an attempt was made to guess at this by a description of various 'choirs of angels'. Thrones and Dominations are names of such groups of angels, intended to indicate that God, for the salvation of man, shares his power.

Satan: In various places in the Bible the evil one is called '*Satan*' (Hebr. = adversary, antagonist); also *Lucifer* (= the morning star fallen from heaven; cf. Isaiah 14:12) or *Beelzebub* (according to 2 Kings 1:2, name of an idol of one of the pagan gods) → 8.3 *devil*.

Exorcism (Gr. = swearing out): Since the third century, prayer (e.g. in the context of baptism) requesting that Christ would release man from the power of evil.

12.2　　　　　　　　　　　　　　　　　　　　　　　　　　**76**

12.3 Man as God's creature

→ 14.1 he became man; 23.1 finiteness

If one compares the age of the world with the twenty-four hours of a day, mankind's age is only a few seconds. We might ask ourselves whether the whole *evolution* of the world is directed towards mankind.

Faith, as expressed in the Bible, says that man is God's favourite *creature*, the crown of creation. True, he is 'dust from the soil' (Genesis 2:7) — '*Adam*' means 'man from the earth' — but at the same time he is created in God's image. With these words the Bible introduces us to man. It thus makes clear that God wants man to share in his own activity. This is the basic fact that runs right through the Bible. As God's image man is to act creatively (Genesis 1:27).

Christians, in common with the *Jews*, believe that God created man out of love and called him to respond to his *love* and to live in *communion* with him. When man and woman in love give birth to new life, this creative act makes it especially clear that man is created in God's image. Man is to investigate, dominate and so shape the world that everyone can live there in a way befitting human dignity. As a partner with his brothers man is not to let himself be dominated by the things of this world, nor is he to misuse them selfishly or upset the order and beauty of creation, for he has been called to be the guardian of creation. What he finds there, from water to the power of the atom, and what he himself discovers, from bread to spacecraft, all is to be used as gifts and possibilities for which he bears *responsibility* before God and man.

In Psalm 8, in praise of the creator, the psalmist says of man:
When I see the heavens, the work of your hands,
the moon and the stars which you arranged,
what is man that you should keep him in mind,
mortal man that you care for him?
Yet you have made him little less than a god;
with glory and honour you crowned him,
gave him power over the works of your hand,
put all things under his feet.   *Psalm 8:4–7*

Soul: The word has great breadth of meaning; biblically 'breath of life', a gift from God. Nowadays soul is often described as 'the self'. The distinction between soul and body is intended to express that man is more than mere body, mere matter. Therefore traditional Catholic teaching holds firmly to speaking of the human soul as a direct creation on the part of God. Moreover, it is difficult to dispense with the Christian concept of 'soul-body' when one has to explain the personal nature of man. Yet the distinction between soul and body must not be allowed to obscure the idea of man as a complete whole. His 'bodiliness' is inherent in his being as man (→ 23.1 immortality).

12.4   God can be found in our world

→ 4.3 the mighty deeds of Jesus; 10.3 God reveals himself

Sun and moon, thunder and lightning, springs of water and trees, were often honoured as gods. The Bible rejects this kind of honour paid to the powers of nature and calls it idolatry. For, however powerful nature may be, the one who made these things is even greater. The biblical and Christian belief is that the *creator* can be known through his *creatures* (Romans 1:20).

In *suffering* and disaster, in *happiness* and joy, the believer looks for signs pointing to the creator. The course of the stars tells us something of God's wisdom. Air and water, plants and animals proclaim to us God as life-giver. Every creature is for the believer a work of art indicative of the Artist.

In what men fashion, too, in technology, art and science, God's power and greatness can be glimpsed. For if man is the likeness of God, the greatness of the creator will be clearly seen in what man does. God's love can be seen above all in those people who know how to love, in the affection of parents, in the loyalty of a friend, in the union between husband and wife, in the goodness of many towards those in need.

The believer discovers in the world special *signs* and symbols of the *presence of God*. In the traditional language of faith God's powerful deeds are called *miracles*. When, for example, sick people, in the power of faith and in the experience of love, are healed, this may be for them a positive sign of God's presence. In the lives of exemplary Christians there are many striking events: what is decisive is always that they are seen and explained by faith in God. Such wonderful signs of the beneficent closeness of God, his presence in the midst of our lives, are precious for the believer, for they make him realise that he has good reason to believe. The powerful deeds of Jesus, of which the gospels tell us, presume faith and confirm it; at the same time they give rise to it.

Miracles are not something sensational to satisfy curiosity, or an area of experiment to confirm or reject scientific results. In a miracle the believer sees his conviction confirmed — that God can freely dispose of the powers of nature to give his people surprising signs of his *fidelity*.

The opinion of science, that everything in nature and history happens according to definite laws, and the Christian understanding of the wonderful works of God, are not irreconciliable. In the laws of nature, made known and examined by man, one and the same faithful, creative God is at work; the believer recognises and praises his unexpected concern for him and finds it surprising beyond measure.

The writer of the book of Wisdom says that the world bears the imprint of God:
Through the grandeur and beauty of the creatures, we may, by analogy, contemplate their Author.

Wisdom 13:5

Idols: Derogatory description for statues or other representations of pagan gods (demons); *idolatry* means making something material or human into God, i.e. honouring it as a god and considering it as of supreme value in one's life.
Book of Wisdom: Book of the Old Testament, probably dating from the first century B.C.; it combines Jewish wisdom and Greek philosophy.

12.5 World order and its enigmas
→ 22.2 power of sin; 5.3 misfortune; 12.2 power and violence

Life is full of contradictions; some people are happy, others experience one *misfortune* after another; some are constantly disposed to laughter, others have — so it seems — nothing to laugh at; some are hale and hearty, others weak and sickly. Why is this so?

Much that is beautiful in the world helps us to recognise the signs of God's presence. We are ready to accept these as pointing to the creator. Side by side with them we meet with what is sad and terrible, and this is an obstacle to belief in a good God. Such experiences lead to doubt rather than to belief.

Every human being must, in his own way, try to conquer the world, to know and understand it. One is successful, broadening the sphere of his knowledge; the insights of the other do not go far, the horizon of his interests remaining narrow. Even the most clever person must sooner or later experience his limitations. Perhaps his most brilliant ideas even prove harmful for man and the world. Then it is hard to believe that this world is God's good creation.

There are situations when we feel sheltered in the affection and love of another; we can also experience being left alone and betrayed by our best friend. *Love* and hatred, human kindness and evil are found side by side, even in the same individual: 'Instead of doing the good things I want to do, I carry out the sinful things I do not want' (Romans 7:19), says the apostle Paul. We share the good gifts of the creator and at the same time are entangled in the *power of evil*.

From all this we conclude that things are at odds with man and the world. In a puzzling way a lack of harmony runs right through everything. In essential questions we grope in the dark. This inner strife is also experienced by the believer. Yet, in *hoping* against all hope, he maintains that eventually God's presence leads to all that is good.

Huub Oosterhuis, a Dutch writer of our times, says:
I stand before you empty-handed, Lord;
all your ways are as strange to me as your name.
Since the beginning of time, men call on God;
my lot is death, have you no other blessing?
Are you the God who promises me a future?
I want to believe — come towards me!

13   And in Jesus Christ, his only Son, our Lord

→ 25 Amen

Not everyone believes in one good God. Many are *afraid*, they fear his omnipotence and think he has to be appeased by sacrifice. Among many peoples, even human beings used to be sacrificed to the gods. Even the Israelites, who experienced in a special way God's concern and nearness, had repeatedly to come to grips with the image of a threatening God, an angry God, ready to punish his people for all their offences.

Who, then, is God? What is he like? What does he think of us? Who will bring us news of him? Who will give us reliable information about him?

Even Christians have difficulties with these questions in their everyday life. And yet they believe in a good God. Where do they get their *confidence* from? How do they know with certainty about a God whose works in creation often conceal rather than reveal him?

In these matters Christians trust in Jesus Christ. They are confident that they can tell from him what God is like. Faith in Jesus Christ is therefore the very heart of the *creed*: Jesus is the *Christ*; he is in a unique way the *Son of God* and our Brother; he is our *Lord*.

God's anger: In the Old, as in the New Testament, mention of God's anger is quite common (cf. Genesis 32:23-33; Psalms 75; 76; 88; Romans 1:18-3:20; John 3:36; Revelation 12:14); it is an attempt to express the fundamental aversion of the all-holy God to all that militates against the happiness and salvation of man and therefore the glory of God (→ 18.2 last judgement; 18.1 Christ's second coming).

13.1   Jesus is the Christ
→ 29.2 service in the world

In his letters Paul often speaks of *Christ* Jesus (e.g. 1 Corinthians 4:17). Here he draws our attention to the fact that Jesus Christ is not a 'double-barrelled' name. 'Christ' is not, as it were, his own name; it expresses a characteristic, a title for Jesus. It means:

Jesus is the 'anointed one' — i.e. he has a special task; he is filled with the *Holy Spirit*, 'anointed' (Luke 4:18), and he is the *Saviour* for whom the chosen people were always praying. When Christians acknowledge that Jesus is the Christ, they are convinced that in him the *hopes* of Israel for a royal Saviour have been fulfilled.

It is true that this *fulfilment* was completely different from what many had expected. They hoped for a saviour who would come with pomp and power; the way of God's anointed Son was one of *service* and helplessness.

It is significant that the title 'Christ' has, in practice, become the name for Jesus. This means that Jesus is fully at one with his mission. There is never a moment when he is not the Christ — the *Messiah* — the Saviour of his people. Jesus Christ means then that Jesus is wholly at God's disposal in the mission assigned to him. Those who follow him are called *Christians* after him — a challenging title with certain consequences.

In the Acts of the Apostles we read how the apostles preached Jesus as the Christ. Peter's sermon at Pentecost ends with this sentence:

The whole House of Israel can be certain that God has made this Jesus whom you crucified both Lord and Christ.

Acts 2:36

Christ: Greek translation of the *Hebrew* word '*Messiah*'; in English 'the anointed one'. In the Old Testament kings and priests were anointed as a sign that they were performing a special mission for God; of a future prophet it is said (Isaiah 61:1) that he was anointed not only with oil but with the spirit of Yahweh (cf. Luke 4:18).

Acts of the Apostles: Book of the New Testament (a kind of 'continuation' of Luke's gospel); relates how the Good News of Jesus spread from Jerusalem to Judaea, Samaria, Antioch and to churches founded by Paul as far away as Rome.

13.2 Jesus Christ is the Son of God

→ 14.2 brother — son; 25.1 Father/Son/Spirit

In the Old Testament all the Israelites were called *sons of God*. God chose them and gave them the superior rights of a first-born child, above all other nations (Exodus 4:22). The Bible also speaks of the king of Israel as the 'son' (Psalms 2:7). God adopted him as his son; he rules in God's place.

In the story of the Passion according to Mark, the high priest asks Jesus: 'Are you the Christ (Messiah), the son of the blessed One?' (Mark 14:61) and the word 'son' is understood in this sense. And 'I am', the answer of Jesus to this question, leads to a charge of blasphemy.

When the story of the Passion was preached to the Christian *church*, they understood the high priest's question differently. This is noticeable from the way in which the fourth gospel speaks of the sonship of Jesus: 'God loved the world so much that he gave his only Son' (John 3:16); this is how it is expressed in the conversation with Nicodemus. And in the discourse at Capernaum the disciples are told: 'Not that anybody has seen the Father, except the one who comes from God: he has seen the Father' (John 6:46). The clearest words are those in John's gospel: 'The Father and I are one' (John 10:30).

At first the same may well have happened to the disciples of Jesus as to others; they were struck by the way Jesus spoke of God. They asked: 'Who is this man, that he even forgives sins?' (Luke 7:49). Only after *Easter* did it dawn on them who Jesus really is. They realised that he is in a unique way one with God, he is the only Son of God. Matthew's gospel summarises this in Peter's confession: 'You are the Christ (Messiah), the Son of the living God' (Matthew 16:16).

When, in the fourth century, Christians appeared who denied that Jesus is truly Son of God, a text was formulated in the General Councils at Nicaea (325) and Constantinople (381) as a *profession of faith* for the Church: the Son is 'one Being with the Father'.

This text is used at *Mass* in the Nicene Creed:
We believe in one Lord, Jesus Christ,
the only Son of God,
eternally begotten of the Father,
God from God, Light from Light,
true God from true God,
begotten, not made,
of one Being with the Father.

13.2

13.3 Jesus Christ is the Lord

→ 17.2 glory of the Father; 18.1 Our Lord will come; 1.1 model one's life on Jesus

'Lord' is a title which, according to the Old Testament, belongs to God alone. 'I am Yahweh (RSV: 'the Lord'), unrivalled; there is no other God besides me' (Isaiah 45:5). When Christians use this title to describe Jesus, they acknowledge their faith in the fact that in Jesus, the Christ, it is God himself who is present and who is at work.

'*Lord*' was also a title attributed at that time to the Roman emperor. When Christians claimed this title for Jesus they thereby confessed: 'our authority is that of *Jesus Christ*, not that of the emperor'. For many Christians this was so important that they accepted death rather than deny this *belief* (martyrdom).

For us the description 'Lord' is connected with the idea of power. We perhaps think of one who crushes others. Jesus wishes to give proof of a different kind of power. He says: 'I am among you as one who serves' (Luke 22:27). In John's gospel Jesus says to his disciples at the Last Supper: 'You call me Master and Lord, and rightly; so I am' (John 13:13). But at the same time he washes the feet of his disciples. He makes his new kind of lordship clear: it does not oppress, it raises up. Jesus is Lord and he shows his greatness through the example of his *service*. In him *God's greatness* is made visible; he humbles himself that man may become great.

In many hymns and prayers the Church acknowledges Jesus Christ as her Lord. At the end of the *Gloria* in the Mass she prays:
You alone are the Holy One,
you alone are the Lord,
you alone are the Most High,
Jesus Christ,
with the Holy Spirit,
in the glory of God the Father.

Kyrios (Gr. = Lord): The ancient invocation 'Lord, have mercy' is frequently retained in the original Greek form: Kyrie eleison. Even in the Latin Mass the Kyrie of early Christian times is retained in its Greek form. — In the early Christian Churches Jesus Christ, invoked as Lord, had a special significance and for the Greek-speaking Jews it sounded provocative. For, in the Greek translation of the Old Testament (the so-called Septuagint), Yahweh, the Hebrew name for God, a word difficult to translate, was rendered as Kyrios.

Litany (Gr. litaneia = prayer of petition): The Kyrie is the original answer, always the same, of the people to all the prayers — which varied according to situations — said aloud by the 'reader'. Later, it became customary to use other answers: 'Lord, in your mercy, hear our prayer' or 'Lord, hear us'. When the saints are invoked, the people's answer is 'pray for us'.

14 Who was conceived by the Holy Spirit, born of the virgin Mary

→ 19.1 the Holy Spirit gives life

Can a person who believes in Christ, the *Lord*, the *Son of God*, add anything else to his belief? In his Letter to the Romans Paul says: 'If your lips confess that Jesus is Lord and if you believe in your heart that God raised him from the dead, then you will be saved' (Romans 10:9). Here it is made quite clear what is the heart of our faith.

In the creed this core is further explained. There is an ancient saying: The *Church*'s faith is revealed in her prayer, which, in its turn, reveals her faith. So we ask what the Church teaches in the creed about the beginnings of the life of Jesus. What does this sentence mean: 'who was conceived by the *Holy Spirit*, born of the *Virgin Mary*'?

14.1 He became man

→ 13.2 Son of God

Every human being is a *mystery* — for himself and for others. Jesus is for us a fathomless mystery as no other person ever was. The creed describes the mystery of his origin in a twofold manner.

He is 'conceived by the Holy Spirit' and this means: his origin is wholly from God; he is 'born of the virgin Mary' and this means: Jesus is completely one of us, he is our Brother. Both facts are inseparably related. He is wholly Son of God and wholly man, not something of each, half-god, half-man. *Christian tradition* emphasises this by saying that, in the conception of Jesus, Joseph did not assume the role of a natural father: it was the *Holy Spirit*, the power of God, that 'overshadowed' Mary.

The *infancy gospels* of Matthew and Luke tell of this origin of Jesus in the mystery of God by writing of his 'roots from above'. They play upon sayings in the Old Testament. When the angel says to Mary: 'The Holy Spirit will come upon you and the power of the Most High will cover you' (Luke 1:35), the reference is to the words of Scripture about creation. When God calls the world into being, his Spirit hovers over the waters (Genesis 1:2). What is to take place in Mary is a *new creation*: God's Son will be born of the virgin. In Jesus God brings about a new beginning for man.

Both the gospels call Mary a *virgin*. The Old Testament often speaks of Israel as a virgin, a bride. God chose the people of Israel for himself as a young man chooses his bride; she belongs to him and to him alone. The virgin Mary is the essence of such *fidelity* and openness to God. In answer to the angel's words she says: 'I am the handmaid fo the Lord, let what you have said be done to me' (Luke 1:38).

Those who, using their reason, say these words of the creed, will never completely understand the mystery itself. That *God* became *man* in Jesus, 'conceived by the Holy Spirit, born of the virgin Mary', can be believed and acknowledged only by one who trusts: 'for nothing is impossible to *God*' (Luke 1:37; cf. Genesis 18:9–15).

Luke the evangelist expresses the angel's message of the mystery of the person of Jesus:

'You are to conceive and bear a son, and you must name him Jesus. He will be great and will be called Son of the Most High. . . .' Mary said to the angel, 'But how can this come about, since I am a virgin?' 'The Holy Spirit will come upon you' the angel answered, 'and the power of the Most High will cover you with its shadow.' *Luke 1:31–32; 34–35*

Jesus: Greek form of the Hebrew name Jehoshua = Yahweh is a help; a frequent name, e.g. for Moses' successor Joshua (Deuteronomy 31:14) and the author of the Old Testament book sometimes called Ecclesiasticus, *Jesus Sirach* (Sirach 50:27).

Incarnation (Lat. = taking on human flesh): Technical term used by theologians for the Son of God becoming man in Jesus Christ (→ 14.2 brother — son), born of the virgin Mary.

Infancy narratives: The introductory chapters of Matthew's and Luke's gospels (Matthew 1:1–23 and Luke 1:5–2:52) are usually called the infancy narratives. The name can be misleading, for they are not an arbitrary selection of stories about the infancy of Jesus. These passages are, in fact, a kind of 'miniature gospel'; moreover, we can gather from them who Jesus is ('infancy gospels').

God-man: In order to express the truth about God and the truth about man in Jesus Christ, the Council of Chalcedon says (451): 'We . . . confess . . . one and the same Christ, Son, Lord, Only-begotten, to be acknowledged in two natures, without confusion, without change, without division, without separation'.

14.2   Man's Brother — God's Son

→ 13.2 Son of God

People who met Jesus of Nazareth during his life experienced both facts: that he is the Son of Mary, that is, of a human being, and that he belongs to God's 'side' as no other human being does. Only after his *glorification* did his disciples reflect correctly on this; for they had to preach and defend the faith that in Jesus Christ the reality of God and the reality of the man Jesus are distinct and yet one.

In order to come a little closer to his uniqueness the *New Testament* speaks of the relationship between the divinity and manhood of Jesus Christ in two ways; he is wholly God's Son and wholly our Brother. On the one hand it says: God has filled one of us, namely Jesus, his servant, with the *Holy Spirit* (e.g. Acts 2:32–36). On the other hand, there is the statement: the Son of God, true God like the Father, existing from all eternity — ever with him — became wholly man in Jesus of Nazareth.

In John's gospel the eternal *Son of God* is called '*Word of God*' (John 1:1), who was always with God and is God himself. And this 'Word' became man. We read in this passage: 'The Word was made flesh, he lived among us, and we saw his *glory*, the glory that is his as the only Son of the Father, full of grace and truth' (John 1:14).

In his Letter to the Philippians Paul has handed down to us a very ancient Christian hymn:
His state was divine,
yet he did not cling
to his equality with God,
but emptied himself
to assume the condition of a slave,
and became as men are.   *Philippians 2:6-7*

Glorification: The so-called 'hymn' in the Letter to the Philippians (2:6-11) speaks of Jesus Christ who 'emptied himself', and was therefore 'raised on high' by God. Glorification means that Jesus Christ is placed in a position of honour in heaven; by this expression the 'resurrection' and 'ascension' are described as a single, comprehensive process.

14.3   Mary, Mother of our Lord
→ 36.4 mother of the faithful; 5.2 God's will

The *New Testament* does not tell us much about Mary, but at the important stages of the life and work of Jesus she is mentioned: in the few scenes in the infancy narratives which reveal who he is (Matthew 1:18-2:23; Luke 1:26); at the first sign of his glory at the wedding feast in Cana (John 2:1-12); at his death on the cross (John 19:25-27); and at Pentecost in the midst of the first assembly of the early church in Jerusalem (Acts 1:14).

At a very early date the *Church* began to reflect about *Mary*, in connection with the mystery of the person of Jesus and above all with the wonder of his birth. In the religious controversy of the fifth century about Jesus Christ, about his being God and man, Mary was given the bold title of 'God-bearer'. Nowadays we frequently use the title 'Mother of God'.

Because Mary was called to be *God's mother*, the Church believes that God sanctified her from the very beginning of her life. He preserved her from the taint of sin in which mankind is involved. What the whole of Israel hopes for came to pass in Mary, the *virgin*: she belonged wholly to God as a bride awaiting her bridegroom. Innumerable witnesses in Christian art throughout the ages depict Mary; hymns sing of her loveliness, her grace and her 'Yes' to God's call.

In a canticle ascribed to her by the Bible (Luke 1:46–55), the Magnificat, Mary is shown as true mother of her Son whose sympathies are with the deprived, who regards powerlessness as a blessing and calls peacemakers the children of God (Matthew 5:3–11). Mary sings of the God who puts down the mighty from their thrones and raises the lowly, who gives the hungry good things and sends the rich away empty (Luke 1:52–53).

The 'humble maiden' of Nazareth comes to be depicted by Christian artists — with all human charm — as a *woman of power*. She is honoured in this way in Christian devotion and has become a model for the Church.

The *Magnificat* begins with praise of the greatness of God which Mary experienced in her life:
My soul glorifies the Lord,
my spirit rejoices in God, my Saviour.
He looks on his servant in her lowliness;
henceforth all ages will call me blessed.
The Almighty works marvels for me.
Holy his name!   *Luke 1:46–49*

Mother of God: A startling title that springs from the fact that Mary is mother of the whole Christ, who is both God and man. Therefore, although she gave him only his human nature, she is rightly described as God-bearer (Gr. Theotokos; Lat. Deipara) or Mother of God.

Magnificat: First word (= glorifies) in the Latin translation of this hymn of praise, which, according to the words of Luke's gospel (Luke 1:46–55), Mary spoke when she met Elizabeth. The Magnificat is often used as a prayer in the Church's liturgy.

15 Suffered under Pontius Pilate, was crucified, died and was buried

→ 16 he rose again from the dead

The creed tells us nothing about the life and work of Jesus. After the statement about his birth it moves immediately to the end of his life. The whole *way trodden by Jesus* is thus seen in retrospect. Jesus meets with rejection. His whole life is marked by the sign of the *cross*. Even in the first chapter of John's gospel we are told: 'He came to his own domain and his own people did not accept him' (John 1:11).

This rejection is perplexing for anyone unfamiliar with the outcome of Jesus' life-history. Why did his life and work lead to this end? How could it come to this? Was it *God's will*?

15.1 A person who lives in this way causes unrest

→ 5.2 God's will; 4.1 kingdom of God proclaimed; 8.1 God's gamble; 27.2 Last Supper

The gospels see Jesus in the light of Easter faith. If this is disregarded and Jesus is considered purely from a historical point of view, this is roughly what we know: Jesus was a *Jew*. He was born in Palestine about 6 B.C. The Bible names Bethlehem as his birthplace. He came from a humble background and grew up in Nazareth in Galilee. That is why he is often called 'Jesus of Nazareth'. About the year 28 or 29 A.D. — after the imprisonment of John the Baptist — Jesus began, first in *Galilee*, to work as an itinerant preacher. The manner of his public appearance caused a stir. People were 'astonished', they 'wondered'; but also 'they were annoyed', 'they were upset', for they noticed that he spoke, unlike the scribes, the professional interpreters of God's law, as one coming directly from God (Mark 1:22). This is so new and so shocking that his hearers are swayed this way and that: some follow him, others reject him.

The special *fullness of power* of Jesus causes the demons, hostile to man, to tremble. They sense the presence of God in Jesus (Mark 1:23–26). When Jesus begins to forgive sins, as God alone can, some of the scribes say: 'He is blaspheming!' (Mark

2:7). When he sits at dinner with people who do not live according to the law, the Pharisees say: 'Why does he eat with tax-collectors and sinners?' (Mark 2:16). And when Jesus helps a man on the Sabbath and heals him, they plot 'with the Herodians against him, discussing how to destroy him' (Mark 3:6).

Even his relatives keep their distance from him, convinced that he is 'out of his mind' (Mark 3:21). His opponents tell the people: 'An unclean spirit is in him' (Mark 3:30); and those who come from his home town of Nazareth 'would not accept him' (Mark 6:3).

Jesus became a bone of contention for many. His claim to speak in God's name and to act in his place must have struck them as scandalous. They sensed something of his claim to be, in a unique manner, one with God (Matthew 11:27) and this aroused their opposition. Moreover, his policy of *non-violence* weakened the force of their *hostility* to the Romans; his proclamation of *God's kingdom* might become a threat to Roman domination.

In what concerns Jesus 'people go their different ways'.

What Jesus preached about God was new, and this annoyed those among his Jewish contemporaries whose profession it was to interpret authoritatively the will of God. Anyone who speaks in so unusual a way of God, who is so attentive to man's needs and who at the same time maintains that this is what God wants, was for them unbearable. Those in authority feared that unrest might arise. Then the Roman occupying powers would intervene. Therefore they demanded that Jesus be done away with.

About the year 30 his *trial* began.

Belief in Jesus can divide families; in what concerns Jesus 'people go their different ways'; his opponents take up their swords. Matthew's gospel gives us the following words of Jesus:

Do not suppose that I have come to bring peace to the earth; it is not peace I have come to bring but a sword. For I have come to set a man against his father, a daughter against her mother, a daughter-in-law against her mother-in-law. A man's enemies will be those of his own household.

Matthew 10:34–36

15.1

Pharisee (lit. one separated): Religious-political party in Judaism whose members were very strict in the interpretation and following of the divine law (*Torah*).

Scribe: Teacher with the honorary title of '*Rabbi*'; theologians and lawyers skilled in biblical law; lay people (as distinct from the priestly scholars); at the time of Jesus many scribes were followers of the Pharisees.

Herod: In the large family of the *Herodians* two rulers are particularly significant for the New Testament: Herod the Great (or the elder, 37–4 B.C.), mentioned in Matthew 2 and Luke 1; and Herod Antipas, a son of Herod the Great (4 B.C.–39 A.D.): as governor of Galilee, he was Jesus' local ruler.

15.2   The powerless one is removed by power

→ 22.1 being reconciled; 16.3 we are redeemed

Pontius Pilate, Roman governor of Judaea from 26 to 36 A.D., is mentioned by name in the creed; he is the ultimate judge in the *trial of Jesus*. He condemned Jesus to death by crucifixion — for the Romans the most despicable and the most cruel form of execution. Under the Roman occupying powers many Jews suffered death by crucifixion. Had the Jews completed and executed their condemnation of Jesus, presumably they would have stoned him to death. The Romans condemned slaves and non-Romans to death by crucifixion for murder, temple robbery, high treason and rebellion. The crime of the condemned person was written out and displayed on a placard. In the case of Jesus the inscription was: Jesus of Nazareth, *king of the Jews* (John 19:19). This is intended to mean that Jesus merited death because he set himself up against the Roman authorities as 'king of the Jews'. Among Christians this title, intended to be contemptuous, has become one of honour for Jesus.

For the Romans anyone hailed by the people as prophet or *Messiah* was a source of danger. For the Jewish authorities Jesus was a thorn in their flesh because he attacked their interpretation of the *law* and their Temple worship. Guilt for his death cannot therefore be assigned only to one party: Jews and pagans (in this case the Romans), religious and civic authorities worked together to do away with Jesus.

When Jesus was staying in Jerusalem for the *Passover*, his opponents had him arrested. Like any human being, Jesus was afraid when confronted with his passion and death (Luke 22:44), but he did not flee. He remained faithful to his mission, even when faced with death.

Jesus is brought before the 'high court', the supreme Jewish court in Jerusalem. The high court finds him deserving of death and therefore hands him over to the Roman emperor's governor for condemnation and execution of the sentence (Matthew 27:2). And the governor has him crucified as a rebel (Mark 15:15). This happened on the hill of Golgotha, outside the walls of Jerusalem. The friends of Jesus took his body and buried it in a tomb in the rock (Matthew 27:60).

A believing Christian recognises himself as a sinner when he gazes on Jesus on the cross; therefore he acknowledges himself guilty of the death of a just man. This is expressed as follows in the Authorised Version of the Bible, as sung in Handel's *Messiah*:

All we like sheep have gone astray,
we have turned everyone to his own way,
and the Lord has laid on him (Jesus)
the iniquity of us all.

Anti-Semitism: In the New Testament there are harsh accusations against 'the Jews' (e.g. John 5:10–18). Since it is always a question of faith and not of racism, it is incorrect to speak of 'anti-Semitism', though one could certainly speak of 'anti-Judaism'. However, it is important to know that, at that time, the rival groups within Judaism were always quarrelling with one another and using hard words. This attitude was, to a certain extent, taken over by the early Christians who had to fight for their independence against ancestral religions. At the same time we must remember that throughout the Bible Israel is considered the typical example of the chosen people of God; and the whole of Scripture, both Old and New Testaments, bears witness to the fact that God does not rescind his promises to the chosen people. In the New Testament it is Paul who expresses this most clearly in his Letter to the Romans (chapters 9–11), where he speaks of the salvation of the whole of Israel. — However, Christians and non-Christians have at all times drawn on the Old and New Testaments as ostensible 'evidence' and 'motive' for anti-Jewish words and actions.

Passion (Lat. = enduring, suffering): Account of the Passion = account of the sufferings of Jesus; the Passion of Jesus = his death on the cross suffered for mankind; the account of the Passion was often set to music, usually in the words of one of the four evangelists (e.g. the St Matthew Passion by Bach).

Sanhedrin: Highest judicial court for religious (and, as far as possible under the Roman occupation, political) trials: 71 members (elders = aristocracy; priests =

those from the house of Aaron; scribes = theologians) under the presidency of the *high priest* (at the time of Jesus his office was no longer hereditary).

Stations of the Cross: In memory of the way of the cross of Jesus in Jerusalem, the Stations of the Cross were erected, from the Middle Ages onwards, in churches and out-of-doors; they were popularised by the Franciscans. In fourteen Stations or stages, the Passion of Jesus from his arrest to his burial is portrayed. More recently — as in many older Stations — the resurrection has sometimes been added as a fifteenth Station.

Pietà (Ital. = devotion): Mary depicted as the Mother of Sorrows holding Jesus on her knees.

15.3   Scandal or folly?

→ 16.3 we are redeemed; 22.1 being reconciled

A message with a crucified person as its content would seem to have little likelihood of success. And yet the apostle Paul is not afraid to make the message of the *cross* the centre of his preaching. No one can overlook the cross; here 'people go their different ways'. For God's action cannot be measured by human standards. For one who advocates human standards, the *message* of the cross is either scandal or folly. This is why Paul writes in his first Letter to the Corinthians: for Jews, preaching about a crucified Messiah is a *scandal*, an *insuperable obstacle* (cf. 1 Corinthians 1:18-25). Is a crucified person not cursed by God (Deuteronomy 21:23)? And to Paul's educated Greek audience this message seems to be completely absurd. For them it is *folly* to see the Saviour in a crucified person.

Yet even on the cross it is clear to the believer how matters stand when God reveals himself. What, according to human standards, is weakness and *powerlessness*, what is considered foolishness and naïveté, is revealed by God as *strength* and wisdom. Through the cross God throws open man's way to *salvation*. On this road we are led not by prudence and knowledge, but solely by *faith* and trust.

In his first Letter to the Corinthians Paul summarises the message of the cross thus:

We are preaching a crucified Christ; to the Jews an obstacle that they cannot get over, to the pagans madness, but to those who have been called, whether they are Jews or Greeks, a Christ who is the power and wisdom of God.

1 Corinthians 1:23

Scandal: In the Bible = an obstacle to the faith, to the way to salvation. Human beings are usually the ones who give scandal; but scandal may also arise if God acts differently from the expectations of pious people.

Folly: A lack of astuteness, often arising from presumption.

16 He descended into hell. The third day he rose again from the dead

→ 23 the resurrection of the body

In an obituary notice, beside the deceased's date of birth there appeared the words: 'born to die', and beside the date of death, the words: 'died to live'. A Christian truth is reflected in both phrases: the fact of death which comes to us all and our *Christian hope of eternal life*.

From earliest times Christians believed in the *resurrection* of their Lord as the centre of their faith. Yet what was revealed to the Christians of earlier times under the picturesque image of the descent of Jesus Christ into the *kingdom of the dead* and of his resurrection on the third day as the central truth of their faith, seems for many Christians today obscure and difficult to understand. What do Christians mean when they acknowledge the resurrection of Jesus Christ? a return to his former life? his being taken up into the fullness of God's life? What does the Bible mean by a glorified body?

16.1 God raised Jesus from the dead

→ 18.1 our Lord will come; 23.2 faith gives courage

With the death and burial of Jesus his 'case' was to all appearances settled. The disciples went into hiding for fear that they might suffer the same fate as their Master. But later they became *witnesses* to the fact that he is alive, that God has raised him from the dead.

Nowhere does Scripture relate how the resurrection took place. It cannot be described. That Jesus was executed and that since his resurrection he is alive, remains concealed from non-believers; but for his friends (Acts 10:45) a meeting with the risen Christ is a very real experience. Jesus is risen, that is the extraordinary event.

In Paul's first Letter to the Corinthians, without any attempt to look for proof, the ancient *Easter creed* testifies to the resurrection: Jesus died, he was buried, he was raised to life and he appeared (cf. 1 Corinthians 15:3-5).

In arguments with Jews and pagans the first witnesses try to cling to their experiences and describe them. They tell of *appearances* of the risen Lord, how he ate and drank with them, how he suddenly stood among them. He showed himself to them in Jerusalem (Mark 16:10-14), met them on the road (Luke 24:13-35), appeared to them beside the lake of Galilee (John 21:1-14). The *traditional accounts* are as varied as the experiences.

People speak of the *raising to life*, or of the *resurrection* of Jesus. There are further accounts of the empty tomb (John 20:1-10; Matthew 28:11-15), and the rumour that the dead body had been stolen and the disciples were lying (Matthew 28:13-14).

In all these different statements about the empty tomb and the appearances of the risen Lord, there is very clear testimony: men rejected and executed Jesus, the messenger of God's love and of the dawning of his kingdom. But God did not leave Jesus among the dead, he raised him to *new life*. The one who was crucified is alive. He lives with God for our sake. He it is who has shown himself to us, even though in a new way: glorified, no longer subject to time. And a second fact becomes clear: those to whom the risen Lord appears become his witnesses, witnesses of his life, his death and his resurrection (Acts 3:15).

On Good Friday, during the Solemn Veneration of the Cross, the Church sings;
We worship you, Lord,
we venerate your cross,
we praise your resurrection.
Through the cross you brought joy to the world.

Resurrection, raising to life: Both expressions are found in the New Testament (e.g. Acts 2:23-24 and 4:33). Both are attempts to express a unique event: the delivery of Jesus and his glorification with the Father. On the one hand, 'the Lord is truly risen' expresses this fact, as it were, from Our Lord's side; it refers to the Son's power to live; on the other hand, 'God has raised Jesus', is expressed, as it were, from God's side, that is, it is the Father's will that he should live. The same fact could be worded thus: when we look at the man Jesus, we say that he was raised; when we look at him as the only Son of God we say: he is risen. The reality that we are considering is a completely new form of life into which Jesus enters, and he offers it to all who believe in him; it cannot be adequately expressed in words.

Witness (Gr.: martyros): In the New Testament someone who, because of his own experience, can speak of the resurrection of Jesus. Later, one who, by shedding his blood, bears witness to the truth of the gospel (a *martyr*).

16.2   The power of death is broken

→ 22.2 power of sin; 19.1 gives life

Easter pictures in the Eastern Church do not show, as ours do, the risen Lord coming out of the grave holding a banner of victory, or an unknown person recognised by the woman who worships him. The Eastern icons show Jesus as he 'descends into the *kingdom of the dead*'. He bows to the shadowy beings there, stretches out his hand and draws them to himself. Here faith is told in picture-form: the death and resurrection of Jesus extend *salvation* not only to those who are to come after him, but also to those who preceded him. Therefore it is usually *Adam*, the progenitor of the human race, to whom the 'last Adam', Jesus *Christ*, holds out his hand (1 Corinthians 15:45).

Such a representation is quite unlike the peace of the tomb as contemplated by our church on *Holy Saturday*; it depicts *victory*.

According to primitive ideas no way ever led back out of the kingdom of the dead. In Sheol, the Jewish underworld, the dead live an unreal, shadowy existence and God takes no interest in them. Like all the dead, the one who dies on the cross goes there. But he bursts open the kingdom of the dead and he leads out with him all those imprisoned in the power of death.

The Christian community sees in the resurrection of Jesus a triumph over the power of death; this is expressed in the creed, in the statement about Jesus descending to our ancestors in the kingdom of the dead.

It resounds as a *song of joy* when Paul writes to the

Corinthians: 'Death, where is your victory; death, where is your sting?' (1 Corinthians 15:54–55); therefore, even before an open grave, Christians can intone the Easter *Alleluia* and full of hope say: the death of Jesus is the gate to life for all.

In the conversation between Jesus and Martha, the sister of Lazarus, John's gospel points to the meaning Jesus gives to our lives:
I am the resurrection.
If anyone believes in me,
even though he dies he will livè,
and whoever lives and believes in me
will never die.   *John 11:25–26*

The third day: In the Old and New Testaments often the end of a time of misfortune, and a time of waiting for salvation; God intervenes for man's salvation (cf. Genesis 40:10–19; Hosea 6:2; Jonah 2:1). Moreover, in the New Testament 'the third day' emphasises the fact that the resurrection took place at the time appointed by God.

The last Adam: In some of Paul's Letters the name for Jesus Christ (e.g. 1 Corinthians 15:45; Romans 5:12–19); 'last' in the old order and 'first' in the new; a term too for the new creation of those who believe through Jesus Christ (cf. 2 Corinthians 5:17).

Underworld/kingdom of the dead: According to primitive ideas the world consisted of three 'storeys': heaven, earth and the underworld. The storey under the earth was considered to be the kingdom of the dead. The Greeks named this place Hades, the Romans Orcus. 'Kingdom of the dead' is an expression for the power of death which we experience even in life — and for its finality.

Sheol: In the Old Testament and above all in early Judaism, the place of the dead. Here, so the Jews imagined, the dead lead a gloomy, joyless existence, far from God and true life. Later, they distinguished a place for the good and a place of punishment for the wicked. In the concept of Sheol the Old Testament expresses the confidence that with death all is not over. Death is described as a puzzle which God alone can solve.

Hell → 18.2

Eastern Church: Collective title for the churches which arose in the eastern half of the Roman empire. The most important are the Orthodox (= correct belief) churches (→34.9). The Patriarch of Constantinople holds primacy among them; each is independent. In addition to them there are other churches which have become separate because of different concepts in their teaching, e.g. the Ethiopian and Armenian churches. Some of the Eastern churches are in communion with Rome. These are sometimes called 'Uniate Eastern Churches'.

Icons (Gr. = picture): Pictures of Christ (Mary, the Saints, the prophets) in the artistic style of the Eastern Church; generally painted on wood, often adorned with silver and precious stones. Icons are much loved and venerated.

16.3 Through him we are redeemed
→ 22.1 being reconciled; 15.3 scandal or folly? 22.3 life in Christ

The death of Jesus was a shock for his disciples and for all who had placed their *hopes* in him. Was his end not a sign of his complete failure? Did he not die calling out: 'My God, my God, why have you forsaken me!' (Matthew 27:46)? Only after he had shown himself to them as the risen Lord did the disciples realise: here something crucial for the world has taken place; a new era has dawned; death is conquered; Jesus is alive; God has raised him up.

Through this *Easter experience* the early Christian *Church* knows: as Jesus lived to preach *God's love*, so too did he die (John 15:13). He was put to death because he upheld the message that God loves man unreservedly. He allowed himself to be executed rather than be deflected from his *message*.

Therefore Christians see an inner relationship between what Jesus taught and did, and their faith in the resurrection: in the name of God Jesus preached God as one who does not cease to love man; he gave his life for this and remained true to this message — even to death. God therefore showed himself faithful and confirmed this message by his death; and by raising his messenger to life he reiterated the message: he raised Jesus to life. Here God's will for our salvation was revealed; he it is who brings about man's salvation. This is what he has done for us.

Now it is obvious that the person who is open to accept God's will for him to be saved will be free from the obligation to attain his salvation through his own efforts. Whoever is ready, as Jesus was, to pass on, in the name of God, his love with all that this entails, will be set free from turning in on himself, a process which leads only to *guilt* and *sin*. He is redeemed. So Christians believe that Jesus, by his life, death and resurrection, has become our redemption. On the cross the redeeming love of God was revealed.

> In many hymns, above all in the joyful Easter Alleluia, Christians profess their belief in the resurrection of Christ:
> **Jesus Christ is risen today, alleluia!**
> **Our triumphant holy day, alleluia!**
> **Who did once, upon the cross, alleluia!**
> **Suffer to redeem our loss, alleluia!**

Redemption: According to the New Testament, the saving of man through Christ from his fallen condition of being far away from God.

Deliverance/setting free: A word with many meanings, usually concerned with distress within the world. There is, however, a link between redemption and deliverance: redemption brought about by Christ urges the faithful to be fully committed to non-violent deliverance of their fellow-men from misery unworthy of man's dignity.

Alleluia (Hebr. = praise Yahweh): Prayer from the Old Testament, especially from the psalms; taken over into Christian liturgy, especially in connection with Easter.

God's servant: The book of Isaiah contains several songs about 'God's servant' (Isaiah 42:1-4; 49:1-6; 50:4-9; 52:13-53:12) who brings the truth to all and suffers, as representative of 'many' (i.e. all); raised up by God he becomes the beginning of the salvation of all. The New Testament has referred these songs to Jesus Christ (cf. Acts 3:13, 26; 4:27, 30; 8:32-33).

Lamb of God (Lat.: Agnus Dei): In the Old Testament the lamb is often mentioned as a sacrificial animal. God's servant is compared to a lamb, since he takes the place of sinners and gives his life for them (Isaiah 53:7). John the Baptist singles out Jesus as the 'lamb of God who takes away the sins of the world' (John 1:29). In the celebration of the Eucharist, at the breaking of bread, we pray: 'Lamb of God, you take away the sins of the world, have mercy on us' (cf. Revelation 5:6). Since the fourth century, the lamb has been used in Church art as an image of Christ.

Heart of Jesus: The expression is intended to indicate with what love Jesus concerned himself with the fallen human race (heart = centre of one's being, of a person). The heart of Jesus, pierced by a lance (cf. John 19:34-36), is honoured as a sign of his love even to death. Special devotion: on the feast of the Sacred Heart, the first Friday of each month and throughout the month of June.

Rosary: A prayer in which Catholics 'contemplate' the life, death and glorification of Jesus Christ through the 'eyes' of his mother Mary and in union with her. Similar to this is the 'Jesus prayer' in Eastern devotion (→9.3). Since the rosary is a repetitive prayer and at the same time a prayer which can be said by a group, beads are used. Each part (decade) begins with the Our Father, followed by ten Hail Marys, sometimes with an additional phrase expressing a mystery of the faith, e.g. 'Jesus who was crucified for us', and ends with the Glory be to the Father.

16.3

16.4 The God of life is the basis of our faith

→ 24 life everlasting; 12.1 the world

The apostles never *preach* without speaking of their meeting with the risen Lord. This meeting gave them the certainty that to follow him does not mean passing into a vacuum. It is the risen Lord who gives them their mission. The Christian faith stands or falls with the *resurrection* of Jesus. The resurrection of Jesus is the guarantee for his life and work. Therefore Paul writes to the Corinthians: 'If Christ has not been raised then our preaching is useless and your believing is useless; . . . if Christ has not been raised, you are still in your sins' (1 Corinthians 15:14, 17).

For one who believes, Jesus is infinitely more than a human ideal or someone anxious to improve the world. In him God has proved himself an enemy of death and a friend of life. In him is the *new life* which is guaranteed in our passage through death. Jesus is God's life for man.

We can also say that, since the resurrection of Jesus, death no longer means falling into the nothingness of an *eternal death* but a call into a new, eternal life with God. Each of us can say: My life will not be meaningless in death; it contains, and it takes on a completely new meaning by my passage through death.

The meeting with the risen Lord left the disciples their freedom; it did not force any of the disciples to believe. At the end of Matthew's gospel we read: 'When they saw Jesus, they fell down before him' (Matthew 28:17). But some of them had *doubts*. This gives grounds for confidence for Christians today. If *hope* in this new life with God is obscured, if doubts abound, it is good to remember the many *witnesses* who, in the course of the Church's long history, have lived in the light of this faith, people for whom the message of the death and resurrection of Jesus Christ has been a decisive stimulus to *action*. The consciousness that we are commissioned as witnesses enables us to serve others without fear of thereby losing something for ourselves. It enables us to attempt to live with others a life bearing the imprint of Easter hope.

> When threatened in their lives by the thought of death,
> Christians set their hopes on the risen Christ:
> **Had Christ, that once was slain,**
> **ne'er burst his three-day prison,**
> **our faith had been in vain:**
> **but now hath Christ arisen.**   *G. R. Woodward*

17   He ascended into heaven, sitteth at the right hand of God the almighty Father

→ 13.3 the Lord

The *Ascension* of Jesus and his place at the *right hand* of the Father are a development of the Easter mystery. The risen Lord does not only live with God: he is 'seated at his right hand'. This metaphor explains that he has been established by God as *Lord* over all creation. To him 'all authority in heaven and on earth has been given' (Matthew 28:18). All decisions are referred to him.

'Ascension' does not mean that Jesus renounces his humanity. He remains 'one of us'. His manhood extends into the *glory* of God. Was his life on earth then more than a brief interlude? Is his 'being seated at the right hand of God' in no way a 'departure' from us and from the world? How is his 'return' to the Father, of which Matthew speaks, compatible with his abiding presence among us: 'I am with you always; yes, to the *end of time*' (Matthew 28:20)?

Ascension: In this age of space-travel the Ascension is easily misunderstood, if thought of as a departure within the sphere of our world. In the language of faith the word means that the man Jesus (and the faithful, the first of whom is Mary) 'enters' (and this too is a metaphorical word) into eternal communion with God. **At the right hand of God**: In the Old Testament 'the right hand of God' is a metaphor for his power and goodness towards man. 'The Lord's right hand has triumphed' (Psalm 117(118):16). God gives the king of Israel this promise: 'Sit on my right' (Psalm 109(110):1). Jesus says in the high court: 'From this time onwards you will see the Son of man seated at the right hand of the Power and coming on the clouds of heaven' (Matthew 26:64; cf. Acts 7:55–56).

17.1 He has preceded us

→ 23 resurrection of the dead

Forty days after Easter the Church celebrates the feast of 'Christ's Ascension'. The liturgy follows the account in the Acts of the Apostles, where the *Ascension* is the conclusion of a forty-day period during which the risen Lord appeared to the disciples and they were permitted to experience his closeness to them (Acts 1:3).

The other New Testament writings do not 'date' Christ's ascension in this way; without giving any specific time, they say that Jesus was 'taken up into heaven' and 'withdrew from the disciples'. It is clear that by the 'ascension' no movement in space is meant. Mark relates that Jesus was taken up into heaven (Mark 16:19). Matthew says nothing of the Ascension but tells, on the contrary, of Jesus remaining with his disciples (Matthew 28:20). In his gospel Luke does not mention forty days; he gives the impression that Jesus rose from the dead and was 'taken up into heaven' on the same day (Luke 24:50–53). John sees the beginning of his *being raised to the glory of the Father* already in the crucifixion of Jesus (John 17:4–5).

From this rather 'vague' manner of speaking on the part of the evangelists it is obvious that what happened to Jesus after the crucifixion is beyond human imagining and cannot therefore be expressed adequately.

Good Friday, *Easter*, Ascension and Pentecost are closely related. These feasts comprise a reality concerning the risen Lord: Jesus, crucified (Good Friday), shows himself as the *risen Lord*, he is close to us and at the same time he is with the Father (Easter); he has gone before us and has prepared the way for us (Ascension); but our Lord does not leave us behind 'as orphans' (John 14:18), he sends the Spirit from the Father so that we can follow him (Pentecost). *Christians* believe that the life of Jesus with the Father is a beginning for all of us: with him we have a 'homeland' (Philippians 3:20); *heaven* is our home. This gives us strength so to act in this world that many others as well as ourselves can come to hope and trust.

Faith in the risen Lord remaining close to his Church is
expressed in this hymn:
Lo, the heaven its Lord receives;
yet he loves the earth he leaves;
though returning to his throne,
still he calls mankind his own.   *Charles Wesley and others*

17.2 Jesus Christ in the glory of the Father
→ 2.2 our Father; 4.4 glory is revealed; 25.1 Father/Son/Spirit

'Jesus is with the Father' — this is a brief summary of what
Christians believe: Jesus has entered into the *fullness of life*;
precisely because he is with the 'Father' — his Father and
ours — he remains close to us human beings. This is expressed in
the New Testament in various ways:

The expression 'Jesus is in the glory of the Father' means that
he has a share in God's power and fullness of life. In him shines
out once and for all God's greatness and *glory*. Another expression is: 'Jesus is the risen Lord'; this means that, because he
emptied himself and served men as a slave, God raised him up and
gave him divine honour (cf. Philippians 2:6-11). It is above all
John's gospel which emphasises that the *'lifting up'* of Jesus on
the cross — although apparently the 'lowest point' — is really
the climax of his life (John 12:32). The belief that Jesus is seated
at the right hand of God expresses in metaphor that Jesus is in
God's keeping and acts in God's power and strength. This image
goes back to the psalms used for the installation of the kings of
Israel (e.g. Psalm 109(110)).

All these metaphors paraphrase this one important fact: in
Jesus Christ the human race, the world, indeed the whole of
creation, remains united with God. With the *resurrection* of Jesus
began the process of the transfer into God's new creation of the
former creation alienated by sin. It is of this risen Lord that the
Church reflects when she *prays* to God the Father 'through Jesus
Christ . . . who lives and reigns with you . . .'.

The ancient greeting 'Praised be Jesus Christ — now and for ever. Amen' has been expressed in a hymn:

Praise, my soul, the king of heaven!
To his feet thy tribute bring.
Ransomed, healed, restored, forgiven,
Who like me his praise should sing?
Praise him! praise him!
Praise him! praise him!
Praise the everlasting king!

Henry Francis Lyte

Glory: One of the keywords used by biblical writers to express their experience of God. Glory is often compared to a very brilliant light; this experience is simultaneously rapture, fear and challenge. To 'glorify' God means to rejoice in his beneficent presence and to pass this joy on with and for others to the glory of God. To glorify God means to recognise him as Lord, to honour him by acknowledging him in our life (cf. John 17:4) and trusting him in prayer. In a unique manner the glory of God has been 'revealed' in Jesus (cf. John 1:14; 2 Corinthians 3:18) so that it can be accepted in faith. Christians believe that this glory is even now at work in them. They hope that God will bring to completion what he has begun; they await the revelation of the 'glory of the children of God' (cf. Romans 8:21) (→ doxology I; 9.1).

Christ the King: The authors of the New Testament use comparisons to clarify what took place when Jesus was raised from the dead; e.g. they call him 'king' (the Church celebrates the *feast of Christ the King*); however, Christ's reign is different from that of other kings. His kingship is one of *service* and all the faithful are to share in this kingship (cf. Revelation 22:5).

18   From thence he shall come to judge the living and the dead

→ 24.1 metaphors for eternal life

Fear and anxiety, but also expectation and *hope*, are mingled with the message of a *general judgement* for all men at the end of time. The biblical *metaphors* indicate both sentiments: there is mention of a catastrophe of world-wide proportions — of hell-fire, where there is weeping and grinding of teeth — of fields ripe for the harvest — of a final separation of wheat and chaff, of sheep and goats — of the destruction of the Temple — of graves opening and the dead coming to life again. But there is also mention of an invitation to a heavenly wedding-banquet with wine in abundance — of a city coming down from heaven where neither sunlight nor moonlight will be needed — of the peace of paradise. Are these images intended in their different ways to express the same fact? What is the final *end* they indicate? What is the norm according to which we shall be judged? What are our *responsibilities*? What do the words of Jesus in Matthew's gospel mean: 'In so far as you did this to one of the least of these brothers of mine, you did it to me' (Matthew 25:40)?

18.1   Our Lord will come
→ 4.4 glory is revealed; 35.1 God loves us first

The first generation of Christians hoped to experience the *second coming* of Christ, and with it the end of the world. They prayed: 'Marana tha', meaning 'Come, Lord!' *Expectation* or *waiting* and being on the watch for Jesus Christ were the hallmark of their lives. The members of the infant Church had to learn that they could not calculate when the Day of Christ would come. They were reminded of the words: 'as for that day and hour, nobody knows it . . . but the Father only' (Matthew 24:36). Christians recognised in this delay in the second coming a sign of God's patience with man (2 Peter 3:9).

Paul journeyed in haste through the parts of the world known at that time so that he might prepare as many people as possible for the expected coming of the Lord. Little by little the Church realised that she must go on living longer in this world, that her *mission* remains a continuing task.

However, the question of Christ's second coming remained alive in the Church. In the course of her history fanatics repeatedly wanted to announce an accurate date for the end of time and the day of *judgement*; they were always wrong. In our present time, when people can plan and calculate ahead, the parable told by Jesus is still apposite: 'If the householder had known at what hour the burglar would come, he would not have let anyone break through the wall of his house' (Luke 12:39).

Each year in *Advent* the Church reflects on the fact that she is always awaiting the coming of her Lord in glory. She looks back over the history of the Israelites and renews in the faithful their longing for *salvation* and fulfilment through God. She rejoices that the Saviour has come. She exhorts the faithful to be ready for the final encounter with Jesus Christ. In every *celebration of the Eucharist* the Church reflects on the way traced out by Jesus 'until he comes in glory'.

> The call to rejoice over the coming of the Lord is always accompanied by a warning to be watchful:
> **You too must stand ready, because the Son of Man is coming at an hour you do not expect.** *Luke 12:40*

Second coming of Christ (or final revelation of Jesus Christ; Gr. parousia – presence, arrival): The immediate, early expectation of the *parousia* is reflected in the letters to the Thessalonians; Mark 13:32 ('as for that day or hour, nobody knows it') and Matthew 25:1–13 (parable of the bridesmaids) testify to the fact that the first generation of Christians knew they must plan their lives as a time of waiting. The question of the future arouses much anxiety on the part of man, but a person who has faith can overcome this anxiety. He is convinced that, at the end, whatever happens, he, Christ, is coming (the Second Coming) and will bring to fulfilment what he has begun.

End of time: Expression with twofold meaning: the fulfilment of time; the end of the old world and the dawning of God's new world — or: the new age which has already begun with Jesus Christ. It introduces a momentous element, an opportunity given us by God to make a firm decision for our salvation (Matthew 11:6).

Marana tha: Aramaic ejaculation; taken over into the Greek New Testament (1 Corinthians 16:22 and Revelation 22:20), meaning: 'Our Lord has come' or 'Come, Lord Jesus!' These ideas of the 'already' and 'not yet' of Christ's presence are very closely related.

Advent: → 27.6

18.2 Christ will judge the world

→ 24.1 metaphors for eternal life; 22.4 God's love; 36.2 freedom; 24.2 the last days

For many people the description of the last judgement causes anxiety rather than confidence. Yet Christ's *judgement* will prove that *love* is more than mere *justice*. The message concerning judgement is Good News. God establishes justice where injustice reigns; justice for the poor, the insignificant, the outcasts and those who are deprived. In him and in his presence everything is arranged as he wills. Holy Scripture speaks unequivocally of the fact that God in Jesus Christ will bring the world to fulfilment. Human beings do not have the last word with their *plans for the future* and their judgements; God has the last word with his plan to reconcile this world with himself in Jesus Christ and to bring it to fulfilment. Therefore the disciples of Jesus should avoid setting themselves and others to rights. God alone in Jesus is the just judge. No one can evade God's plan for the world.

God's love will be experienced by each individual at his death ('personal judgement'). But as each one is in many ways involved with the fate of others and so with that of all the world, he will also *see* the full extent of *God's love* bringing the whole world to fulfilment ('general judgement', 'last judgement'). The victory of God's love will be revealed bringing all to its appointed end. Every human being will meet him; no one is excluded from his love. But God does not force his love on man. The gift of *God's forgiveness* in Jesus Christ and the seriousness of the *responsibility* of each individual exist side by side. For those who have definitively rejected God's love it will lead to condemnation (*hell*); for those who have not been sufficiently open to that love it will lead to suffering (*purgatory*/purification) — and for those who have trusted in God it will lead to eternal bliss (*heaven*).

We find these things difficult to imagine because instinctively we carry our concept of time over into life after death. So we connect 'purgatory' with the idea of duration of time and we distinguish between personal and general judgement. As to when heaven, eternity, 'begins', we fail to make headway if we use our *ideas of time*. Here we have to acknowledge the limitations of our way of thinking. In reality death removes us from time and brings us before the eternal God. For him there is only the 'present', only a timeless 'now'.

God's love for his creation permeates the whole of history and reaches its *goal* in the final fulfilment of the world.

In his speech to the Council of the Areopagus in Athens Paul says of God's judgement:

Because he has fixed a day when the whole world will be judged, and judged in righteousness, and he has appointed a man to be the judge. And God has publicly proved this by raising this man from the dead. *Acts 17:31*

Eternal happiness: The happiness people experience in this life is usually of short duration; the happiness promised by God is without limit — and we shall never tire of it.

Final judgement: Because by this the Bible means the fulfilment of the kingdom of God, it is also called *'last judgement'* and 'last day' (the day that will never wane because it will have no end) or 'day of Yahweh', 'day of the Lord' (God's final victory over all his enemies) and 'day of judgement'. Associated with it is the image of God's judgement of all men and all nations: in this *last judgement* the meaning of human history will be revealed.

Purgatory: Metaphorical expression for the purification of the dead; since 'nothing unclean may come into the new Jerusalem' (cf. Revelation 21:27), all shortcomings must be 'swept away' as rust is 'swept away' from iron by fire. The Council of Trent (1563) says: 'There is a place of purification and the souls who are detained there are helped by the intercessions of the faithful but above all by the sacrifice of the altar, a sacrifice well-pleasing to God' (→ 24.1). Kierkegaard says that purity of heart is to love one thing and that purgatory is caused for us by our loving things other than God: purgatory is the process of weaning ourselves from those other objects of love.

Hell: Biblical word for the place of eternal damnation (cf. Matthew 25:41) (also called *Sheol* or Gehenna); this takes up the description of an underworld such as fitted in with primitive Eastern ideas of the world (→ 16.2). God does not will hell to exist; man prepares it himself when he knowingly and expressly rejects what God wants to give him. Cardinal Newman thought that the vision of God could be hell for one man and heaven for his neighbour, depending on their choice, of God or not.

18.3 Norms for the general judgement

→ 37.1 loving one's neighbour; 5.2 God's will; 39.10 praying to God

'Courage! It is I! Do not be afraid' (Mark 6:50). These words hold good too for the time when we meet him at our *judgement*. Jesus will apply different norms from those to which we are accustomed: prestige, fame, influence, riches, 'a following', a great name — none of these will count. The measure of *love* on which our life is based is what is decisive. The one who has experienced what the love of God is will find a thousand ways of *passing on* that love to others. Love is inventive. It will work in various ways with various people, for each has different abilities and possibilities of putting love into practice.

Matthew's gospel points the direction: food for the hungry, drink for the thirsty, shelter for the stranger, clothing for the naked; visiting the sick and those in prison, burying the dead (Matthew 25:34–36). These are examples of the words: 'In so far as you did this to one of the least of these brothers of mine, you did it to me' (Matthew 25:40).

Even in countries where people are adequately 'provided for' materially, it is often obvious that such provision does not suffice for them to live lives of human dignity. To experience personal concern from one's fellow human beings is often much more important than material help. Jesus showed his disciples the way. He showed real affection for people; he lived his love for them. In so doing he gives us the *norm for action* and at the same time the norm according to which he will judge us.

Many will realise only at the judgement that, without being aware of it, they have served Jesus Christ. They will ask: 'Lord, when did we see you hungry and feed you . . .?' (Matthew 25:37). Then Jesus himself, as Paul writes, will 'light up all that is hidden in the dark and reveal the secret intentions of men's hearts' (1 Corinthians 4:5).

In his Letter to the Romans Paul writes of trust and confidence:
For I am certain of this: neither death nor life, no angel, no prince, nothing that exists, nothing still to come, nor any power, or height or depth, nor any created thing, can ever come between us and the love of God made visible in Christ.
Romans 8:38–39

Norm for action: In addition to the examples in Matthew 25:34–36 (→ 37.1), other New Testament words can be helpful on this subject: e.g. the Beatitudes in Matthew 5:3–11 (→ 5.2) or Matthew 7:21 about our entry into the kingdom of God; equally important is the parable of the two sons who acted differently (Matthew 21:28–32).

19 I believe in the Holy Spirit

→ 34 the Church in the concrete

Contemporary man often finds it difficult to speak of the *Holy* *Spirit*. Perhaps this is due to the fact that a personal relationship is not easily established by using the biblical images for God's Spirit — breath, fire, storm, dove. On the other hand the word 'spirit' is in current use among us. For example, we say of a group 'there is a good spirit here' or 'there seems to be a bad spirit among them'. This is really saying that there are *communities of people* where they are kind to one another and there are others where discord, hatred and malice prevail.

It is said of Jesus that he is completely filled with God's Spirit; he is conceived by the Holy Spirit (Luke 1:35); the Spirit of God comes down on him (Matthew 3:16), he is driven by the Spirit (Mark 1:12); he promises his followers the Spirit of truth who will glorify him (John 16:13-14). Christians are convinced that all who believe in *Jesus Christ* can live in this Spirit.

The Holy Spirit is the *Spirit of the Father*, by whom Jesus was wholly possessed; it is through the *Spirit of Jesus* that we human beings have access to God as our Father. But if we recognise the good or evil spirit of man by its work among us, we might well ask: How do we recognise *God's Spirit*? How do people united in the Spirit of God live, speak and think?

19.1 The Holy Spirit gives life

→ 22.3 life in Christ; 26.1 sign of salvation

In chapter 2 of the Acts of the Apostles Luke describes, by the attitude of the disciples, what it means to be 'filled with the Holy Spirit' (Acts 2:4). After the death of Jesus the disciples were disappointed, perplexed and timid. Some returned to Galilee, others — struck by the revelation of the resurrection of Jesus — did remain in Jerusalem, but behind closed doors. They were as a lifeless remnant, lacking in initiative, turned in on themselves and busied about their own concerns.

And then Luke tells us of the *effect* of the Spirit. 'When

Pentecost day came round' (Acts 2:1), he bursts in on them like a storm, like a fire: he brings new life. Doors are flung open; Peter begins openly to *preach* the Good News of the crucified Messiah. With courage, determination, enthusiasm and the power of strong conviction the disciples set out and win people to follow Jesus Christ. The Church grows (Acts 2:47) and needs additional helpers in her service (Acts 6:1–7). Paul passes beyond the confines of Israel and goes out to the pagans; he begins to preach Christ throughout the Mediterranean. The success of their mission and the life of these new churches is proof of the working of the Spirit.

A similar *Pentecost* is ever breaking out afresh in the *Church*. The *Holy Spirit* wakes Christians from their sleep, bursts open frontiers, fills with new life empty words and dead formulas. The working of the Spirit makes *forgiveness* possible and *transforms* men's lives. Therefore Christians believe that God's Holy Spirit is poured out 'on all flesh' (Joel 3:1–5 and Acts 2:17–18, *RSV* translation); each one can be possessed by this Spirit.

A Latin hymn of the ninth century, the *Veni Creator Spiritus*, begins thus:
Come, Holy Ghost, Creator, come
from thy bright heavenly throne,
come, take possession of our souls,
and make them all thine own.

Galilee: District in the north of Palestine: the lake of Genesareth and the towns of Nazareth, Tiberias and Capernaum are in Galilee.
Joel: One of the twelve so-called 'minor' prophets of the Old Testament (→ 19.2 prophet).
Flesh: in Hebrew means simply 'mankind' as found in the world, man of flesh and blood (cf. John 1:14); all flesh = everyone (Isaiah 40:5 = Luke 3:6).

19.2   The Holy Spirit is the Spirit of God
→ 25.1 Father/Son/Spirit; 24.2 God's love

When the Bible tries to explain that God is at work in this world it often speaks of the Spirit of God. But to express the many-sided concern of God for us, more than one idea is used. The comparisons and metaphors vary, the expressions are not fixed; but all are attempts to describe the ways in which people experience the *Spirit of God* as a driving force in their *lives*.

God's Spirit breathes where it wills (John 3:8). It breathes as creative power over the waters of creation (Genesis 1:2); as Spirit of the Lord it falls upon seers and prophets and makes them *witnesses* of God's word (Ezekiel 11:5). As God's life-giving breath the Spirit gives man life (Genesis 2:7). The Holy Spirit is given by Jesus to his disciples to make a *new beginning* possible for them through forgiveness of sins; as a sign of this he breathes on them (John 20:22). God's Spirit rests on Jesus (Luke 1:35 and 4:18); this Spirit of God is also promised to his followers (Luke 12:12).

But one difference must be clear: the Spirit of God is not the spirit of this world (John 14:17) and this is why he is called the Holy Spirit. He comes upon the disciples like a storm (Acts 2:2); he makes himself felt, he is the powerful Spirit of the Lord (Acts 6:10). Like fire he upsets what is opposed to God's work (Luke 12:49); he lightens the darkness, warms the cold (Acts 18:25), makes out of hearts of stone hearts of flesh (Ezekiel 11:19), gives a new heart (Ezekiel 36:26). *Jesus* was known, even more than the prophets, as one who was wholly 'driven' by the Spirit of God (Mark 1:12). The demons are aware of this when they — as Mark (1:24) writes — call out: You are the holy one of God. God's Spirit moves in him (Luke 1:17), is at work in him (Matthew 12:28). God's Spirit guides the first messengers of the faith when, in the Spirit of Jesus (John 15:27), they go out to preach the *gospel* (Acts 8:29–39).

Those who *follow* Jesus have had the experience that God's Spirit gives life, that even today he transforms people and gives them new life (2 Corinthians 3:6). They experience him as Advocate, as Comforter, as John's gospel says (John 16:7). Because in this experience God himself is present, the Church calls upon the Holy Spirit as a person and asks him for his gifts. 'You have revealed your glory as the glory also of your Son and of the Holy Spirit: three Persons equal in majesty, undivided in splendour, yet one Lord, one God', the Church says, in the ancient Preface of the Blessed Trinity. We express the same truth every time we recite the Nicene Creed.

An Irish folk prayer has the following words:
Three folds in cloth, yet there is but the one cloth.
Three joints in a finger, yet there is but the one finger.
Three leaves in the shamrock, yet there is but the one
shamrock.
Frost, snow and ice . . . yet the three are only water.
Three persons in God likewise, and but the one God.

Translated by Thomas Kinsella

Prophet: In the Old Testament, one who preaches a message from God and knows himself called by God, God's Spirit, for this work. Prophets appeared above all in the time between the eighth and fifth centuries B.C. There were prophets like Elijah who only preached; others also wrote down their prophecies. According to the length of their writings, four 'major' prophets are distinguished (Isaiah, Jeremiah, Ezekiel, Daniel) and twelve 'minor' prophets.

Divine Persons: God, by becoming man in Jesus Christ, has shown himself as he is. Since the resurrection and glorification of Jesus, in the Holy Spirit, he, Jesus — and with him God the Father — continues to be experienced by us. Because of this, the Church concludes, in faith, that there are living relationships within the Godhead. She therefore professes belief in three Divine Persons: Father, Son and Holy Spirit.

19.3 The Holy Spirit is at work in man

→ 22.4 God's love; 36.3 the Saints; 1.2 following Jesus

Everywhere where people live according to the example, and in the Spirit of Jesus, *God's Spirit* is at work — whether the individual knows it or not. The working of the Holy Spirit does not restrict a person, does not oblige him to do what he does not accept. The Holy Spirit can work effectively in us only when we are open to Jesus and his message. Our *freedom* is experienced not as a right, on which we must insist, but as a *gift*.

If we open ourselves to the Holy Spirit we discover — often to our surprise — capabilities in ourselves of which we had hardly a suspicion. We succeed in inspiring others.

Paul writes in his first Letter to the Corinthians that no one can *believe* in Jesus Christ without the Holy Spirit (1 Corinthians 12:3); moreover, no one can live as a Christian without him, no one can *pray* without him. Christians are convinced that when someone speaks or thinks well of another, the Holy Spirit is at work. When a person does not think first of himself but treats others as his brothers, when he does not give up *hope* in the fulfilment of mankind and the world, God's Spirit is at work. The Spirit inspires *trust*, *confidence* and the energy not to be satisfied with what one has already done. The Holy Spirit gives man the wisdom to avoid self-importance.

Paul sees in the Holy Spirit the source of true freedom. He says to the Galatians: 'The proof that you are sons of God is that God has sent the Spirit of his Son into our hearts: the Spirit that cries, "Abba, Father", and it is this that makes you a son, but you are not a slave any more; and if God has made you son, then he has made you heir' (Galatians 4:6–7). So Paul is saying that the Holy Spirit makes men *'children of God'* and brothers to one another.

There are characteristics by which we can recognise that the Holy Spirit is dwelling in us: love, joy, peace, patience, kindness, goodness, trustfulness, gentleness and self-control (Galatians 5:22): these qualities, summed up by Paul as *'fruits of the Spirit'*, grow in the one who believes. They are gifts which one does not 'possess', but they are 'caught' and make a full human life possible.

The following prayer is ascribed to St Augustine:
Breathe in me, Spirit of God, that I may think what is holy,
Drive me, Spirit of God, that I may do what is holy,
Draw me, Spirit of God, that I may love what is holy.
Strengthen me, Spirit of God, that I may preserve what is holy,
Guard me, Spirit of God, that I may never lose what is holy.

Gifts of the Holy Spirit: At the end of Isaiah 11:1–3 (where the Messiah is described), Christian tradition recognises seven gifts of the Holy Spirit: the spirit of wisdom, understanding, counsel, fortitude, knowledge, piety and fear of the Lord.

Fruits of the Holy Spirit: The qualities summarised by Paul (Galatians 5:22) under this title indicate attitudes where the gifts are effective; it is difficult to distinguish the various 'gifts' and 'fruits' in detail.

Children of God : Ultimately, everyone is a child (a son or a daughter) of God; God wills salvation for all. Paul speaks of the Christians as children of God because in them, through the working of the Holy Spirit (in faith and baptism), the love of God has become especially effective. They are to show themselves children of 'their Father in heaven' (Matthew 5:45) in loving others as children of God (→ 2; 22.2).

Sect: 'Children of God': Members of one of the so-called 'new religions'; a misleading name for an influential group whose members do not seem to possess the freedom of the children of God (Ephesians 1:14) but rather seem to be coerced by questionable methods. Secrecy is imposed on them within a very authoritarian structure to which membership commits them. There is no spirit that 'sets them free' (→ 10.1 'New religions')

Charismatical Renewal (movement): Widespread Church movement for renewal — originating in the USA — in various groups in Europe, including England; e.g. the Catholic Pentecostal Movement. These groups wish to contribute to a renewal of parish life by trying to let the working of the Holy Spirit be experienced in spontaneous prayer in groups, 'baptism in the Spirit', certain life-styles, and a critical view of some entrenched Church institutions.

20   The holy Catholic Church

→ 26 sign of salvation; 34 the Church in the concrete

The word *'church'* is used in many different senses: to mean a building, a *parish*, a *denomination*, the leadership of the Church, the *universal church*, often too for a *church service* ('going to church'). What is meant in this chapter? In what sense can the 'holy Catholic Church' itself be part of the content of the faith? Can one really speak of 'belief in the Church'? What is meant in the creed?

In the creed the Church is separated from the *Holy Spirit* literally only by a comma. Does this mean that one cannot live in the Church without believing in the Holy Spirit? Or does it mean that faith in the Holy Spirit is, in practice, faith in the Church? Irenaeus of Lyons (*c.*200), one of the Fathers of the Church, said: 'Wherever the Church is, the Spirit of God is also present and where God's Spirit is present, there too is the Church and all *grace*'.

Father of the Church: Title of honour for early Christian theologians whose way of writing about the faith and life-style have lasting significance for the Church (→ 10.1 Doctor of the Church).

20.1 The Church — work of the Holy Spirit

→ 19.3 the Holy Spirit at work; 26 sign of salvation; 34 the Church in the concrete

The Spirit of Jesus is concerned not only with people as individuals; it is he who also brings them together and unites them. This is what happens in each separate Christian *parish* and in the whole *Church*; the work is not first and foremost that of human beings. Christians are convinced that Jesus Christ in the *Holy Spirit* unites all the members of the Church with one another and works through them.

The Acts of the Apostles tell of Peter's sermon at Pentecost: a sermon so persuasive that thousands joined the *disciples* of Jesus. They *believed* his words and accepted *baptism*. They remained together, had all things in common and shared with those who were in need. They were of one mind in prayer and praise of God, held fast to the teaching of the apostles and broke bread together (cf. Acts 2:41–46). What exactly the Church is supposed to be can hardly be more aptly described. Because the Church is assembled and filled with the one Spirit of Jesus, there can be only '*one church*'. It is therefore deplorable that, in the course of her history, through human frailty, there have repeatedly been divisions in the Church. Yet, trusting in the working of the Holy Spirit, Christians hope that the Church will be moved and led towards unity.

Because the Holy Spirit of God unites and fills the Church, we speak of a '*holy church*'. Christians believe that God's sanctifying power works through them, even though they are a 'church of sinners'.

Because what the Church teaches and passes on concerns the whole world, she is the *Catholic Church*. This means that she is open to all who are ready to accept the message that she hands on and to be moved by the Spirit of Jesus Christ to accept baptism.

Because the Church is rooted in the belief of the apostles and continues their mission, she is called an '*apostolic church*'. She is built on the 'foundation of the apostles'; Jesus Christ is the cornerstone (Ephesians 2:20), the Holy Spirit unites her.

Already, at the beginning of the second century, Christians prayed for the Church in these words:

Be mindful of your Church. Deliver her from all evil. Perfect her in your love and gather her together from all the ends of the earth into the kingdom which you have prepared for her. Yours is the power and the glory for ever and ever.

From the *Teaching of the Twelve Apostles* (the *Didache)*

Marks of the Church: The Nicene Creed does not speak of the holy Catholic Church, but names four marks or characteristics: 'the one, holy, Catholic and apostolic Church'.

one church: → 20.4

holy church: First, it is a fact that God alone is holy (→ 3.2); but through his Spirit he transforms people who belong in faith to his Son; he sanctifies them. By their baptism they are 'set apart' and belong to God, which is another meaning of holiness.

catholic (Gr. = all-embracing, world-wide): The Church knows she has been sent by Jesus Christ to all men, to serve all by the proof of her love and by her message of joy. Therefore, all cultures must find their home in her. — Since divisions occurred in the Church, the word 'catholic' is used in a restrictive sense. In current speech it has lost something of the splendour of its breadth and richness. Nowadays people speak of the 'Catholic' Church as distinct from 'Protestant', 'Evangelical', 'Orthodox' Churches.—Because the word 'catholic' has thus become a denominational sign (→ Roman Catholic 34.9), others understand the word 'catholic' differently in the creed. Another meaning of the word is 'universal' in the sense of 'total' and it is applied to the totality of the Christian faith.

apostolic: The connection of the Church with the apostles is expressed above all in the office of bishops (in unbroken succession since apostolic times). It also implies fidelity to the teaching of the apostles.

20.2   Tradition in the Holy Spirit

→ 21.1 Church as community: 19 the Holy Spirit; 1.3 in the community of the faithful

For a community like that of the Church a good memory is essential. Memories are to be kept alive to ensure strength for the present and *hope* for the *future*. The Church, by her memory, hands on the experiences of the *community of the faithful* from her early beginnings down to the present day. She hands on what God has done for us, above all through his Son, in the first centuries and at the present time. In so doing the Church relies on being led by the Spirit of God who preserves her from being unfaithful to all that has been entrusted to her.

Even in *Israel* in ancient times people related how God acted with their elders. Before the *traditions* of God's deeds in Israel were written down, they passed by word of mouth from generation to generation, in the services in the synagogue, in national feasts, in their family circles. In this way they handed on legends and sagas, laws, sayings and accounts of various events. The particular character of the group, in which a certain text originated and was handed down, determined its form. Only gradually were these *testimonies* to their common faith written down and collected together. We find them now in the *Old Testament*.

The *traditions about Jesus* went through the same process as the traditional faith of Israel. At the beginning there were personal *witnesses* to the faith: those who had *seen* and *heard* and believed in Jesus. Here and there what they handed on in their 'church' services, their conversations about the faith, in religious instruction or in missionary sermons, was written down. In addition there were letters written by the apostles to the Christian churches, letters suitable for reading aloud during their *services*. All this material was collected in the *New Testament*. Thus the recollection of what God has done for us through Jesus Christ brings to life the faith of Christians, and, together with the experience of Israel, it gives us hope and courage when we recall the *mighty deeds of God*.

The Church, as community of the faithful, understanding herself as the work of the Holy Spirit, is confident that the 'Spirit of truth' will lead her 'to the complete truth' (John 16:13). Therefore she takes to heart her *commission* to preserve and hand on what she has recognised as her tradition in the Holy Spirit. In the *history of the Church* Christians tell too of men and women — the *Saints* — who have modelled their lives wholly on Jesus Christ. Another part of these living Christian memories are our feasts and customs, our pictures and our hymns. So there is a long chain of tradition in which the Church of today is the most recent link. The Church must bear the responsibility of ensuring for the Church of tomorrow that this chain is not broken.

> Christians recall, as did the Jews, God's deeds and they
> sing:
> **Come and see the works of God,**
> **tremendous his deeds among men.**
> **Come and hear, all who fear God.**
> **I will tell you what he did for my soul.**
>
> *Psalm 65(66):5, 16*

Tradition (Lat. = handing on): The Second Vatican Council says (1965): 'What
was handed on by the apostles includes everything which contributes to the
holiness of life, and the increase in faith of the people of God; and so the Church,
in her teaching, life and worship, perpetuates and hands on to all generations all
that she herself is and all that she believes' (*On Revelation*, para. 8). The living
tradition of the Church as source of the faith was a point of disagreement in discussions concerning the faith at the time of the Reformation. The Reformers
referred to the Bible only (*sola Scriptura* = Scripture only). But because the Bible
without the community of the faithful is unthinkable, the Catholic Church
emphasises the close connection between Scripture and tradition.
Patriarchs: 'Elders' of the tribes of Israel; frequent description of Abraham,
Isaac and Jacob (our *'fathers in the faith'*). To be distinguished from patriarch as
title of an ecclesiastical office (→ 34.8).

20.3   The Bible — the Church's book

→ 10.3 God reveals himself; 1.4 reading the Bible; 19 the Holy Spirit

The believing *community* — i.e. the *Church* — existed before
the book which we call the *New Testament* came into being, just
as *Israel* existed before the *Old Testament* was written down.
Without the believing *people of God* of the old and of the new
covenant, anxious to keep alive their remembrance of God's
mighty deeds, there is no *Bible*.

The composition of the Old Testament lasted a long period,
about 1,000 years. The last books to be accepted for the collection
of these sacred writings were written about 150 years before
Christ. The Jews call the collection 'the sacred writings of Israel'.
They are divided into 'laws', 'prophets' and 'writings'. Christians
call the same collection the Old Testament. In this reciprocal
recognition of the sacred writings of Israel as Holy Scripture we
see the relationship between *Christianity and Judaism*. Israel's

experience of God is, as it were, the matrix of Christian faith.

Nor was the New Testament the work of a single drafting process; here too there are various kinds of testimony to the faith. They stem from the second half of the first century. The collection of all the writings of the New Testament and the collation of them with those of the Old Testament was virtually completed by the middle of the second century. The resulting collection is called the *canon* of Holy Scripture.

The Bible is therefore the book of the community of the faithful, of the Church, of the group of people who know they are led by God's Spirit. Therefore, the Church claims for herself the reliable interpretation of this book. From her knowledge and experience of the Holy Spirit she trusts that she understands the language of the *Holy Spirit* and that she is able to express, preserve and interpret validly this calling to witness. For, with the faithful of Israel, Christians share the conviction that the Holy Spirit was at work when the books of the Bible were written down (*inspiration*).

However, the Church cannot freely dispose of Scripture. In establishing the canon she has once and for all bound herself to her origins. Thus the message is safeguarded from additions and omissions. The Church exists, it is true, 'before' the Bible, but at the same time she is 'subject' to it.

The Church hands on the word of God and knows that she is directed by this word:
The word of God is something alive and active: it cuts like any double-edged sword, but more finely; it can slip through the place where the soul is divided from the spirit, or joints from the marrow; it can judge the secret emotions and thoughts. *Hebrews 4:12*

Inspiration (Lat. = breathing in): The Holy Spirit of God was at work during the editing of the writings of the Bible, according to the faith of Jews and Christians; he inspired the authors, i.e. their writings testify to God's word for the Church. **Canon** (Gr. = guideline): What was recognised by the community of the faithful as sacred (i.e. inspired) writings could be read at church services; these writings were accepted in the canon (= register, index) of Holy Scripture. — Which books belong to the Bible and into what groups they are divided can be seen from any complete edition of the Bible.

Apocrypha (Gr. = hidden; secret writings): In addition to the books belonging to the canon there are others which were omitted by the Church as not genuine; they were said to be written by prophets (Old Testament apocryphal writings; not accepted by Jews either) or they told of words and deeds of Jesus (New Testament apocryphal writings). Apocryphal writings may be compared with pious fiction; they were not completely forbidden by the Christian churches, but they might not be read aloud at Church services. The same word 'Apocrypha' is also used for a section of the Bible called Apocrypha (or the deutero-canonical books). In non-Roman versions this section is usually printed separately between the Old and New Testaments. At the beginning of the Christian era these books were accepted by Christians and Jews; later, controversy between Christians and Jews arose and led to the drawing-up of the canon (cf. note above). From this canon the Jews excluded the deutero-canonical books because they originated among the Jews of the Dispersion. Some Christians now accept them as inspired, others do not.

20.4   Unity in diversity

→ 34.2 leadership in the Church; 34.9 Christian unity

The *Church* has to bear witness to and hand on to all nations God's salvation as experienced in Jesus Christ. But Christians can give this 'recruiting' witness only in the measure that, in unity and harmony, they rely on Jesus Christ. There should be no quarrelling among themselves. It is not by chance that John's gospel hands on to us, before the passion and death of Jesus, his great prayer for *unity* (John 17:20–26).

The Church has only one *foundation* and that is *Jesus Christ* (1 Corinthians 3:11). However, this foundation is not something static, it is characterised by liveliness and diversity. In the New Testament it is clear in what a variety of ways people speak of the one Christ; correspondingly, the life of the early churches offers a variegated picture. In the variety of cultures and of religious assumptions in these churches there are, quite naturally, discussions concerning the preservation of Christ's teaching and its interpretation. This is substantiated by the Acts of the Apostles and by Paul's letters. The variety of views of the different witnesses is seen in the characteristics of the *four gospels*. In early Christianity different view-points were discussed, but the Church never divided into *denominations* and 'camps' at strife one with the other. She possessed the strength to hold firm during these tensions but at the same time knew how to engage in lively dialogue with the different groups.

In Church history there are numerous examples of positive solutions in such *discussion on matters of faith*. When the unity of the Church was not at risk, when no mania for always being in the right prevailed, when all those taking part did not ignore one another's goodwill, the Church came through such tensions enriched, and with her faith strengthened. But it is also true that conflicts sometimes had a tragic outcome, ending either in *heresy* and *schism* or in general lack of interest.

The abundance of experiences in faith, as voiced from time to time in dialogue concerning the faith, the fund of fresh inspiration and ideas, as expressed in books written by theologians, the *variety of charisms* shown in the churches — all this is enriching for the Church, provided it remains within the unity of the Church (→ 34.2).

Unity in freedom and freedom in unity is what nourishes the Church. *Variety* must be allowed to develop for the sake of *truth*. And this happens best when the Church is loved as the Church of Jesus Christ, not when one picks and chooses what one fancies in the *Good News* or what is according to one's taste, but when one accepts the whole Church and her gospel. In other words, safety consists in accepting the whole canon, the whole gospel; there is danger in making one's own selection of a canon within the canon.

At the beginning of the second century the following prayer, or hymn, is found:
As grain, once scattered on the hillside,
was in this broken bread made one,
so from all lands thy Church be gathered
into thy kingdom by thy Son.

From the *Didache*; translation
versified by *Francis Bland Tucker*

Mark's gospel (Gospel according to Mark): Oldest gospel, giving a connected account of the traditional words and stories about Jesus from his baptism to the discovery of the empty tomb: written for Gentile-Christian readers, as is clear from the confession of the pagan officer who believed in Jesus as Son of God (Mark 15:39 — the climax of the whole gospel).
Matthew's gospel (Gospel according to Matthew): Chief source for it is Mark's gospel, the order of which is, in general, maintained; there are some discourses

(e.g. Sermon on the Mount), about half of which material stems from a source which has not come down to us, but which was known also to the author of Luke's gospel. Chief statement: Jesus is the Messiah sent to Israel, bringing salvation to the world and showing himself as Son of God. Great interest in formation of new churches. Probably written for a Gentile-Christian community (after 70 A.D.) which was in conflict with Judaising trends.

Luke's gospel (Gospel according to Luke): Account of the author: 1:1–4. More than half of Mark's gospel (reworked) is taken over; in addition, the oral tradition used by Matthew and other traditions known only to him are worked into the gospel; twice the length of Mark. Written for Gentile-Christians unfamiliar with the Jewish background. The Christian's 'way' is a continuation of the 'way of Jesus'; warning to be on the watch. Jesus as Saviour of sinners brings salvation for all nations. Same author as that of the Acts of the Apostles; written in the nineties A.D.

John's gospel (Gospel according to John): Is different in outline and language from the other three (so-called *synoptic*) gospels (→ 1.2); influenced by a Jewish milieu but also by late Greek (= Hellenistic) philosophy. Chief emphasis: revelation of God's glory in Jesus; symbolism of the actions of Jesus interpreted in their meaning for faith and life in the Church community; presence of the risen Lord in his church. Written at the turn of the century (certainly before 120).

Schism (Gr. = tear or division): Separation from the Roman Catholic Church united under the Pope (→ 34.9), without necessarily rejection of the teaching of the Church. Especially far-reaching was the separation of the Greek Church of the East (Byzantium) from the Latin Church of the West (Rome) in 1054.

Heresy (Gr. = choice, preference, being selective): Teaching (or erroneous teaching) deviating from that of the Catholic Church, falsifying, or abbreviating it, on a point of faith.

Division in the churches: Often used with the same meaning as 'schism', but sometimes distinct. Usually to be understood as separation in the churches for reasons of faith.

Reform: Renewal or new order in some parts of the Church's life (e.g. liturgy, etc.); occasionally also a fundamental new arrangement of Christian life (or of a religious order) in keeping with the example of Christ. In this sense the Church is continually in need of reform (not to be confused with the Reformation → 34.9).

20.5   I believe in the Church

→ 10.4 I believe; 34.2 leadership in the Church; 20.1 Church as community; 1.3 in the community of the faithful

A Christian can say: 'I believe God' as he may say to a human person: 'I believe you'; this means that I trust you; one can believe what you say; you are a trustworthy witness.

In the creed there is the formula: I believe *in God*. The one who says this with conviction says: God is the object of my faith; my faith, i.e. my life, depends on him. I trust him utterly and completely.

We cannot understand in the same sense 'belief in the *Church*'; she is not the object of Christian belief; God alone is its object. A Christian can however say: I trust that the Church will give me the message of Jesus Christ, that she will hand on to me reliably what God has done for us; the *Church* is for me a trustworthy *witness*. I can even describe her as 'pillar and foundation of the truth' (cf. 1 Timothy 3:15).

On the other hand the formula 'I believe the Church' is very unusual. And yet this is what is found in the creed as literally translated from the Greek and Latin. We can say in English: 'I believe history'. This means that I accept history as true, that is, I believe the content, the facts related. Whoever says 'I believe the Church' acknowledges that the Church, despite all shortcomings, remains the work of Jesus Christ. He himself lives on in her, i.e. the Church is for the Christian not only a useful organisation, a meaningful gathering of people who believe, but the Church is an essential part of the Christian faith. Therefore 'I believe the Church' means: I believe that the Church is part of being a Christian. *One* Christian on his own is not a Christian at all. For the Christian faith can live only in the context of a *community* and can develop effectively only in this way. This enables me to see the origin of the Church; she grows out of the people of Israel and the community of the disciples of Jesus, who, through *Jesus* and his *message*, came to a new relationship among themselves. 'I believe the Church' means: with regard to the Church I count myself as someone who is concerned with her interests, as someone who, with her, exerts himself for the kingdom of God brought about by Jesus Christ.

The Second Vatican Council writes about the Church as the people of God:
Among all the nations of the earth there is but one people of God. For all the faithful scattered throughout the world are in communion with each other in the Holy Spirit. He it is who, on behalf of the whole Church and each and every one of those who believe, is the principle of their coming together.

cf. *Constitution on the Church,* para. 13

---

21 The communion of saints

→ 27 centre of life

A *communion*, or *community*, arises when people are brought together through a common interest. The deeper the interest, the more stable the community, the stronger the ties that bind it together. Regarded from outside, the Church herself is such a community, a social group among others.

From within the *Church* understands herself differently; she is the communion, or community, of *saints* (i.e. holy people) and *salvation*.

What is meant by these two statements? That the Church is called holy is understandable; but that Christians should describe themselves as holy? Are they less sinful than other people? And what does '*communion of salvation*' mean? Can the Church be said to 'possess' salvation? for herself? for the world? Hasn't much harm been caused in the world by representatives of the Church? What grounds has the Church to speak of herself in such high terms?

21.1 Church as communion or community

→ 4.1 kingdom of God proclaimed; 20.1 work of the Spirit; 26.1 sign of salvation; 1.3 in the community of the faithful

Christians are convinced that God himself builds up *communities*; he has established communities or associations with human beings: by leading Israel out of Egypt and becoming their faithful companion; by calling into being the new people of God, his *Church*, through Jesus, and leading her on her way.

The Christian lives in the community of the Church, in the community of those who believe in Christ. Without his fellow-Christians his faith would be stunted. The Church is his 'home', his 'family', his 'mother'. The faith of a Christian is supported by his predecessors and his contemporaries; he himself hands it on to those who will come after him.

Therefore the community of the Church does not exist for itself; it is at the service of the coming of the *kingdom of God* and is unlike any other organisation. In the creed Christians profess that the Church lives through the Spirit of God, she is the work of the *Holy Spirit*.

The prophets spoke of the working of the Spirit of God: for example, Ezekiel, who hands on God's word to ages yet to come, says: 'I will put a new spirit in them; I will remove the heart of stone from their bodies and give them a heart of flesh instead, so that they will keep my laws and respect my observances and put them into practice. They will be *my people* and I will be their God' (Ezekiel 11:19–20). This can be for the Church a promise and at the same time an accusation against her. For there are hearts of stone in the Church and they detract from her life and vigour. The Church needs a *'new spirit'* to move men's hearts. And this process is continually repeated. For example, religious congregations and various movements in the Church give proof of such renewal, as indeed do all who are open to a new life in a spirit of fraternal charity. From such people a spark will spread over the whole Church.

Christians anxious for a strong spirit of community among themselves and with Christ pray:
Bind us together, Lord,
bind us together, Lord,
bind us together in love.

Author unknown

Excommunication: Exclusion from the community (Lat. communio) of the Catholic Church on account of serious offences against her ordinances or teaching.

21.2   Church of saints
→ 36.3 the Saints; 3.2 the all-holy One

Paul often calls Christians 'holy' or 'beloved saints' when he addresses them in his letters (e.g. Romans 1:7; 1 Corinthians 1:2). In so doing he is not boasting of the excellent moral life of the Christians in Rome or Corinth; for in the course of his letters he mentions their misdeeds by name, and upbraids them (e.g. 1 Corinthians 5:1-6, 20). Christians are 'saints' because of their *calling* through Jesus Christ who 'sanctifies' them in baptism and gives them a share in his own *holiness*. This union with Christ challenges Christians to live according to their calling: 'I implore you therefore to lead a life worthy of your vocation' (Ephesians 4:1).

In the course of Church history the word 'saint' has become more and more restricted to those who show especially clearly to what holiness of life they aspire in virtue under the influence of the Spirit of Jesus Christ. Because their form of *following Christ* is an example — through acts of *love of their neighbour*, through their whole-hearted love of God or through their readiness to die for him (*martyrdom*) — they are honoured as Saints. Christians know themselves to be united with them on their way through life. They ask the *intercession* of those who are very close to God. They pray that God will bring the dead near to himself. And they pray for one another and help one another to reach their goal.

Because all Christians know themselves to be so closely united in the Spirit of Jesus Christ, and through this Spirit with one another, they speak of the '*communion of saints*' and this is seen very clearly in the *celebration of the Eucharist*: the assembled faithful pray for the living and the dead, they ask the intercession of those holy people who have completed their lives in Christ, and they come to pray before God as one large community sanctified by him.

> In Paul's first Letter to the Corinthians he sums up with a metaphor what all Christians believe:
> **You together are Christ's body; but each of you is a different part of it.** *1 Corinthians 12:27*

21.3   Communion or community of holiness

→ 27.2 centre of life; 26 sign of holiness; 26.3 Church as Sacrament

Christians are convinced that very little has been understood about the *Church* if she is considered merely as a human institution. Organisation, rules and money certainly play their part — and are obviously necessary — yet the essence of the Church is much more than their sum-total. Catholics believe that what the Church is and stands for and what has to be developed in her does not derive its origin from human decisions. It is above all what her Lord claims from her that is important.

The Church is best described as the *community assembled round the table of the risen Lord*: she is gathered from many nations, united through the working of the *Holy Spirit* and held in being by the salvific gifts of the *word of Christ* and the *body of Christ*.

The Eucharist unites these two elements: Jesus Christ shows himself alive in his word and in the bread of the *Eucharist*. In these salvific gifts God's Spirit is at work; thus through the Spirit the community grows in holiness. These gifts are at the disposal of the Church and are entrusted to her to be offered to all and to be shared by all. It is for this reason that the Church lays so much emphasis on the regular celebration of the Eucharist by all her members. For the Eucharist is the expression of the visible community of all the *baptised* throughout the world.

The community of the Church has its foundation in the celebration of the Eucharist: therefore the Church prays:
Lord,
may this Eucharist
accomplish in your Church
the unity and peace it signifies.
We ask this through Christ our Lord.
Concerning prayer at Mass,
11th Sunday of the Year

'Communion of saints': The expression 'communion of the holy' was used in the early Christian centuries; its primary meaning was that of the community of the Eucharist (then called 'the holy'); its secondary meaning was a recognition of the community of those who, as 'saints' or 'holy', were called to a holy life.

22 The forgiveness of sins

→ 28 baptism

If one looks through the third part of the Apostles' Creed, it is difficult to see the connection between one statement and another. Why does forgiveness of sin have to be mentioned at this point? Must we always be talking of *sin*? Is it necessary to recognise oneself as a sinner before one can genuinely believe in God's goodness? Would it not be preferable to conduct one's life in trust and optimism without constant self-reproach?

The line of thought in the *Apostles' Creed* follows a different direction: by comparing it with the text of the Nicene Creed we are given further enlightenment; there we are told: 'We acknowledge one *baptism* for the forgiveness of sins'. We have to remind ourselves that the creed is originally related to baptism. Are we then here concerned with baptism? Is it so important that it has to be expressly mentioned in the creed?

22.1 Being reconciled with him

→ 16.3 we are redeemed; 30 guilt; 28.1 new life

Experiences of *happiness* and *suffering*, of overwhelming joy and of incredible pain, of boredom and longings — far from being exceptional situations in human life, these are quite normal experiences. Reaction to them can vary: we can come to grips with the tension between helpful and devastating experiences; we can close our eyes to them; we can go to pieces.

Christian faith does not remove this tension, on the contrary: the one who believes has perhaps a clearer perception and gives more serious consideration to what he sees, for at the centre of Christian faith is the cross.

People who believe dare to bracket together their good and bad experiences and ultimately they see the *cross* as an advantage. In spite of all their dreadful experiences they are people who see in Jesus Christ an opportunity and a reason for making the good which they experience the driving force in their lives. And they dare to do this because they know they are accepted. They are convinced that *life, love* and goodness are stronger than all the *powers of evil*, stronger than the evil one himself, stronger than sin, hatred and death. Those who believe stake all on Jesus Christ, in spite of harmful experiences, in spite of denial and evil, in spite of their own *guilt*.

This attitude is rooted in the belief that God in Jesus Christ has concerned himself unconditionally with man. This *interest on God's part* shows that he has said 'yes' and 'Amen' to us (2 Corinthians 5:18). In his great love God has *reconciled* man with himself (Romans 5:10). Because God in Jesus Christ has ranged himself on man's side, because he went with him to the deepest abandonment and withstood even to death the powers most opposed to man and those threatening his life, Christians have the courage to accept the cross as a sign of reconciliation. Despite all other kinds of experience they commit themselves whole-heartedly to goodness and account it an advantage for their own life and the *life of the world*.

This hymn is suitable for use in Lent and at other times:
Walk with me, oh my Lord,
through the darkest night and brightest day.
Be at my side, oh Lord,
hold my hand and guide me on my way. *Estelle White*

Reconciliation: After a person has been baptised, it is the sacrament of penance that reconciles a sinner with God. The sinner receives from God reconciliation and the forgiveness of his sins.

22.2 Freed from the power of sin

→ 12.5 world order and its enigmas; 7.1 no one is without sin; 8.3 deliver us from evil; 12.2 power and violence

Through Jesus Christ 'we have been *reconciled*' (Romans 5:11), we have been 'freed from the *slavery of sin*' (Romans 6:18); God gives us 'eternal life in Jesus Christ our Lord' (Romans 6:23). Such statements shed a strong light on human life. But the stronger the light, the darker the shadows.

One would have to close one's eyes to say that everything is in order with man and the world. Even in earliest times in the Old Testament man tried to find a solution to the problem of *evil*. For there is no denying it: we are born into a world dominated by injustice and malice, and although we suffer from it, we also contribute to the influence exercised by the power of evil. We contribute to a history teeming with stupidity and meanness. We suffer in unjust circumstances and at the same time we help to spread them further. This is our inheritance and everyone takes them upon himself, no one can escape them. As long as the world exists, *sin* and *injustice* proliferate. The faith of the Church therefore speaks of 'original sin' weighing on the whole of mankind. My own conduct, for which I am responsible and shall be made to answer, bears the impress of sin and injustice. Each one experiences it: 'I fail to carry out the things I want to do, and I find myself doing the very things I hate' (Romans 7:15) and I gladly seek elsewhere for the guilt for them and often find people who are guilty. And yet I cannot absolve myself from my own guilt.

There have been many attempts to clarify this terrible situation. The Old Testament describes the reason thus: man — Adam — sins against God (Genesis 3) and the curse for this deed rests on his descendants. The New Testament says more clearly that we are born into a world characterised by sin; we are *heirs of sin*. The slavery of sin weighs heavily upon us; how heavily, we realise through the man *Jesus Christ* — the counterpart of Adam (Romans 5:15). In him it is clear how much we human beings need what the Church calls 'sanctifying grace'; it becomes obvious what it means for us to be freed from the power of evil through Jesus Christ and given grace. He faced the power of sin and was condemned to death because of it. Yet God's power proved stronger and God did not abandon his Christ to death; he wrenched him away from death. Now it is clear that victory belongs, not to the power of the one who is for ever involving man in demands which admit of no solution, but to the power which, in love, goes the way of helplessness in order to open to man the way of trust in a God who is always greater than sin and thus to *set him free* from the slavery of sin.

This throws light on our situation. Only in this light will the *power of darkness* be recognised (Colossians 1:13) and removed. Man's destiny is no longer determined by his involvement in sin, but by *salvation given* to us by God in Jesus Christ. Therefore

Paul can write in his Letter to the Romans: 'However great the number of sins committed, grace was even greater' (Romans 5:20); 'those who are moved by the Spirit are sons of God' (cf. Romans 8:14), and 'therefore heirs of God too, that is *co-heirs with Jesus Christ*' (cf. Romans 8:17) — and no longer heirs of sin.

The Church prays:
God our Father,
you redeem us
and make us your children in Christ.
Look upon us,
give us true freedom
and bring us to the inheritance you promised.
We ask this through Christ our Lord.   *Opening Prayer,*
                                                  23rd Sunday of the Year

---

Original sin: A name for the experience shared by all men from the beginning — 'since Adam' — under the influence of the dominating power of sin in their environment; no one relying on his own strength can avoid it. The Church by her teaching on universal, original sin emphasises the power of Jesus Christ; for God through Jesus Christ has 'snatched us from the power of darkness' (Colossians 1:13).

The Second Vatican Council says (1965): 'All of human life, whether individual or collective, shows itself to be a dramatic struggle between good and evil, between light and darkness. Indeed, man finds that by himself he is incapable of battling the assaults of evil successfully, so that everyone feels as though he is bound by chains. But the Lord himself came to free and strengthen man, renewing him inwardly and casting out that prince of this world (cf. John 12:31) who held him in the bondage of sin (cf. John 8:34). For sin has diminished man, blocking his path to fulfilment. The call to grandeur and the depths of misery are both a part of human experience. They find their ultimate and simultaneous explanation in the light of God's revelation' (*The Church in the Modern World*, para. 13).

Power/slavery of sin: Another expression for our involvement in sin; this expression puts greater emphasis on the deep mystery of sin and the universal state of sinfulness than on the part played by the individual; moreover, it is an attempt to avoid the misunderstanding that might arise from the use of the word 'inherit'.

22.3 Life in Christ Jesus

→ 28.1 new life; 7.2 a God who forgives

The concluding part of the creed speaks of the working of the Holy Spirit in the *community of the Church*. What God has done through Jesus Christ is experienced by the believer through the mediation of the Church. This is obvious in *baptism*. Here the one who believes receives the gift of *reconciliation* with God so that he may live in the Spirit of Jesus Christ.

The New Testament understands the 'plunging' into the waters of baptism as being buried with Christ (Colossians 2:12). This metaphor is saying: To die with Christ and live with him (Romans 6:8) means death to sin and life for God (Romans 6:11) and this is being rescued from the *slavery of sin* and reconciled with God.

For a Christian this is not merely a pleasant-sounding play on words. We learn to understand that the *new life* growing out of reconciliation with God has consequences for our lives. If we are accepted by God we can also accept ourselves, we have no need to be depressed by our darker side. Reconciled with God, we can learn to be reconciled with the conditions of our life. And when we have experienced reconcilation with God we can look on the whole of the world with conciliatory eyes; not in mere resignation and not with aggression but circumspectly and in the full light of day. We know that the power of evil has been crushed and that God's power is greater; thus we can live in the Spirit of Jesus Christ.

This 'new Life', given to us in baptism, has a very clear *object*. The creed expresses it thus: the *'resurrection of the dead and life everlasting'*.

An Easter hymn shows the connection between resurrection, baptism and life in Christ:
The day of resurrection!
Earth, tell it out abroad;
the Passover of gladness,
the Passover of God!
From death to life eternal,
from earth unto the sky,
our Christ has brought us over
with hymns of victory.   *St John of Damascus;*
                    translated by *J. M. Neale*

Justification: A theological concept, especially in Paul's letters: everyone is under pressure to prove that he is 'good' and to show himself as positive; he looks for recognition, love and justification through his achievements and his actions. To this end he often does harm by overtaxing himself and others. However, the one who believes finds recognition and justification not in what he does but in the grace God wills to give him in Jesus Christ. The Council of Trent says (1563): 'Faith is the beginning of salvation for man, the foundation and root of all justification'. It is God who justifies us through the gift of faith, and indeed *gratis*, out of pure love, without any 'payment in advance' from us. It is part and parcel of faith in justification through God that man gives up all opposition to God's goodness; that he is prepared to accept God's gift in his word and in the signs of salvation (→ 26.3 Sacraments).

New life: This is how the early Christians tried to express their experience of a life of faith; related to: kingdom of God, salvation, grace. The expression can also indicate the final life of the resurrection, or our life on earth as transformed by faith and baptism, or, because of one's faith, a different outlook on life.

22.4 God's love in the Holy Spirit

→ 28.1 new life; 19.3 the Holy Spirit at work; 35.1 God loves us first

'Grace and peace be with you!' — this is the way many letters in the New Testament begin. The authors do not wish their listeners or readers something special which man may accept or not. They express once and for all the relationship, through Jesus Christ, between God and man: God turned in love towards man; Jesus Christ has revealed this. The person who does not close himself to *God's love* has experience of it 'in the Holy Spirit': those who believe are new men, *children of God*, members of Christ's body; they share in the life given by God; as the Bible says, they have received 'grace' (1 Peter 2:10).

In the Bible 'grace' has many meanings: God is merciful and he forgives; this is his response to our *sin*. God takes the initiative, he turns towards us without previous efforts on our part. God so works in us that we let ourselves be loved and transformed. We move out of the devil's sphere of achievement and counter-achievement. We become active in the way God wants. Grace is new life.

The love of God is available for each and all completely. His *Holy Spirit* leads us out of our isolation; he gathers us together; we become a community in the *Church*. However, *God's love* is not at work in a dream world; it is interwoven with the whole of reality; it is met with in people, in everyday things and situations, sometimes in seemingly unlikely events and meetings. But God's love shines out above all in the community that is the Church and especially in the *Sacraments*. They are signs of his love that speak to us, visible signs of his grace.

God's love in the Holy Spirit is the reason why Christians praise him:
Praise to the Father most gracious, the Lord of creation!
Praise to his Son, the Redeemer, who wrought our salvation!
   O heavenly Dove,
   praise to thee, fruit of their love,
Giver of all consolation!   *James Quinn, SJ*

Grace (Lat. gratia): A keyword in the New Testament; it means God's love for us. The Old Testament too is permeated with wonder at the goodness, the grace of God (Exodus 34:6; Deuteronomy 7:7; 9:4); the psalms are in many ways hymns of thanksgiving for God's grace (e.g. Psalm 36; 63; 136). The salvation that came with Jesus is simply the gift of God's grace; it is given 'gratis' (i.e. without previous efforts on our part). God's grace makes man just before God and men and gives him a new life which endures (Romans 6:23). Because the fullness of grace given by God is so great, theologians distinguish different kinds of grace (e.g. helping, sanctifying). The well-wishing is not only on God's part, but is expressed in what is going on in man (e.g. being a child of God, sanctification). In such distinctions we must beware of the danger of speaking of God's love as a 'thing'. It is primarily God giving himself to us as a gift, and secondarily the change in ourselves — our character, actions, attitudes, etc. — brought about by this presence of God within us. At the time of the Reformation Protestants had a 'war-cry' 'sola gratia' (= 'by grace alone'). They wished to emphasise that man's good works are only the fruit of God's grace. Nowadays this is no longer a bone of contention between the churches (→ 33.1 charism).

23   The resurrection of the body

→ 16.4 basis of our faith; 12.1 the world

The fact that human beings themselves do harm to life on this earth has only recently been recognised. To understand this we have only to think of atomic warfare, the increasing pollution and poisoning of air and water, interference with the balance of nature, the ruthless consumption and misuse of the resources of our earth — these are crucial matters.

In view of these problems, which concern the *survival* of mankind, the statement 'I believe in the *resurrection of the dead*' may look like escapism. 'Leave the dead alone and give this life a chance' is what non-Christians may well say to Christians. And *Christians* too must ask themselves what faith in this *truth* does in fact mean for them. What do they answer when people question them at an open grave? Do they really live according to this truth? Can they cope with death better than people who do not believe in the resurrection? Is there a reality to correspond with their faith? Is it more than an old-fashioned metaphor for the uncertain *hope* that 'somehow' perhaps all is not over at death? And what does this truth mean for the here and now? For the after-life of mankind?

23.1 In the sign of 'finiteness'

→ 12.3 God's creature; 31.3 Christian death; 10.1 questions

Human beings bear within themselves the sign of an end. They must pass away. Sickness and *death* are painful signs of this. Man is not his own master. Jews and Christians say that man is a *creature*; someone else is his creator. Man is a finite being. Therefore he is not self-sufficient; he is obliged to receive fulfilment at the hands of another who is unending life.

It is true that people make great efforts to improve the quality of their lives so that they may have a better life and live longer; but increasingly they experience in these efforts that life on this earth is not *perfect*; it is threatened in many ways. One's sphere of life is limited; one person's desires stand in the way of those of others. And not only this. Everyone experiences sickness and increasing frailty. As a person grows older he feels the weakening of his powers, he stands *helpless* before deterioration and decay. All these are sure signs of his *finiteness*. From the beginning life goes on its way towards death.

Mankind has never as yet succeeded in coming to terms with

this knowledge. Myths and fairy stories dream of people who outwit death. In the most varied ways, in different religions, the continuance of life, new life, *immortality* is expressed. Legendary figures seek for herbs capable of making them immortal. Are these only pious wishes?

In Scripture the word *'life'* becomes a fascinating keyword. The life given by God puts an end to finiteness. God presents mortal man with *immortal* life. He has a 'burning desire' to do this.

There is a hymn which expresses what man feels:
From the deep I lift my voice,
hear my cry, O God;
listen, Lord, to my appeal,
none but you can help.
Night and day my spirit waits,
longs to see my God,
like a watchman, weary, cold,
waiting for the dawn.   *Luke Connaughton*

Immortality of the soul: The immortality of the soul appears in the Greek, Egyptian and Iranian religions and in the Greek philosopher Plato. The Bible, above all the New Testament, says more: it speaks of eternal life for the *whole* man. In order to indicate the interim condition of man between his death and the resurrection promised on the last day, the Church adopted the expression 'immortality of the soul'. It is well-nigh impossible to find a better expression. The Fifth Lateran Council (1512–17) stressed this idea in order to explain the unique character of each individual and to emphasise that man is more than mere matter. But it is important for the faith of the Christian that complete salvation should include the *whole* person, and this is sometimes indicated by stressing that, since the human soul is intrinsically orientated towards giving life to a human body, the immortality of the soul implies the resurrection of the body.

Finiteness: A theological expression of the fact that everything created has an existence limited in one or more dimensions and is, to that extent, imperfect.

Myth (Gr. = story): Statements about the origin of the world, of the gods, of heroes used to express fundamental concepts and problems of certain nations and cultures.

23.2 Faith gives courage

→ 16.1 risen; 16.2 power of death; 10.4 I believe; 21.1 metaphors for eternal life

The *hope* of human beings to survive death is almost as great as their *fear* of death. This is surely inherent in life. Why do people defend themselves against death? They obviously feel it is something that should not be, and they refuse simply to subordinate their life to the law of 'death and new life' which they find so natural in plants and animals.

Christian *faith* in the *resurrection* of the dead is an answer to this puzzling longing of man for a life that will never end. This faith, however, does not result from long philosophical reflection, but grows out of trust that God will not allow man to go under in death. This hope finds confirmation in an event: the *resurrection of Jesus*. It is at the same time an indication as to how one should *not* describe the resurrection of the dead.

Resurrection does not mean returning to an earthly existence, as if the one awakened to life 'somehow or other' lives on as he lived before. Nor does resurrection mean a 'return of the immortal soul to God' comparable with the waves flowing back into the sea.

The *Easter witnesses* in the New Testament help us further in this matter. They speak of the body of Jesus bearing the marks of his wounds; they tell us how the risen Lord ate and drank, how he came and went. They are trying to say that the same person who died on the cross is alive, and that there is continuity between the body his disciples had known in the years of his ministry, that seen on the days after the resurrection, and now that of the ascended Christ. The Bible speaks too of '*glorified*'; this means a body freed from its transitory quality, a body in which God's life shines forth.

Although our words fail and biblical pictures should not be taken 'literally', many artists have expressed their faith in pictorial form, showing the dead rising from their grave on the last day. These *pictures* explain our *faith* as saying: the whole of our corporal, mortal life will be preserved and pass as everlasting into God's '*new creation*'.

Paul explains the resurrection of the dead to the Corinthians by using the image of corn: 'The thing that is sown is perishable, but what is raised is imperishable . . . when it is sown it embodies the soul, when it is raised, it embodies the spirit' (1 Corinthians 15:42, 44).

Christ's resurrection is described by a Latin writer about the year 800:
By these same scars his men
beheld the very body that they knew. . . .
They knew their Master risen, and unfurled
the hope of resurrection through the world.
By these same scars, in prayer for all mankind,
before his Father's face
he pleads our wounds within his mortal flesh . . .
> *Theodulf of Orleans,*
> translated by *Helen Waddell*

23.3   Life in the sign of hope

→ 37.3 taking the world seriously; 1.5 through the eyes of Jesus; 24.2 the last days; 31.2 anointing of the sick

Perhaps there are people who think that, if someone believes in the *completion* of his life in the *resurrection*, the *suffering* and distress he sees in this world do not matter. This thought would be correct only if this earthly life had nothing to do with the 'new life'. But faith in God's new creation, in the 'corporal aspect' of the resurrection, expresses great *hope*: this passing world will be transformed into the future world, it is already in process of becoming God's new world. Therefore, when Christians with all men of good-will struggle for a more just world, they do this not merely for moral reasons binding on Christians too, but because they hope in the transformation of the world, the resurrection. Therefore they try to fashion this world, at least in some respects, according to God's promises; for they know the *validity* of what is lived and brought about here; nothing that happens is in vain before God. Christians do not act as if they relied on their own strength; they know their weakness, but they are resigned and do not despair when, for example, in their struggle against dangerous illnesses, they come to realise: we can do no more. They manage to live with the *limitations* of their earthly existence and to endure them. They can be at peace and yet with all their strength try to stem the tide of suffering and meaninglessness. This is different from closing one's eyes to the misery of the world and acting as if it were not there.

The man who believes sees reality as it is. But he hopes that what man cannot *complete* will be brought by God to a fitting end. His efforts are a vivid, courageous *belief* in the fact that God will fulfil his *promises*.

We pray for strength to act rightly:
Lord, open my eyes to see the needs of others;
open my ears to hear their cries;
open my heart so that they may not be left without help.
From the German prayer book *Gotteslob*

Transformation of the world: The transformation of the world awaited by Christians means no annihilation of the old. The Bible speaks of 'glorification' and 'new creation'. Paul uses a metaphor for this: the seed becomes a tree; seed and tree are, in a way, identical, yet different in form (cf. 1 Corinthians 15:42–44).

24 And life everlasting

→ 29 do the same

No one can live without thinking of the *future* — immediate, or final. Freedom, progress, *hope*, are all geared to the future. There is a future which man in his planning can prepare and shape; this is the work of scientists, politicians, poets, visionaries and 'soothsayers'. But the strange thing is that the more man has the future 'within his grasp', the more do fresh and weightier problems appear; man cannot overlook the fact that 'future' is always what human beings cannot plan and carry out: it is something that *happens to him*.

The end of the creed deals with this kind of future. What is said of the *working of the Spirit* is summarised and concluded with the short statement: I believe in *life everlasting*. Is this the Christian expectation of the future? Or can we say that whoever belongs to the Church has eternal life? Or does eternal life begin only after death, with the 'resurrection from the dead'? If this is so, is this sentence in the creed, as far as content is concerned, mere repetition of what has already been said?

Expectation for the future: In addition to its meaning in everyday speech, the future has, for Christians, another dimension: here we do not mean what we can control by our planning; the future is — from a Christian viewpoint — first and foremost what comes to us from God, whatever part of God's plans for the end of the world is already brought about in this world and — only partially — what can be effected by human beings. All this is for the Christian a preview of the new creation, of the end of the world to be brought about by God.

24.1 Metaphors for eternal life
→ 17.2 glory of the Father; 18.2 judge the world; 23.2 faith gives courage

The Old and New Testaments often speak of the coming of the *kingdom of God*, of life with the Father, of *eternal life*. Even Jesus has spoken only in metaphors of what it is and what it will be like 'there'. This need not be a disadvantage: where a reality is so great that it surpasses our understanding, it has to be described in metaphors. It is true that metaphors do not convey the reality itself but they can say something significant about that reality.

In the *Bible* there are several *metaphors* concerned with the *judgement*. Here again, in what concerns Jesus Christ, people go their different ways. Allusions to suffering are included in the statements about eternal life; they warn us to be *on the watch* (Mark 13:35). There is mention of harvest and winepress (Joel 4:12–15; Revelation 14:15–20), of natural catastrophes, wars, persecution (Joel 2:1–11; Mark 13:3–8). These will come as a thief in the night (1 Thessalonians 2:5), i.e. there is no last respite: it is now — and always — necessary to be ready (Matthew 24:43). These metaphors tell us that eternal life is a gift and yet man can freely decide whether he wishes to accept it.

With this possibility of a *decision* for God there is also the possibility that we can exclude ourselves completely from God's will and therefore exclude ourselves irrevocably from union with God. The following metaphors refer to a decision of this kind:

hell-fire (Matthew 25:41) and darkness (Matthew 22:13), wailing and gnashing of teeth (Zephaniah 1:14–18; Matthew 8:12).

The Church's teaching on *purgatory* is not proved directly from the Bible, but it is communicated to us by certain hints in the Bible. In metaphorical statement the conviction of the Church is expressed that even for people who were in no way 'saints', but who died fundamentally open to God, there is the possibility of purification after death. So the word 'purgatory' means something completely different from the word 'hell-fire'. In explaining words and metaphors such as these we quickly realise the limitations of our language. It is hard to speak of them and at the same time avoid inadequate statements.

Other images in the Bible speak of eternal life itself; the images of the end are similar to those of the beginning: a *'paradise'* of unending *joy* and of nearness to God that is taken for granted, with springs of water in abundance — the essence of life for one dwelling in the desert (Revelation 22:1–2). It is a 'place' of *peace*; lamb and wolf lie down together (Isaiah 11:6); babes play near a viper's nest (Isaiah 11:8), swords are beaten into ploughshares (Isaiah 2:4). It is like a joyful feast, a feast of *reconciliation* (Isaiah 55:1–3; Luke 15:32), a *new creation* (Isaiah 35:1–9; Revelation 21:5), a city, the heavenly Jerusalem (Revelation 21:10): the beauty and security of this life are portrayed in rich colours. The centre of this beautiful city is God himself; he is their light (Revelation 21:23); he will wipe away all tears; there will be no more sorrow, no suffering, *no death*. For the old world has passed away (Revelation 21:4), the *new world* is complete.

The Second Vatican Council summarises some of the biblical statements:
We are taught that God is preparing a new dwelling place and a new earth where justice will abide, and whose blessedness will answer and surpass all the longings for peace which spring up in the human heart.
The Church in the Modern World, para. 39

Paradise: The word stems from the Greek translation of the Old Testament (the so-called Septuagint) and means 'God's garden'.
Purgatory: → 18.2

24.2　The last days

→ 4.4 glory is revealed; 18.1 Our Lord will come; 35.2 God worthy of our love

It is an ever-recurring subject of surprise that after 2,000 years of Christianity so little change for the better is to be seen in human beings. Therefore even Christians are sometimes tempted to say: *perfection* will come only '*on the other side*', 'in the hereafter'. When no one any longer sins, when all obstacles and dangers in people's lives are overcome, there will be perfection, for then *eternal life* will have dawned and the new world will have come into being. Yet God's Spirit does not allow any today or tomorrow, any here or there to be thrust upon him by human beings. Always and everywhere, where men do not oppose his working, the beginning of the last days is present. What in the eyes of man grows only very slowly, what is repeatedly affected adversely by serious setbacks, is already in existence for God. God has already brought perfection wherever man uses his best efforts. Therefore the gospel says: 'The *kingdom of God* is (already) among you' (cf. Luke 17:21).

This does not in any way mean that in the last analysis nothing depends on our actions — on the contrary. We live in time and it depends on us whether something of the kingdom of God is already visible among us. In the last days too we should not think of this kingdom only as the action of God coming upon us like a gift from a distant planet. The kingdom is already '*among us*', God brings it about and he wants our collaboration.

When we believe in 'the resurrection from the dead' we mean that what we do in the Spirit of Jesus will rise again with us as our new 'body' and take on a form that is lasting. In other words: Christians believe that all the good that happens here is not lost, but accompanies us into *God's new creation* when he comes to bring the world to perfection. The Revelation of John says: 'their good deeds go with them' (Revelation 14:13). What God has prepared for those who love him will surpass all our imagining. Perhaps the metaphor of the wedding feast best describes the unending *joy* of the *communion of saints* (Isaiah 25:6-9; Revelation 19:7-9).

> Jesus was asked by the Pharisees when the kingdom of God would come and he answered:
> **The coming of the kingdom of God does not admit of observation and there will be no one to say, 'Look here! Look there!' For, you must know, the kingdom of God is among you.**
> *Luke 17:20–21*

'**The other side**': This expression has become customary for the 'place' where the righteous go after death; often the expression means 'beyond this world', i.e. the world that will dawn at the last day. This concept leads to the misunderstanding that 'the other side' has little to do with 'this side'; for Christians there is only one reality of God and it already extends into our world. It is visible in Jesus Christ and in those who believe in him. But we see only in 'dim reflections' and as 'in a mirror'. Seeing 'face to face' is something for the future (cf. 1 Corinthians 13:12).

25 Amen

→ 10 I believe in God

The creed is a hymn in praise of God: we thank him as our Father for all that we are and all that we have; in Jesus Christ he has given the world *salvation* and *peace*: in the working of his Spirit he urges us to pass on by word and deed his kindness to us human beings. The creed is enclosed, as it were, by the words '*I believe*' and '*Amen*'. It cannot be recited without expressing trust in God's relationship with man and without a strengthening of our own life. It is this trust in the living and life-giving God that we express by 'Amen', the last word of the creed.

The basis of the creed is the *baptismal profession of faith*. The person who confesses belief in God: the Father, his Son Jesus Christ, and the Holy Spirit can be baptised. And he is baptised 'in the name of the Father and of the Son and of the Holy Spirit' — the fulness of salvation which God has prepared for man is promised to the one baptised.

When Catholics make the sign of the *cross*, they say the same words. They are absolved from their sins in the name of the Father, the Son and the Holy Spirit. When Catholics promise one another *fidelity* in the sacrament of matrimony, they do so by professing their *faith* in the Blessed Trinity. At the graveside priests and faithful make the sign of the cross and pronounce the same words.

And yet — when Christians are questioned as to what they mean when they pray 'in the name of the Father and of the Son and of the Holy Spirit' — who does not begin to falter?

Baptismal profession of faith: The form of the creed is easily recognised in the questions asked at baptism (cf. the rite of baptism).

25.1   God — Father, Son and Holy Spirit

→ 19.2 Holy Spirit — God's Spirit; 10.4 I believe

The Church's teaching on the *Blessed Trinity* appears for many strange and difficult to understand, even for Christians who quite naturally pray 'in the name of the *Father*, the *Son* and the *Holy Spirit*'. The impression may arise that one needs to be very learned to understand this Christian truth.

Faith in the Blessed Trinity is not the outcome of complicated processes of thought. It grows out of one's relationship with Jesus of Nazareth. Jesus Christ is so completely moved by, and at the disposal of God that in him a believer recognises: this man is wholly with God and God with him: this man and God are one. The New Testament speaks of this when the Son says: 'to have seen me is to have seen the Father' (John 14:9), and when the Father says: 'This is my Son, the Beloved' (Matthew 3:17).

Those who have a relationship with Jesus experience something wonderful: *the same God*, who is at work in Jesus, is also at work in his followers. The Spirit of Jesus is the Spirit of God and those who believe in him are filled with the same Spirit. The Holy Spirit is the driving force in the lives of individual believers and in the whole Church.

This force is not something but somebody, a person to whom we can relate. In the Nicene Creed we say: 'We believe in the Holy Spirit . . . with the Father and the Son he is worshipped and glorified'. Jesus calls the Holy Spirit the 'Advocate' whom he will send to his disciples after his glorification (John 14:15; cf. 8:39).

And when the disciples have received the Holy Spirit they begin to preach the *Good News*: about the Father whose love for men is infinite; about the Son who, in the power of this love, sets men free from the power of evil; about the Spirit who dwells in the faithful with the fullness of life of Jesus Christ.

The following conclusion can be drawn from God's action in Jesus Christ and through his Spirit in the faithful, who recognise him as the author of life: God himself is life, a life rich in relationships. Just as God in Jesus Christ and in the faithful reveals himself as unqualified goodness, so is he truly in himself, just as he is present in Jesus Christ for us. We human beings can speak only falteringly of this *greatness of God*.

The second Letter to the Corinthians ends with this prayer:
The grace of the Lord Jesus Christ, the love of God and the fellowship of the Holy Spirit be with you all!
2 Corinthians 13:13

Trinity: The central mystery of the Christian faith is belief in one God in three Persons. The expression 'three-in-one' stresses the unity of the Divine Persons, 'one-in-three' the fact that they are distinct. This belief in a triune God is special to Christianity, and separates Christians from Judaism (and from Islam). Nevertheless, Christians are at one with the Jews and Muslims in their belief that there is only one God. However, the failure of Jews and Muslims to grasp that belief in the Trinity of Persons is not belief in three gods is a challenge to Christians not to make their faith in a triune God into belief in three gods.

Sign of the cross: Since the end of the second century a familiar formula with which to bless oneself or others (and objects too). The relationship between the sign of the cross and belief in the Trinity refers to the connection between the baptismal profession of faith and the rite of baptism. The sign of the cross is made with the right hand, and the Church distinguishes between the 'large' sign of the cross (on forehead, breast and shoulders with outstretched hand; this means: I am completely under the power of the redeemer) and the 'small' sign of the cross (made with thumb only on forehead, mouth and breast which means: God bless my thoughts, words and desires). The words said with the sign of the cross are: 'In the name of the Father and of the Son and of the Holy Spirit. Amen.' Many Christians use this prayer and the sign of the cross when beginning a fresh piece of work or a new day.

Images of the Trinity: An early symbol was a triple monogram of Christ. In the twelfth century the first pictures of Father, Son and Holy Spirit (in the form of a dove) appeared in Ireland. In the Eastern Church the Trinity is often depicted in the form of three angels (cf. Genesis 18:1–33).

25.1

25.2   The known and unknown God

→ 11.2 the great God; 4.1 kingdom of God proclaimed

It is a fact that many people believe in *God*, but for them he is very far away; they cannot imagine that he is concerned with the problems of the world and their own lives. Many accept that God holds the threads of the world's history in his hand, but are insistent that we cannot know how this happens. Others say: God did indeed create the world but since then it is governed by its own laws. Others again are of the opinion that there is something of God to be found in everything in nature.

The *distant God* and the *God near to us* — this remains for us human beings a mystery. In a mysterious way God is very near, more intimate than we are to ourselves. Paul can say: 'It is in him that we live, and move, and exist' (Acts 17:28). But at the same time God is for us always greater than our understanding, our feelings and our heart. If God had not shared himself with men through *Jesus Christ*, his Son, he would have remained incomprehensibly distant. But in Jesus Christ he has come close to man and has made his *love* seen and felt. By the working of his *Spirit* he stimulates the faithful. For the person who believes a way has been opened for him to meet his God.

And yet God remains a mystery — and this is something different from a problem. We can find a solution for the latter, the former remains. People who love one another, for example, come ever closer to each other, but they experience that their love remains all the more mysterious. So it is with the love of God. It is clearly seen in Jesus Christ and in his followers, and yet it is an inexhaustible mystery. God is open and approachable — but as the hidden one. More we cannot say.

Therefore, no matter how much we speak about God, words in the end fail us — fail to express the mystery with which we are dealing. Even a person very closely united with *God* realises that he soon comes to the end of his reflection and meditation, that he must be silent in *adoration of God's greatness*.

> One who prays, trusts God and honours him; this is why
> many prayers end with praise:
> **Glory be to the Father and to the Son and to the Holy Spirit,
> as it was in the beginning, is now and ever shall be, world
> without end. Amen.**

Mystery (Gr. = secret). Something that takes place in faith, through which we experience healing and salvation; it surpasses man's thought and planning and at the same time fulfils his deepest longing (→ 4.1).

Amen: With this Hebrew word the faithful confirm that they want to 'establish their lives wholly in God'. It is not just a pious wish: 'so be it', but a firm belief that 'it really is so'; 'we are convinced that it is so'. In the Old as in the New Testament the word is customary in the liturgy of the Church and in the prayers of Jews and Christians. 'Amen' is the expression of a firm faith that God will fulfil his promises. When Jesus wants to underline with special emphasis what he is saying, he begins with 'Amen' (Matthew 5:18-26; 6:2-5). Jesus himself is called 'the Amen' (Revelation 3:14) because he is the 'faithful and trustworthy witness' of God. Paul says of Christ: 'However many the promises God made, the "Yes" to them all is in him. That is why it is through him that we answer "Amen" to the praise of God' (2 Corinthians 1:20).

Part III : Church and Sacraments

The Church celebrates seven Sacraments:
Baptism, Confirmation, Eucharist,
Penance, Anointing of the Sick,
Holy Orders and Matrimony.

The fundamentals of the Christian life
are laid by the reception
of the first three Sacraments.

Introduction

Christians naturally tend to talk about the *Our Father* and the *Creed* when they want to justify what they believe; it is important that they should also speak of the *daily practice of their lives* as Christians. For the Christian faith is more than teaching truths about God and man. It is a specific way of life and view of the world. It is a particular attitude to personal and social matters; it is living out the Christian life as a member of the Church.

Living one's life and seeing the world from a Christian viewpoint is not a private affair. In the Our Father we pray to God as 'our Father', as Father of all the faithful, indeed of all men. It is a question of his kingdom, his rule, his goodness to all. The creed is not first and foremost a private *witness*; it is the expression and practice of the faith of all Christians, that is, of the *community of the faithful*, the *Church* and *life in a Christian community*. The practice of the Christian life takes place in a community and is intended to promote the well-being and salvation of all men.

In the community of the faithful the working of God's Spirit becomes visible in the world in a special way: through the centuries the reason for the coming of Jesus and for his death is present in this community, though in veiled fashion; *God's kingdom* is in process of 'coming'; God is present and comes in Jesus Christ and in *his followers*. Christians are 'on the way' to a life where God will be all in all. *The sign of this salvation* is the church; she is for Christians a special place where God's closeness to us is experienced 'for ourselves and for our salvation'. She is the *'sacrament'* of the union of mankind with God and with one another; that is, she is an advance sign *indicating the world to come*, a sign in which this 'coming' is already at work.

The fact that the community of the faithful is a central and all-embracing sign of salvation can become visible if the faithful live according to the gospel. It can become obvious in what the Church is doing. It is experienced where Christians show and celebrate, in perceptible signs, their relationship with God, that is, in the Sacraments, especially in the *Eucharist* and *baptism*. Specific mention of these two sacraments is therefore made in the creed when we reflect on the communion of saints and the forgiveness of sins.

26 Sign of salvation

→ 21 communion of saints; 22 forgiveness of sins

The Church is a believing community professing its faith. We can also say she is a community that 'recounts', for she preserves and passes on what has been entrusted to her. Since *faith* comes from *hearing* (Romans 10:17), this is first of all expressed in response to the profession of faith and in thanksgiving.

Yet faith does not depend only on words. As words do not suffice to explain the most important things in life, so too *signs* and *gestures* are needed for the expression of our faith. The most important forms of this expression are the sacraments. They are more than mere outward forms, they are signs which show the reality of what we are talking about. Christians believe that the Church herself is a *sign* for the truth that, with Jesus Christ, the 'new time' has begun, during which God's world is in 'process of coming'.

These are big words. Can Christians who are familiar with the *Church* in the concrete take them seriously? Isn't the Christian community more often a sign of sin in the world? Can the *love of God*, shown in Jesus Christ, be experienced in the community of the Church? How can the Church become for the world a *sign of salvation*?

26.1 A sign of salvation for the nations

→ 10.2 all nations; 34.1 the people of God; 20.2 tradition; 21.3 community of holiness; 20.5 I believe in the Church

The Israelites, Yahweh's chosen people, were continually in danger of restricting the choice exclusively to themselves, in spite of the words spoken to Abraham concerning his vocation: 'All the tribes of the earth shall bless themselves by you' (Genesis 12:3). Israel was not chosen for its own sake — it was to give *witness* to the other nations of Yahweh's greatness and *fidelity* so that they might come to know who God is.

Even the early Christians had to come to terms with the question whether *Jesus* had come only for the people of Israel or whether he was proclaiming *salvation* for all. Many letters in the New Testament, especially that to the Romans, many places in the gospels (Mark 7:24–30) and some passages in the Acts (10:1–48 and 15:1–35) tell us of the discussions the early Church had to cope with before arriving at the conclusion that the Church as the 'new people of Israel' is open to all, Jews and pagans. She is called together from all *nations*.

A person to whom salvation comes through Jesus cannot keep it for himself. An insight into what Jesus has brought stimulates him to pass on this gift to all. Everyone is to experience what God has done, through Jesus, for the world.

By *words* and the *testimony* of their lives Christians down to the present day try to tell others of God's love and enable them to experience it. They show concern for the poor, the sick and the hungry; they talk to people of their queries and their troubles. They instruct those who have come to believe and baptise them. They live simply with them, sharing the lives of others and thus witnessing to their Lord who, throughout his life and after, is present for others.

Thus new *communities* or *parishes* come into being; the *Church* grows among all nations. She is, as it were, in Christ, the Sacrament, that is, the effective sign for God's union with mankind and for the unity of all mankind; each and every nation must experience, through her, that God wills salvation for everyone. That is why the Second Vatican Council calls the Church the 'all-embracing sign of salvation for the world'.

The whole people of God is charged with sharing the Church's mission:
But you are a chosen race, a royal priesthood, a consecrated nation, a people set apart to sing the praises of God who called you out of the darkness into his wonderful light.
1 Peter 2:9

Mission (Lat. missio = sending): The derivative of the corresponding Greek word is *apostolate* (→ 33.1). — All the faithful are commissioned to pass on to others the Good News of God's truth which they themselves have received. The Second Vatican Council says (1965); 'As members of the living Christ, all the faithful have been incorporated into him and made like unto him through baptism, confirmation, and the Eucharist. Hence all are duty-bound to co-operate in the expansion and growth of his body, so that they can bring it to fullness as swiftly as possible' (*Missionary Activity in the Church*, para. 36).

Mission in a more restricted sense means passing on the message to other countries (*'foreign' missions*).

Missionary: A Christian who proclaims the gospel to non-Christians in a foreign country; often used in a narrower sense: missionary = member of a religious congregation active in missionary work. The word is increasingly used to describe the spirit of people who desire to share the treasures of the faith with others — even in their own country.

Missionary methods: In the course of history these have changed to correspond with general ideas about religion, faith, freedom, etc. Problems arise because of identification with certain aspects of Western culture; intolerance, on the part of missionaries, of local cultures and religious practices; and a compulsion to make converts indiscriminately.

Parish Mission: Arrangements made in a parish to strengthen and renew the spiritual life; usually conducted by members of religious orders. Less frequent today in this form.

26.2   Images of the Church

→ 21.1 Church as community; 20.1 work of the Spirit; 13.3 the Lord; 27.4 Christ celebrates with us

In Christian tradition there are many expression and images for the relationship of the Church with her Lord. They are all saying that anyone who contemplates the Church in *faith* comes up against a reality which cannot easily be summarised by concepts. Just as the *people of God* in the Old Testament is called *'holy people'*, so the Church in the Acts is described as *'God's people'* and *'holy priesthood'*, called wholly to God's service (1 Peter 2:9–10).

The Church is also God's *vineyard*. As the vinedresser tends a vine so that it may bear fruit, so God cares for his Church (Isaiah 5:1–4; John 15:1–5). As the *Temple* was built of many stones, so God builds his Church of 'living stones', the faithful (1 Peter 2:5); but the cornerstone and keystone is Jesus Christ (Matthew 21:42).

The *flock* is another image of the Church; John's gospel speaks of Jesus Christ as the good shepherd. As a shepherd tends his flock and is ready to give his life for it, so Christ is concerned for his Church (John 10:1–18; cf. Ezekiel 34). In the Letter to the

Ephesians the Church is compared to a *bride* (Ephesians 5:26; cf. Hosea 2:18–22). loved by Christ as by a bridegroom (cf. Vatican II document *On the Church*, para. 6).

The early Fathers saw in the Church the *new Eve*, the woman who gives life, the mother of the living (Genesis 3:20), chosen by the 'last Adam' — Christ (cf. 1 Corinthians 15:45). Many Fathers of the Church have described Mary too as the prototype of the Church; she showed what is meant by faith; she lived in complete union with Jesus Christ and was made perfect by him. St Augustine says of Mary, 'In the Spirit she is mother of the members of Christ's body, for by her love she brought it about that the faithful who are members of Christ the Head are born in the Church'. The Letters to the Ephesians, the Colossians and the Corinthians compare the Church with a *body* (1 Corinthians 12:12–31) consisting of many members and a head: Christ (Ephesians 1:22; 4:15; Colossians 1:18). By him all is gathered together and made new. In faith we can describe the close relationship between Christ and his Church by saying that the Eucharist, like the Church, is called the *Body of Christ*. It is in many ways significant that the Church is said to come to her full stature in the celebration of the Eucharist; *Catholics* emphasise that whoever belongs to the Church and is one of her living members, is at the same time even more closely knit with her: he is a member of the body of Christ.

In Christian tradition numerous metaphors are used to describe the nature of the Church: bride, body, organism, new Eve, vineyard — these are all images and signs for a reality which cannot easily be explained — a reality too great for human language to express.

At the beginning of the Letter to the Colossians there is an important hymn about Jesus Christ:
Before anything was created, he existed,
and he holds all things in unity.
Now the Church is his body,
he is its head.   *Colossians 1:17–18*

26.3 Church as sacrament

→ 20 Catholic Church; 21 communion of saints; 13.1 Christ; 4.2 kingdom of God in parables

By the word 'Church' many understand first and foremost a huge organisation with its own buildings, administration, laws, funds and investments; they think of power and authority, officials and solemn festivities. True, there is all this and the Church cannot exist without these things; but it is not the whole Church. She is more than an institution.

The truth about the Church can be learnt only through Jesus Christ. He proclaimed the kingdom of God. It is for the sake of this kingdom that he gathers people around him, heals the sick, drives out demons, eats with sinners, instructs his disciples and sends them out so that many more people may be drawn to him. This is the beginning of the Church. She is wholly at the service of the *kingdom of God* that he proclaimed. When Jesus Christ comes again at the end of time and the kingdom of God is complete, the Church will no longer be needed. But until that time the Church, in the name of Jesus, continues what he began. He commissioned and instructed her and promised her his support. His *Holy Spirit* fills her with life. Jesus Christ continues to live and work in the Church so that God's kingship and his kingdom may become visible and reach their appointed goal.

Just as Jesus by his *words and deeds* enabled the people of his time to hear and see God's will for their salvation, so the Church commissioned by Jesus Christ must do the same through the ages. The Church is the *sign of the community of salvation* which God, through Jesus Christ and with human collaboration, has established, the *effective sign* of his *nearness*; through her God is brought close to man. This is why the Church is the *fundamental sacrament* of God's love for man. Only a person who sees this relationship between Christ and the Church can understand what Catholics believe: that in the Church we can still see, hear and understand Jesus Christ.

Side by side with the *preaching of the gospel* and *fraternal service*, this is brought about above all in the Church's *sacraments*. They are effective, symbolic actions showing what God does for us through Jesus Christ. The sacraments convey in detail what the Church is as a whole: union with God. The forms

26.3   **158**

of organisation in the Church — in which the message of God's kingdom can easily be lost sight of — must repeatedly be checked, from the point of view of this centre, with reference to their commission and their service in it.

The Second Vatican Council says of the Church:
The Church is a kind of sacrament or sign of intimate union with God, and of the unity of all mankind.
Constitution on the Church, para. 1

Sacrament (from Lat. sacramentum = a firm sealing), usually a translation of Gr. 'mysterium': theologians say that Jesus Christ is the basic sacrament of God's love for man; this means: he preaches it (word), he puts it into practice (actions) and he himself is it (effect). In the same sense the Church is sacrament (and therefore theologians speak of the fundamental sacrament); this means that the Church is commissioned to preach God's love for men, to practise it and to make it effective. This is developed in special, symbolic actions, the sacraments, which enable us to see, hear and understand how God loves us through Christ.

Symbol (Gr. = sign): A sign that points to something else. Pictures, gestures, actions can become symbols. The most important concrete Christian symbol is the cross.

Sacramentals: Actions used in *blessings* which have long been customary in the Church; similar to the sacraments. They are 'sacred signs' by which, in a kind of imitation of the sacraments, effects — spiritual effects — are indicated and obtained through the intercession of the Church (Vatican II, *Constitution on the Liturgy*, para. 60). The word 'blessing' is used of a person (e.g. the Abbess of a monastery) or an object (e.g. church bells) to be devoted wholly to God's service; sometimes 'blessing' means that God's favour is invoked on people (e.g. children) or things (someone's home).

26.4   The sacraments of the Church
→ 21.3 communion of saints; 22.4 God's love

Through the sacraments of the Church we can see, hear and understand what is meant by God's *union* with man for his salvation. The sacraments are rooted in *Jesus Christ*, in his life, death and resurrection, for he is the incarnate *love of God* for man. Pope Leo the Great (d. 461) says: 'Everything that could be seen, heard and understood in the saving event of Jesus Christ is effective later in the sacraments of the Church.'

This is particularly obvious in the *Eucharist*: it not only promises union between God and man but effects it; in the Eucharist new life is not merely a matter of words, Jesus Christ actually gives himself to us for new life. The same can be said of all the sacraments. God effects through them what is said and indicated.

The sacraments have reference to the course of human life. At the climaxes and turning-points of man's life the Church effectively promises him, in the name of Jesus Christ, God's love and salvation, his grace, and she shows through these *symbolic actions* how much God is concerned for human beings. At the beginning of our lives, in *baptism*, union with Jesus Christ and with all our fellow human beings is effectively promised to us. In *confirmation* what began in baptism is ratified by our being strengthened through the Holy Spirit: living as a Christian. There is therefore a close connection between baptism and confirmation.

Even when we are at fault we are not without a sign of God's nearness. In the *sacrament of penance* God offers us reconciliation and again grants us his forgiveness.

When we are seriously ill, courage and hope for salvation in God and his mercy are promised us and given to us in the *sacrament of the sick*.

When someone is commissioned for special service in the Church as deacon, priest or bishop, this charge is mediated to him through the sacrament of *Holy Orders*.

In the *sacrament of matrimony* the bridal couple are promised that God's love will be effective in their reciprocal love for one another. Their union in marriage becomes a sign of the union given by God.

Thus the sacraments show God's loving intention to form a loving community in a way that both our bodies and our minds can experience.

A German textbook for religious lessons says of the sacraments:
They do not merely point to new life, they give it to us.
They do not merely speak of our redemption, they give us redemption.
They do not merely speak of the nearness of the Lord,
he is with us in the sacraments.

Number of sacraments: Reflection about the distinction between sacraments and sacramentals first took place in the Middle Ages (twelfth century), and agreement was reached concerning the number of sacraments. This does not mean that there have been seven sacraments 'only since the twelfth century'; before that time, no accurate distinction was made between sacraments and sacramentals, though both were administered. The Council of Trent (1545–63) — in response to disputes with the Reformers — made the number of seven sacraments binding on all Catholics.

Sacraments in other churches: There is no unified teaching about the number; baptism and Holy Communion (or the Last Supper) and penance (with certain restrictions) are not disputed. According to the conviction of the Reformed churches the sacraments are effective only through faith.

Theological virtues: Faith, hope and charity. They are called theological because they are caused by God himself and have God as their object. They cannot be acquired by man's efforts, but are a gift from God 'poured into our hearts' (cf. Romans 5:5).

27 Centre of the Church's life: the Eucharist

→ 21.3 communion of saints; 27.1 the Church preaches God's message

People on their way to the celebration of the Eucharist say they are 'going to church'. This is not as inaccurate as it might seem, for the Church is, in fact, a reality at the *celebration of the Eucharist* as she is nowhere else. Here the *Christian community* recalls its past, reflects on its present mission and looks forward to its future destiny. In the Eucharist is revealed God's goodwill as it comes to light through Jesus Christ (Titus 3:4). *Thanksgiving, praise of God*, petition and contrition run through the celebration like the themes of a musical composition.

A person who, for the first time, takes part in such a *celebration* will not readily understand the sequence of events, actions and prayers of the Mass; an introduction to the sacred mysteries is needed. In earlier times this was more difficult because, until 1963, the Mass in all Roman Catholic parishes throughout the world was celebrated in Latin.

Why is the Mass so important? Why can it be called the centre of the Church's life? Since when has the Eucharist been celebrated? Did Jesus celebrate it too?

Reform of the Liturgy: The manner of celebrating Mass in the Church — the prayers, texts and books used — are uniformly prescribed in detail in the Catholic Church. After the Council of Trent (1545-63) the Latin Missal (with the exception of Holy Week) was not changed until the liturgical reform of the Second Vatican Council (1962-65). Since then the Missal has been translated into countless languages, and the choice of biblical texts to be read at the Eucharist has been considerably extended — However, Latin remains the official Church language for the universal church, especially at international level.

Missal: The prescribed liturgical book for the celebration of the Eucharist. There are editions for the use of the faithful (Sunday missals, weekday missals, Mass leaflets or missalettes, etc.).

27.1   The Church preaches God's message

→ 20.3 the Church's book; 1.4 reading the Bible; 9.4 kinds of prayer; 4.1 God's kingdom proclaimed

Christians do not cease to talk about their faith. They put into words *God's mighty deeds* so that, in gratitude, they may pass them on to others. A particularly important place where Christians preach God's message is at the celebration of the Eucharist, or Mass as it is often called. It is the great thanksgiving for everything that God has done through Jesus Christ.

The *celebration of the Eucharist* has a long history. Forms and texts have their roots in pre-Christian Jewish times. Above all the form of the *Liturgy of the Word* goes back to the Jewish Sabbath service. The Liturgy of the Word is preceded by a greeting given to the congregation and a general acknowledgement of sin.

The Kyrie and Gloria, the Opening Prayer (Collect) for the day, congregational prayer and singing, form the content of the Liturgy of the Word. The central focus is on the *readings* from the Bible. The first — sometimes the second too — is taken from the Old Testament, the Acts of the Apostles or a Letter from one of the apostles; these readings are also called *lessons*. The last reading is always a passage from one of the *four gospels*. On feast-days the gospel, as this last reading is called, is sometimes sung.

Because the congregation believes that Christ is present in his word, the people stand for the reading of the gospel, and acclaim: 'Glory to you, Lord'; at the end, the priest kisses the book. On feast-days the book of the gospel is accompanied to the lectern

27.1   **162**

with candles and incense. Some of the gospel books are illustrated with valuable illuminations and miniatures. The respect shown for this book is appropriate because of the Person whose word is proclaimed in it.

But the *word of God* is not only the object of a Christian's respect, it is of great importance to him: head, heart and mouth of every Christian should be influenced by it. This is the reason for the sign of the cross with which the faithful sign themselves at the beginning of the gospel.

The *sermon* or *homily* is intended to make the word of God appropriate in our times, to explain it and apply it to our own lives. So the Church hands on what the Bible tells of those who have preceded us and experienced *God's nearness*. In this way we enter into the vast community of those who tell of God's mighty deeds in both Testaments, and who, like us, are believers. We obtain courage, after experiencing God's nearness, to be on the look-out for similar circumstances in our own lives and also to convince non-believers — through our lives and by our words. On Sundays and feast-days, after hearing the word of God and reflecting on the explanation of it, by reciting the *Creed* we profess our faith in God and his saving work.

What is preached in the Liturgy of the Word and handed on serves as a preparation for us to thank, praise and glorify God in the celebration of the Eucharist itself that follows. But first the faithful are reminded that they are part of an immense community where they intercede for one another. In the *bidding prayers* the concerns of the congregation and of the *universal Church*, prayers for those suffering distress, for human troubles and for the salvation of the whole world are offered to God.

The Liturgy of the Word clarifies for us what Jesus meant by the words:
Where two or three meet in my name, I shall be there with them. *Matthew 18:20*

Bible service: Held independently of the Eucharistic celebration. A Scripture reading, or readings, with explanation, forms the centre, and is followed by responsorial singing and prayers.

Eucharist (Gr. = thanksgiving): Name for the whole Mass; in a restricted sense used for the second part of the Mass, where the Eucharistic prayer (or Canon) is the central point. The Canon is a great prayer of thanksgiving for God's working 'through Jesus Christ our Lord'; the word Eucharist is also used for the consecrated bread (host) received and honoured during the celebration (and also outside times of Mass).

Lesson: Description of the reading in the Liturgy of the Word taken from the New Testament Letters, from the Acts or from the Old Testament.

Pericope (Gr. = extract): Passage taken from the Bible. The Catholic Church has made specific arrangements of *pericopes*, i.e. the readings from Scripture, according to the feasts of the liturgical year (in a three-year cycle); these readings are collected in books known as *Lectionaries*. In other Churches there are similar arrangements.

Rite: Regulations according to which a service of a liturgical function (e.g. baptism) is conducted. Through prescribed forms the Church gives her celebrations a definite structure.

Liturgy: All forms of public worship of God or honour of the Saints; e.g. prayers, hymns, celebration of feasts.

27.2 The Church remembers Jesus' Last Supper

→ 16.3 we are redeemed; 15.2 removed by power; 1.3 in the community of the faithful; 20.2 tradition

In the celebration of the Eucharist the Church does what her Lord did on the evening preceding his death. He commissioned her and gave her power to do this: 'Do this in *memory* of me!' (cf. Luke 22:19; 1 Corinthians 11:23–25).

'*Remembering*' or '*memorial*'-is a concept understood by Jews and Christians as more than mere 'not forgetting', more than a happy memory of something in the past, more than something which one is glad to recall. 'Memorial' means that God allows what is past to be *present here and now*, that we are related to that past which is here and now effective. So Jesus' last supper is present in every Eucharistic celebration.

The *congregation* assembles round the table (altar). The leader of the parish, the priest, is also the president at the Eucharist. For the congregation, in the fullness of Christ's power, he says the *eucharistic prayer* with the words that remind us of Jesus' *last supper* with his disciples. Over the bread and wine he pronounces the words spoken by Jesus 'This is my body' — 'this is the cup of my blood' (transubstantiation). The congregation confirms this act of thanksgiving by their 'Amen' and the Our Father. Then priest and congregation receive the consecrated bread, the body of Christ. The congregation assembled round the table of the altar is not only a reminder of the *Last Supper*; here and now it is a community that shares a meal and offers sacrifice with the crucified and risen Lord, and at the same time enjoys a foretaste of the heavenly *wedding banquet*, the feast of everlasting joy, of which Jesus speaks in many of his parables.

Jesus' last supper is not described in detail in the gospels. But we know how the Jewish paschal meal was celebrated. It was a festive meal with bread and wine, singing and prayers, and during it the paschal lamb was eaten. The gospels highlight what is unusual and what is new: when Jesus broke the bread and shared it with his disciples, he said 'Take it; this is *my body*' (Mark 14:22). These are words hitherto unprecedented. As the chalice was passed round he said 'This is *my blood*, the blood of the new and everlasting covenant. It will be shed for you and for all men' (cf. Mark 14:24). With these words Jesus points to his *surrender* to death on the cross. So the Eucharist does not only bring Jesus' last supper into the present; it makes him present, his whole life and his death on the cross 'for all'.

There are four different Eucharistic prayers in the liturgy. However, the words of the priest over the bread and wine are always the same because he says what Jesus himself said:
Take this, all of you, and eat it:
this is my body which will be given up for you.
Take this, all of you, and drink from it:
this is the cup of my blood,
the blood of the new and everlasting covenant.
It will be shed for you and for all men
so that sins may be forgiven.
Do this in memory of me.

Last Supper: Jesus' farewell meal with his disciples on the night before his death. In the Catholic Church the celebration of remembrance of this supper, the Eucharist, is also called *Holy Mass* (Lat. missa = sending). Other Churches use the words 'Lord's Supper' or 'Communion service' or 'Eucharist'.

Manna: According to Exodus 16:4, 15 the 'bread from heaven' for the Israelites on their journey through the desert. Literally a cry of astonishment: Man-hu? ('What is this?'). Edible grains, a secretion of the manna-tamarisk, which look like rice. In the Church the word is also a metaphorical description of Eucharistic bread (→ 6.1).

Pasch: Jewish festival of 'remembrance' (reminder, making present) of the delivery from slavery in Egypt, passing over from slavery to freedom — cf. Christ's passing over from the world to the Father. Date: spring full moon.

Breaking of bread: At the Jewish festival the father of the family breaks the bread in pieces — Jesus did this at the Last Supper. In the early church presumably the whole Eucharistic celebration was described in these words (cf. Acts 2:42). Even today the custom of the breaking of bread in the Eucharist is maintained in a token breaking of the priest's host. The sharing round of fragments of what was previously one piece of bread highlights the one-ness which sharing the Eucharist brings about. What was one is broken in order to bring together the scattered people of God.

Eucharistic prayer: Heart of the Eucharistic celebration; prayer of praise beginning with the Preface and continuing as far as the Our Father. Praise for God's mighty deeds in Jesus Christ.

Transubstantiation: This expression emphasises the words of Jesus 'this is my body', 'this is the cup of my blood', in opposition to all attempts to understand these words as only metaphorical. In the Eucharist, through the power of the words of Jesus and the commission he gave, bread and wine are changed into the body and blood of Christ without any change in their outward form. Here the faithful trust wholly in the words of Jesus. The Council of Trent (1545–63) says on this subject that in the sacrament of the Eucharist, after the consecration, 'Our Lord as true God and truly man is present truly, really and substantially under the form of visible things' (bread and wine).

Communion: That part of the Mass at which the faithful receive the Eucharist. Also a description of the actual food and drink of the Eucharist (to receive 'Communion').

Flesh and blood: In the Bible often found as a formula (e.g. Sirach 17:31 or Matthew 16:17) for the whole earthly 'man' (does not, therefore, mean parts of the body).

Body: As the Bible does not distinguish between body and soul but sees man as an entity that cannot be divided, body means the whole man as he lives and acts. So 'this is my body' means 'this is myself'.

Blood: Means in the Bible, as in almost all religions, 'source of life'. So 'this is my blood' means 'this is my life which will be given for you' — 'this is myself'.

27.3 The Church recalls her Lord's surrender

→ 15 crucified, dead and buried; 22.1 being reconciled; 16.3 we are redeemed; 26.4 sacraments

Jesus devoted his whole life to others. Without showing any concern for himself, and trusting wholly in his *nearness to God*, he was entirely available to others. This surrender also characterises his last meeting with his friends. When he says 'This is my body', he means too: this is *myself* (→ 27.2); I am here *for you* even at the hour of betrayal and suffering, even in death on the cross. Jesus spends himself utterly for God and man. He offers himself in *sacrifice*. When he stretches out his arms on the cross, Christians see in this a sign of his *surrender* and of the helplessness he has freely chosen for himself. In the celebration of the Eucharist not only Jesus' last supper but also his death and resurrection become present here and now. When Catholics speak of the *sacrifice of Christ* or the *sacrifice of the Mass* they do not mean the kind of sacrifice offered to the godhead by many religions, which are human offerings made again and again. The Christian sacrifice describes both the sacrifice of Christ and the sacrifice of the Mass: the Christian sacrifice is the original sacrifice of Christ brought into the present by means of signs and symbols.

The sacrifice of Christ embraces his whole attitude throughout his life, his surrender in life and in death. This surrender of his life seals and strengthens the *union* between God and man; it reconciles man with God and people with one another, making *forgiveness* of sin possible and serving for the *happiness* and salvation of all. It becomes an effective presence when the Church celebrates the Eucharist. 'Do this in memory of me' means then not only that Christ's own attitude and sacrifice are recalled and made effective in our time; it also calls forth from us a similar attitude and therefore also means: Let the surrender of his life, the death of Jesus, become effective in all of you: *go on doing* what Jesus did during his life for God and man.

> When the priest has said the words of Jesus over the bread
> and wine and has shown the congregation the body and
> blood of Christ, the faithful acclaim:
> **Dying you destroyed our death,**
> **rising you restored our life.**
> **Lord Jesus, come in glory.**

Sacrifice: (Lat. sacra facere = to make sacred by setting aside for God): In
nearly all religions people express through sacrifice their awareness that they are
indebted to God for all they are and all that they have. As a sign of this they give
part of their possessions back (through burning = destruction, or by giving away).
In the Temple, in the Old Testament, sacrifice played an important role. In the
New Testament there is only one sacrifice, and it abrogates all others: Jesus, who
gave his life on the cross in the service of mankind, anticipates at the Last Supper
in word and gesture, by the breaking of bread and the pouring out of wine, his
readiness to surrender, even to the sacrifice of his life. The Second Vatican
Council says (1966): 'At the Last Supper . . . our Saviour instituted the
Eucharistic sacrifice of his body and blood. He did this in order to perpetuate the
sacrifice of the cross throughout the centuries until he should come again, and so
to entrust to . . . the Church a memorial of his death and resurrection' (*Liturgy*,
para. 47).
Sacrifice of the Church: As the Church re-enacts in the Mass the memorial of the
life, death and resurrection of Jesus Christ, she is united with the unique sacrifice
of Jesus Christ in that, through the priest, she offers Christ's sacrifice and she
offers herself. She thus becomes 'a living sacrifice' in Christ (cf. the Eucharistic
prayers in the Mass).

27.4   Jesus Christ celebrates the Eucharist with us

→ 16 rose again from the dead; 9.4 kinds of prayer; 9.1 praise and
glorify; 21.3 community of holiness

The violent death suffered by Jesus was at first beyond the com-
prehension of the disciples. Their eyes were opened only when
they met the *risen Lord*. Then they understood what he had said
to them at the Last Supper about his death. Then they knew what
had actually happened on the cross. Above all, they saw the close
relationship between his death and resurrection. Death 'on the
gallows' became for them an expression of *God's love* shown in
Jesus to the uttermost limits. The cross became a sign of victory.
Because of this Easter experience of the first witnesses Christians

believe that God has raised Jesus from the dead; Jesus *Christ is alive*. He is in our midst when we come together to celebrate the Eucharist. He gathers people together. The Church is indebted to him for all that she has. How important Christ is for the Church is shown in the breaking and distribution of bread: he is as necessary for life as bread is. Just as bread broken in pieces is shared, so he is distributed to the people. Under the forms of bread and wine he becomes nourishment for mankind. What he has done for man in his life, death and resurrection he gives him in the Eucharist. From this the *Church* draws her life. So Christians become what they receive: one body, the *body of Christ*.

Hence Christians say of the Eucharist that it is the celebration of the life, death and resurrection of Jesus. It is the memorial of his *Last Supper*. It is the *surrender of Christ* for God and man, made present here and now. It reconciles us with God, it is the coming of the *kingdom of God*; it is the anticipation of future glory in the new world.

This abundance of meanings is not always explicit or ever completely understood or exhausted. Each time one meaning or another takes precedence, without for that reason excluding the others. For contemporary Christians the celebration of the Eucharist is especially familiar as a sacrificial meal in the company of their risen Lord.

The Eucharistic prayer closes with praising the God and Father of Jesus Christ:
Through him,
with him,
in him,
in the unity of the Holy Spirit,
all glory and honour is yours,
almighty Father,
for ever and ever,
which the people confirm by saying:
Amen.

Structure of the Mass: The Liturgy of the Word comprises readings from Scripture and the explanation (*sermon* or *homily*), prayer and the responsorial psalm. — The Liturgy of the Eucharist includes (after the preparation of the gifts) the Eucharistic prayer and Communion. The opening words and the dismissal (with the blessing) form the framework. For further details, consult a missal.

Celebrant (from Lat. celebrare): Priest, president, leader of a liturgical celebration.

Chalice (Lat. calix = cup): The vessel used at Mass for the wine.

Host (Lat. hostia = victim): Baked, wheaten bread, in the form of a thin wafer, used at Mass.

Ciborium (Lat. = cup): Large chalice, usually with a lid, used for the reservation of hosts in the tabernacle. During Mass a flat 'bowl' or plate is often used for them.

Monstrance (from Lat. monstrare = show): An artistic, precious 'stand' used for a large (consecrated) host — Christ present in the Eucharist — shown to the faithful who pray before it (for adoration, Holy Hour, Benediction, Corpus Christi).

Tabernacle (Lat. = tent): A precious 'cupboard' — kept locked — where the hosts are reserved for taking Communion to the sick and for the adoration of the faithful outside times of Mass.

Communion of the Sick: The early Church stressed that the sick in the parish should be able to share in the Eucharist. Priests, deacons or ministers of Communion take Communion to the sick in their homes or in hospitals.

Sacrament of the Altar: A description of the Eucharist frequently used in the past; relates the concept of sacrament with that of the Mass celebrated on the altar and the host reserved on the altar (in the past usually the place where the tabernacle stood).

First Communion: Term used for the first full sharing in the celebration of the (parish) Eucharist by the reception of Holy Communion.

27.5 Each week Easter is celebrated

→ 16.1 raised from the dead; 9.3 pray without ceasing; 39.4
work — celebrate

According to the Jewish calendar the day of the resurrection of Jesus was the *day after the Sabbath*: i.e. the first working day of the week (Mark 16:2). From the beginning Christians made this day of the week the one on which they met together (cf. John 20:19, 26). Later they called it *'the Lord's day'*; for in the celebration of the Eucharist they experienced the presence of their Lord Jesus Christ. In some countries the former Roman name *'day of the Sun'* was taken over. Christians transferred to this day the commandment to keep the Sabbath holy and celebrated Jesus Christ as the 'true sun' (cf. John 1:9; 8:12; Malachi 4:2).

Sunday is the day of Jesus' resurrection. Therefore each Sunday is a *paschal feast* in miniature. This can be sensed at the

Sunday Mass. It is characterised by Easter joy. For most people Sunday is a day free from work. They can show that they are not ruled by a mere occupation, for Sunday exists for them (cf. Mark 2:27). Every Sunday should be a *feast-day* on which people have time for others, for themselves and are free to spend time with God.

In many parish churches Mass is celebrated not only on Sunday but every day. Thus God is continually *thanked* and man's life is associated with Jesus Christ and his *surrender to God*.

The host is reserved in the tabernacle. In this way the sick and dying are able to share in the community of the body of Christ. Above all the faithful can adore their Lord present here outside times of Mass. An outward sign of their adoration is the genuflection. The light of the sanctuary lamp reminds them of the *presence of the Lord* in the form of bread.

The response to the psalm for the Easter Sunday Mass is suitable for every Sunday:
This day was made by the Lord:
we rejoice and are glad.

Responsorial psalm: Psalm, or part of a psalm, after the first reading, with a short phrase (the *response*) repeated between the verses. Content related to the theme of the Mass.

Third commandment: 'Remember the Sabbath day and keep it holy' (→ 35.4 ten commandments; 34.3 precepts of the Church).

Sunday rest: As early as the year 321 the emperor Constantine forbade, by law, work on Sunday for pay. In the Middle Ages infringements of the commandment were severely punished. In our age of the 40-hour-week the legal ruling has become less meaningful. The 'sanctifying of the Sunday' has once more become the responsibility of each Christian.

Eucharistic devotion: Interior attitude of reverence for the Eucharist which finds external expression in e.g. silent adoration before the tabernacle or before the host exposed in the monstrance.

Consecration (= making sacred): e.g. of an altar or a church. This solemn blessing is reserved to the bishop. The word is also used to describe the moment of the changing of the bread and wine into the body and blood of Christ at Mass (transubstantiation).

Parish church: Principal building in a parish in which the Eucharist is celebrated. When it is consecrated by the bishop, the altar and twelve consecration crosses are especially singled out. The twelve crosses are a reminder of continuity with the apostolic tradition. In the *sacristy*, a room, or rooms, adjoining the church, are kept all the things required for services (books, sacred and other vessels, vestments, holy oils for baptism and the anointing of the sick, etc.). The holy oils are blessed by the bishop on Holy Thursday and taken to each church in the diocese.

Sanctuary lamp: Always kept alight as a reminder of the presence of Christ in the form of Eucharistic bread. Christ is the light of the world (John 8:12).

Genuflection: Kneeling on one knee; for Catholics a sign of honour and worship of Jesus Christ as Lord. Expression of faith in his presence in the tabernacle in the form of bread.

Communion under both kinds: After the Middle Ages communion from the chalice was received by the priest only (because of the problem of reserving consecrated wine, and danger of accidents); in the fifteenth century it was forbidden for the faithful (controversy with Jan Hus who maintained that it was necessary for salvation to receive from the chalice). — Since Vatican II communion under both kinds has been restored in principle and strongly encouraged on special occasions (as far as practicable) in order to make the full sign of the Eucharist clear.

Ministers of Holy Communion: After recommendation by the local clergy, specific men and women can be commissioned by the bishop to help with the distribution of Holy Communion.

27.6 The liturgical year

→ 9.3 pray without ceasing; 13 Jesus Christ

By her special feasts during the *liturgical year* the Church reveals what God has done for man through Jesus Christ. In the *liturgy* the effectiveness for our salvation of the life, death and glorification of Jesus Christ is brought within the reach of the people. Anyone who throughout the year celebrates Mass with the Church will be drawn more closely into *union* with Christ and come to share in the reality of the salvation brought by Christ.

The greatest feast in the liturgical year is *Easter*; it continues until Pentecost. The Church prepares for Easter by Lent which begins on Ash Wednesday. There is no fixed date for Easter; it is arranged according to the Jewish Pasch celebrated on the day of the first spring full moon. Easter is usually the following Sunday. Easter and all the feasts dependent on Easter (Ascension, Pentecost, the Blessed Trinity and Corpus Christi) are therefore known as 'movable' feasts.

The principal feast, after Easter, is *Christmas* (25 December). It is celebrated liturgically until the Epiphany (or Manifestation of the Lord), 6 January, or the second Sunday after Christmas. The preparatory time before Christmas is called Advent. The liturgical year begins with the first of the four Sundays of Advent. The Sundays between Pentecost and Advent are numbered, and are called 'Sundays of the Year' or 'Sundays in Ordinary Time'. The liturgical colour for these Sundays is green.

> The liturgical year comprises the various feasts celebrated in the course of the year:
> **In her liturgy throughout the year the Church preserves and reveals the fullness of her faith.**
> From *A New Catechism* ('The Dutch Catechism')

Advent (Lat. = arrival): Preparation for Christmas (liturgical colour: purple). A reminder of our waiting for the Saviour, associated too with waiting for the second coming of the Lord.

Christmas: Feast of the birth of Jesus on 25 December. In the Eastern Church, on 6 January, the feast of the *Epiphany* is solemnly celebrated (as we celebrate Christmas on the 25 December). Liturgical colour: white.

Lent: Forty days (liturgical colour: purple), beginning on *Ash Wednesday*. The signing of the faithful with ashes on the forehead dates back to the eleventh century. For the candidates for baptism, Lent used to be the time of final preparation for their baptism during the Easter Vigil. For the baptised: a time for renewal of one's baptismal promises, for conversion, prayer, self-denial (fasting) in favour of those in need (→ 35.4 works of mercy).

Holy Week: Last week of Lent beginning on *Passion* (or *Palm*) *Sunday* (= entry into Jerusalem); liturgical colour: red. — *Holy Thursday;* day of reconciliation with sinners; memorial of the Last Supper; liturgical colour: white. — *Good Friday*: day of the death of Jesus; liturgical colour: red.

Easter: Victory over death in the resurrection; hope of eternal life. The *Easter Vigil* is in a special way the baptismal feast of the Church (liturgical colour: white). — Forty days after Easter: feast of the *Ascension* of Christ; ten days later, the Easter cycle closes with the feast of *Pentecost* (= 50 days). At Pentecost the Church celebrates the coming and work of the Holy Spirit (liturgical colour: red).

Feast of the Blessed Trinity (or Trinity Sunday): A week after Pentecost. In some Churches the Sundays up to Advent are reckoned from this feast (Sundays after Trinity).

Other feasts of the Lord: On 25 March (nine months before Christmas) the *Annunciation of the Lord*. On Thursday after the week of Pentecost, *Corpus Christi* (further celebration of the institution of the Eucharist). On Friday of the third week after Pentecost, the feast of the *Sacred Heart of Jesus*. On the last Sunday of the liturgical year, the feast of *Christ the King*: Christ is acclaimed king of the whole world.

Days of fasting and abstinence: Ash Wednesday and Good Friday. Fasting: only one full meal; the fast is of obligation for Catholics between the ages of twenty-one and sixty. Abstinence: refraining from eating meat (for those aged fourteen and over). Formerly Catholics might not eat meat on Fridays; now there is a general call to self-denial (denying oneself enjoyment from food, fasting, works of penance, acts of charity) (→ 34.4 precepts of the Church).

Feasts of the Saints: On many days in the liturgical year the faithful remember the Saints who followed Jesus and can be models for us; we ask their intercession. The most important feasts are those of *Our Lady*: the chief one is that of the *Immaculate Conception* (the Mother of God conceived without original sin) (8 December); *Our Lady's Birthday* (8 September) and her *Assumption* into heaven (15 August). Other important feasts include those of the Apostles and Evangelists, that of *St Joseph* (19 March) and the feast of the *Birthday of St John the Baptist* (24 June) (→ 21.2; 36.3; 36.4).

All Saints and All Souls (1 and 2 November): On these days the faithful remember those who believed before them and to whom they owe their faith; on *All Saints* they think prayerfully of those who have preceded them and who tried to live always in God's presence; on *All Souls* they pray that God may complete whatever, in the lives of those who have died, was unfulfilled — through their inability, weakness, failings and sins (→ 31.3).

28   Called into life: baptism

→ 30.4 forgiveness of sins; 1 a Christian

A Christian takes Jesus Christ as his model. One who is prepared to be guided by the *life of Jesus* is ready to be *baptised* into the *Church*. Baptism expresses God's 'yes' to this person and it is at the same time the person's 'yes' to life in the *Spirit of Jesus* Christ. The meaning of this sacrament is more easily understood from adult baptism than from that of an infant.

Is it right to baptise infants? Isn't it incompatible with the essence of baptism which presupposes conversion and faith? Isn't infant baptism incompatible with a free *decision* — especially if baptism is more than a pious custom? Why then does the Church nevertheless baptise the children of Christian parents?

28.1   Baptism as the beginning of new life

→ 10.4 I believe; 22.1 being reconciled; 22.3 life in Christ; 24 eternal life; 29.1 growing up; 26.4 sacraments

Christian baptism is the beginning of a *new life*, a life in union with Christ Jesus and with all who, through him, believe.

As sign of the new beginning the baptised person is called by his name. He may even receive a new name, his baptismal name. The Church's established laws show how radically she understands the *new beginning* brought about by baptism. Baptism validly administered can never be repeated, nor can it ever be revoked. Even someone who turns away from *God's love* and the community of the faithful still remains a baptised person, for God's promise is valid once and for all. God never withdraws his love. The person who is baptised is incorporated into Christ (Romans 6:5), shares in Christ's priesthood (1 Peter 2:9) and is the recipient of God's goodness.

Although baptism is so decisive for one's life as a Christian, it is simple to administer. In case of necessity anyone can baptise. It suffices for the one baptising to pour water over the head of the person concerned, saying at the same time: *'I baptise you* in the name of the Father and of the Son and of the Holy Spirit'. In the early Church the *symbolic action* was even more expressive: the person being baptised was immersed three times in water, and this still happens in the Eastern Church.

Immersion in water is a sign that the one baptised is buried with Christ; coming up out of the water symbolises his rising with Christ to a new life. The remaining symbolic actions of baptism — signing with the sign of the cross, anointing with holy oil, being given a white garment and a baptismal candle (lighted from the paschal candle) — strengthen the fundamental sign. The *Easter Vigil*, when the baptismal water is blessed, is the ideal time for baptism.

Christians believe that the person baptised shares the life of the *risen Lord*. Sealed in the depths of his being by Jesus Christ he has become brother or sister of Jesus Christ, son or daughter of God. Full of trust he can now say to God: 'Abba, Father!' Christians are confident that one who has died and risen with Christ in baptism is *reconciled with God*.

Drawn away from the power of sin, freed from original sin, he lives in Christ Jesus. Thus baptism is the beginning of a life rooted in the strength of Jesus Christ.

> The Letter to the Colossians says of baptism:
> **You have been buried with Christ, when you were baptised; and by baptism, too, you have been raised up with him through your belief in the power of God who raised him from the dead.**
> *Colossians 2:12*

Baptism by water: Immersion in water, as a sign of purification and a new beginning, is also practised in other religions. For example, in Judaism, in Jesus' time, it was not only known through John the Baptist; the Qumran sect (a monastic community near the Dead Sea whose writings were discovered in a cave in 1947) was familiar with baptism by water. Jesus was baptised by John and so were some of the disciples. Jesus himself did not administer the sacrament of baptism (John 4:1–2). Matthew ends his gospel with the 'great command to baptise' (Matthew 28:19), but this became a reality only in the power of the Spirit (Acts 2:41).

Baptism as re-birth (cf. Matthew 19:28; Titus 3:5; 'born again', John 3:3; 3:5; 'new creation', 2 Corinthians 5:17; Galatians 6:15): in the New Testament a metaphorical expression for what is given to Christians through faith and baptism; a completely new life characterised by love for God and one's neighbour. But even the baptised person must painfully experience how much the 'old man' (cf. Ephesians 4:22; Colossians 3:9) is still at work in him.

Indelible character: Because God's love and concern for man in Jesus Christ is once and for all and is irrevocable, the Church teaches that an 'indelible character' is given in baptism. The phrase expresses the unique nature of belonging to Jesus Christ, something which God will never undo.

Rite of baptism: Ordinarily baptism is administered by a priest (or deacon). The rite includes — in addition to the act of baptising — prayer, homily, creed, bidding prayers and singing.

Baptismal water: From the earliest times water (as a life-giving element) was used in baptism. Immersion is a symbol of the death of the 'old man' and the rising again of the 'new man'. Water also has power to cleanse. The symbol of baptismal water therefore further includes the idea of 'washing away' (cf. Acts 22:16). In the course of time the custom arose of a special blessing of water during the Easter Vigil or immediately before a baptism.

Holy water: Water (if possible mixed with a little salt) blessed by the priest; often placed in a 'small bowl' or holy water stoup at the church door or near the entry to a house. As the faithful sprinkle themselves with it they make the sign of the cross as a reminder of their baptism. It is also used for blessings (→ 26.3).

Chrism: Oil (mixture of balsam and olive oil) blessed by the bishop on Holy Thursday and used in the administration of baptism, confirmation and Holy Orders.

Baptism in case of necessity: A person in danger of death may be baptised by anyone. He/she pours water over the head of the one to be baptised, saying at the same time: 'I baptise you in the name of the Father and of the Son and of the Holy Spirit'. If parents baptise their dying child they profess their faith in God, who in

Jesus Christ gives eternal life, and they bring their child into the community which unites the living and the dead in Jesus Christ.

Unbaptised persons: The Church believes that God's love embraces everyone even if — without any fault on their part, or because of insufficient insight — they do not find the way to faith and baptism.

Effects of baptism: By baptism the person is brought out of the sphere of the slavery of sin (Colossians 1:13), he is set free from original sin (→ 22.2) and personal sin (Romans 6:7; Colossians 2:13); he is brought into the sphere of Christ's power (Romans 6:4); the new life given by God's love grows in him, he is guided into the community of the Church and, commissioned by her, takes on the obligation to announce to the world the coming of God's kingdom (cf. 1 Corinthians 15:28).

28.2   Member of the Church

→ 21.1 Church as community; 1.3 in the community; 33.1 offices and services; 34.1 people of God

No one is a believer for himself alone. The faith of an individual is related to the faith of the others who travel with him along the road Jesus travels. The *community of the Church* strengthens the *faith* of the individual.

In the administration of baptism this community in faith is visible. Baptism can be given only when the recitation of the *creed* has confirmed the fact that the one seeking baptism is asking for the traditional faith of the community of believers. In the case of infant baptism the parents and godparent vouch for the child's faith. Representing him, they abjure everything opposed to God and, together with the *congregation* present, profess their belief in God and his work for man's salvation. As many members of the parish as possible should be present at a baptism so that what is taking place may be quite clear: the one baptised is accepted into the Church, the *people of God*, and thus incorporated into the body of Christ. So baptism is no 'private' affair; it concerns the whole parish. Therefore in many places — on the model of the Easter Vigil — baptism is administered during the *celebration of the Eucharist* — the centre of the Church's life.

In the first centuries of the Church the process of becoming a Christian began with the catechumenate; during this time the person learnt and practised life as a Christian. The *catechumens* took part in the Lenten liturgy of the word which was especially orientated to their preparation. Today those adults who want to become Christians and receive baptism are prepared by a fairly long course of instruction in the faith.

At infant baptism the parish, with the parents and godparent, by the example of their faith and by *instruction*, take upon themselves to help the child later to make a *personal decision with regard to the faith*. At the beginning of the ceremonies of baptism, the parents make it clear, in the presence of the congregation, that they are aware of their obligations.

The one baptised begins to share in the new life given him by God and he is welcomed into the community of all baptised Christians; so he can say:
Christ the Lord has chosen me
and I am to live henceforth for him.
I will serve him in the world
and be his witness.
So I no longer live for myself alone
since I am permitted to be his friend and disciple.
I bear his name;
I am his for ever.   *Friedrich Dörr*

Talks with parents: Before baptising a child the priest meets the parents and explains the meaning of baptism and the details of the rite of baptism. This is intended to help the parents to become aware of the obligations they take upon themselves for the child and to encourage them in their own faith.

Godparent or sponsor: The godparent has an obligation to share concern for the religious education of the person baptised (or confirmed). He should therefore be mature in his own attitude to the faith and the Christian life. He must be a member of the Catholic Church. A Christian who is not a Catholic might be allowed to assist a Catholic godparent.

Catechumenate: The word refers to the preparation undertaken by the *catechumens* (from Gr. = those receiving instruction in the faith) and the actual form of instruction. Whereas the catechumenate is for those preparing for baptism, *catechesis* refers to religious instruction for those already baptised (→ 34.2).

Baptismal font: Usually an artistic 'bowl' or basin in stone (or metal) used for the baptismal water; it stands in the baptistery, if there is one, or in a prominent place in the church. In either case the significance of baptism should be emphasised for the parish.

Baptistery: (from Gr. baptisma = baptism). Special part of the church, or sometimes a separate chapel adjoining the church, where baptism is administered.

28.3 Baptism as a way of life

→ 1.2 following Jesus; 7.3 whom God forgives; 36.1 necessary

It is customary in many countries for people to be baptised as infants. This makes it clearer than in the case of adults that the new life and *membership of the community of the faithful* are a gratuitous *gift* of God. But it is easy, in the case of *infant baptism*, to overlook another fact, namely, that baptism and faith are interrelated. Baptism has its consequences. A baptised person should live a different kind of life from someone who has not been baptised. Jesus has become for the baptised the guiding principle of their lives. Therefore for them baptism cannot be an event of the past. They have been assigned a *life-long task* of becoming more and more like Jesus. This means that a Christian takes upon himself, as a basic obligation, making his neighbour's needs his own, considering it a duty to be compassionate towards his weaker brethren, seeking God's will in everything and being united with God in love.

Once a year, at the Easter Vigil, Christians renew their *baptismal promises*. They abjure everything opposed to God, once more they renounce evil and profess their faith in God who wills man's salvation. They trust that God will accept them back even if they have denied him and lost sight of their baptism as source and *foundation of their lives*. In this way they encourage one another to become better Christians.

A person's *patronal feast* (of the saint after whom he was named) can be a special opportunity for recalling his baptism. The name which he received at baptism can guide him along his path as a Christian.

The Letter to the Colossians reminds us of the obligation we have taken upon ourselves by our baptism:
You must live your whole life according to the Christ you have received — Jesus the Lord; you must be rooted in him and built on him and held firm by the faith you have been taught and full of thanksgiving.   *Colossians 2:6–7*

Priesthood of all the faithful: According to Peter's first Letter (2:9) the whole Christian people is a 'kingly priesthood' (cf. Exodus 19:6); all share in Christ's priesthood. Martin Luther reminded people of this important fact; he challenged what at his time was generally accepted that only those in Holy Orders shared in the priesthood of Christ. The Second Vatican Council reaffirmed the tradition of the early Church: 'The common priesthood of the faithful and the ministerial or hierarchical priesthood are interrelated. Each of them in its own special way is a participation in the one priesthood of Christ' (*The Church*, para. 10).

29 The Christian in the world: confirmation

→ 21.1 Church as community; 19 the Holy Spirit; 33.1 offices and services

The *new life* received by the Christian in baptism has to grow and develop. At the beginning this happens for a child by his sharing the life of faith in his family and in his parish and by gradually coming to believe with them.

A day comes when the young person is no longer satisfied with saying: This is what my parents do. The older he is, the more he has to take his own steps in faith. He has to *decide* for himself the path he is going to choose, the plan he is going to adopt for his life and for the object of his endeavours.

As he enters upon this stage of his life he receives the sacrament of *confirmation*. In many places there is an increasing tendency to see this sacrament as closely associated with *coming to maturity*. In keeping with this, the time of preparation is prolonged; young people are confirmed when they are older than was previously the case.

Does this fulfil all the conditions? What can be done to ensure that the *commitment* awakened by confirmation is not stifled? to ensure that confirmation will be effective in the life of the person concerned?

Confirmation: In Protestant churches, this is the public admission of the young Christian to the adult parish. Age: about fifteen years. The time of preparation varies in length; in some churches up to two years. After confirmation (not considered as a sacrament in some non-Catholic churches) the person concerned is admitted for the first time to the Lord's Supper.

29.1 Sacrament of Christian adulthood

→ 28.1 new life; 20.1 work of the Spirit; 22.4 God's love; 28.3 way of life; 34 Church in the concrete; 39 do likewise; 26.4 sacraments

The Church became visible to people only when she was filled with the Holy Spirit (Acts 2:1–47). So it is with the faith of the individual Christian: the new life received in *baptism* is brought to its full power in *confirmation*. Confirmation is the sign for the individual Christian that God's *Holy Spirit* comes upon him and moves him — the Spirit whom Jesus promised to his disciples (John 16:7–13). The word 'confirmation' comes from the Latin and means literally 'strengthening'. Sometimes it is also described as *'seal'*. What began in baptism is sealed and completed in confirmation; union with Christ and his church; working for people in the Spirit of Jesus.

Confirmation is the sacrament of Christian adulthood. The Christian is strengthened for his *work in the world*. Christians believe in the special power of the Holy Spirit which encourages them and enables them to *bear witness* to Christ in the Church and in public.

The effect of this sacrament is clear in the sign by which the *bishop* administers confirmation: first, he stretches out his hands over the persons being confirmed and calls down the Holy Spirit on them all. Then he lays his hand on each individual — a gesture of blessing, of solidarity, and at the same time of taking him into God's service. He calls on the person by name and says: '. . . be sealed with the gift of the Holy Spirit', at the same time anointing him on the forehead with chrism. The Spirit of *Jesus Christ*, the *anointed One*, gives courage to the person confirmed and urges him to do in his life what Jesus the Christ did: to live *wholly for God* and, in his name, *for others*.

In his letter to the church in Rome Paul writes of life in the Spirit of God:
Your interests . . . are in the spiritual, since the Spirit of God has made his home in you. In fact, unless you possessed the Spirit of Christ you would not belong to him.

Romans 8:9–10

Rite of confirmation: The bishop is usually the minister of confirmation; in certain circumstances a priest may confirm.

29.2 Service in the Church and in the world

→ 13.1 Christ; 34.1 people of God; 21.1 Church as community; 34.7 Church in the world; 39 do likewise

Baptism as the beginning of one's life as a Christian is directed towards the Eucharist and confirmation. These three sacraments are described as sacraments of initiation, or those sacraments that establish the *foundation* of the Christian life.

A Christian does not receive confirmation only for himself. The *gift of the Holy Spirit* is intended also to be effective for the good of others. It is through Christians that people encounter the Spirit of Christ, through this Spirit that they should be enabled to experience his power for good.

This is true in the first place within the *parish*. Here the Christian should make his competence and his talents available; for example, by taking an active part in the Mass; by involvement in social problems in his district, by care for the lonely and the aged, by youth work, by work for the parish council. For one who has been confirmed the question is not: 'What have I got from it? What am I going to get out of it? What good does it do?' but 'Where can I be of use?' 'Where, given my competence, can I work with others?' Only in this way will the parish gradually become a 'unity in the Holy Spirit', a fraternal community, attractive to others.

The task entrusted to the one confirmed is not confined to the sphere of the Church. He is confirmed for the world; there he has to become a messenger of the loving *nearness of God*. No hard and fast directions can be laid down in detail. It is a matter of all that concerns the life and actions of a Christian in the world and his *task in the world*.

One or two examples may clarify what is meant. Everywhere there are people who are in despair; to bring the light of God's goodness to such people can make them happier. Anyone who knows he is strengthened by God to commit himself energetically and joyfully can become involved in team work; he can dispense with working for his own satisfaction. A person open to the Holy

Spirit is *expected* to battle against injustice, and to use his talents for social and development work, or to promote work for the missions. Perhaps he may even become professionally engaged in the *service of the Church*.

In any case in what he does a Christian is called to *be a sign* for the God who loves men, the God of whom he has experience — without his having to say very much in everyday life. But if he is challenged to profess the mainspring of his life and actions, he is 'not to worry' about what 'he is to say'. He should quite naturally speak according to his convictions and trust to what is said in Matthew's gospel: 'What you are to say will be given to you when the time comes; because it is not you who will be speaking; the Spirit of your Father will be speaking in you' (Matthew 10:19–20). The person who wants to be a Christian must expect opposition to his convictions about faith.

Words from the Sermon on the Mount shed light on the Christian vocation:
You are the light of the world. A city built on a hill-top cannot be hidden. No one lights a lamp to put it under a tub; they put it on the lamp-stand where it shines for everyone in the house. In the same way your light must shine in the sight of men. *Matthew 5:14–16*

Confirmation: Confirmation belongs (like baptism and the priesthood) to the sacraments which — once received — are valid once and for all. God's mandate to us, in the power of the Holy Spirit, to work as a Christian in the Church and in the world, needs no fresh endorsement at a later date.
Time for confirmation: There is no clear opinion about the appropriate time for confirmation. The Eastern Church administers confirmation at the same time as baptism, thus clarifying the close relationship between the two sacraments. Others stress that confirmation should precede the Eucharist as one of the sacraments of initiation to the Eucharist. Elsewhere the custom has spread of giving prominence to 'growing up' and of appealing to those to be confirmed to accept their responsibilities as Christians; for this reason confirmation takes place some time after the first communion.

30 Guilt in the lives of Christians: the sacrament of penance

→ 7.1 no one is without sin; 22.2 power of sin

Being a Christian means not only forgiving others but first and foremost allowing oneself to be forgiven. Every Eucharist is celebrated for '*the forgiveness of sins*' and in consciousness of our failings and our guilt. The whole of our Christian life has to be supported by the power of forgiveness and by the courage to acknowledge our *failings* and our *guilt*, before God and man, so that we may thereby grow as human beings and as Christians. This is often hard, but where it takes place, it is — as experience teaches — a source of renewal and of setting free. To be absolved from our guilt, make a fresh beginning and go forwards corresponds to our deepest longings.

This experience is expressed in a special way in the sacrament of *penance and reconciliation*; it serves for renewal, joy, reconciliation with God and with the community of the faithful, the coming of God's kingdom. To confess oneself a sinner is painful, but to experience forgiveness of sins is valuable. It contributes especially to renew man and the world for the coming of *God's kingdom*.

These questions are therefore crucial: how do people get quit of their guilt nowadays? Are mental illnesses an indication that there is much guilt which, instead of being acknowledged and forgiven, is suppressed? Why do even Catholics today make so little use of the opportunities for forgiveness and for the sacrament of penance? Is their fear of acknowledging their guilt stronger than their longing for reconciliation?

30.1 Sin and penance

→ 7.2 a God who forgives; 22.4 God's love

Sin does not consist simply of lapses, failings, blunders, bad behaviour towards our fellow-men. Sin is directed *against God*. The more a person knows God, the better he understands what sin is. It is told of many saints that they felt themselves to be great sinners. Some people regard this as exaggeration. In reality the saints are more perceptive than others of the glory and *love of God*. In God's light their own darkness strikes them as frightening.

But *sin* is not only everything expressly directed against God. Even when a person fails another *human being* and does not think of God as he does so, God is affected by his action. Christians are conscious that in all their misdemeanours, whether consciously or unconsciously, they also set themselves against God and his plans for the world. Their sin is an obstacle to the coming of the kingdom of God. They are rejecting God's goodness whether they do so expressly or not.

A person who sins acts as though God did not love him. A person who sins acts as if *God's will* were unimportant or completely unknown. He forgets that since his *baptism* he is united with Christ. A person who sins sets little store on his fellow-men and on a human world, although God has both very much at heart. The sinner weakens the community of the faithful and makes holy Church — as far as he is concerned — unholy Church.

Despite all this, God does not cease to love man; on the contrary he repeatedly offers him the gift of his *pardon*. God says 'yes' even to those who say 'no' to him. Jesus bears witness to this. He is God's 'yes' in person; he is God's total 'yes' to man's happiness and salvation (2 Corinthians 1:20) — in the midst of man's guilt; at the same time Jesus Christ is the unhesitating 'yes' of mankind to God.

When someone 'grasps' God's readiness to forgive, he is so overwhelmed that he suffers when he has done wrong (Luke 7:36–50; 15:11–32). He is determined, as far as possible, to make good the evil he has done (Luke 19:1–10). He wants to make a *fresh beginning* (John 8:11). He abandons his evil path, is converted and turns again to God. *Conversion* does not happen in the twinkling of an eye; it is a long-drawn-out and taxing process. The whole person is involved. But in the one who wants to make a fresh beginning God has already initiated it. God forgives sin and guilt.

> At the beginning of the celebration of Mass a general
> acknowledgement of our guilt may be expressed as follows:
> **To prepare ourselves to celebrate the sacred mysteries,**
> **let us call to mind our sins.**
> **Lord, we have sinned against you:**
> **Lord, have mercy.**
> **Lord, show us your mercy and love,**
> **and grant us your salvation.**
> **May almighty God have mercy on us,**
> **forgive us our sins,**
> **and bring us to everlasting life. Amen.**

Penance: In customary Church language sometimes restricted to the sacrament of penance. In the Old and New Testament the fundamental act, frequently repeated and always necessary, of *conversion*; a decisive turning away from all that is opposed to God and a return to God and all that is good. It is expressed by remorse or contrition, good resolutions and making satisfaction. Penitential acts (→ 30.3)

Remorse: This is more than worrying about human judgement or the consequences of sin; it is more than consciousness that one has done something wrong, and more than 'being in the dumps morally'. Remorse has to do with God; it is brought about by God's Spirit and is related to trust in God's goodness; this trust enables one to look one's guilt in the face, recognise it as sin and turn away from it in contrition tempered with trust and hope.

Resolution or good intentions: This is connected with remorse or contrition. It is an intention to avoid evil and do good in the future; the more accurately it is pinpointed, the more effective it is; with it goes courage always to begin again and trust that God sees one's goodwill.

30.2   Who is a sinner?

→ 36.2 freedom; 22.2 power of sin; 7.1 no one is without sin; 39.6 making decisions

In order to recognise what is, and what is not sin, *distinctions* are necessary. Where weaknesses, failures, mishaps and slips happen, where one unknowingly and unintentionally does something wrong, one cannot accurately talk of sin.

The concept of sin describes the guilt which comes between God and man. The more consciously one decides to do evil and the more important the matter, the more serious the sin is. A person who, with *clear insight*, by a *free decision*, in an *important matter*, sets himself against God's will, says 'no' to God and breaks away from him, commits a grievous sin. 'There is a sin that is death, . . . but not all sin is deadly' (1 John 5:16–17). What is *decisive* is the extent of harm done to the chief commandment of *love of God and of one's neighbour*. No one is without sin, but a person who wants to listen to God and takes pains to know and do his will, despite his weaknesses and faults, is on God's side. One who intends to do good is already on the way to what is good. *Temptation* is not a sin.

It is not only by doing evil that man sins; *omission* or *neglect to do good* can be a sin. One can sin even by one's thoughts and words if one allows these free rein.

But one who without any evil *intention* does something wrong, for example, causes an accident, is not guilty before God even if he is legally penalised for the consequences of his action. With God what we intend to do is considered more important than what we actually do.

No fault is too great for God to be able to forgive it. Even the worst sinner can with *God's help* make a fresh beginning.

At the beginning of the celebration of the Eucharist, the faithful may ask God's forgiveness by reciting the 'I confess':

I confess to almighty God,
and to you, my brothers and sisters,
that I have sinned through my own fault,
in my thoughts and in my words,
in what I have done,
and in what I have failed to do;
and I ask blessed Mary, ever virgin,
all the angels and saints,
and you, my brothers and sisters,
to pray for me to the Lord our God.

Serious sin: A person's natural feelings tell him that in different sins the degree of guilt varies before God. According to this, the guilt before God, the sin, is considered 'weighty' in differing degrees. Repeated attempts have been made to label serious sins and less serious sins. For example, people speak of 'mortal' sin (i.e.

actions leading not to life with God but to everlasting death) and of other sins less serious. People also speak of 'venial' sin, meaning that the sin is not so serious that absolution in the sacrament of penance is essential for forgiveness. Such distinctions exist, but it is not good when an individual Christian wants to use them to decide 'whether he must go to confession or not'. The appreciation of God's boundless love, which precedes all human conversion, should put an end to such 'calculations'. The sacrament of penance is an opportunity to receive God's forgiving mercy; the more a person is conscious that he needs this, the less reluctant he will be to seek it.

30.3 Sin and community

→ 7.3 the one whom God forgives; 21.1 Church as community; 18.3 norms for judgement; 39.3 acting in a spirit of solidarity

No one does evil for the sake of evil. A person often does wrong because at the moment it seems to him advantageous. Yet what is advantageous for one is harmful for another: the person who steals deprives another of his lawful possession. The one who claims for himself something that belongs to everyone harms the *community*. One who, to protect his own name, spreads what is untrue about another, does harm to the personal reputation of the other, poisons the atmosphere and stifles confidence.

Sin is not a 'private' affair. It has evil consequences, even if at first sight no one seems to be harmed. Above all, sin makes people careless with regard to evil. Moreover, *sins committed by Christians* lessen the credibility of the Church and hinder the coming of the kingdom of God. Therefore Christians who have set themselves completely against God's commandments (i.e. against the chief commandment of love), and persist in this attitude, jeopardise their place in the community of the faithful. Their guilt calls for conversion and forgiveness; only then is community once more possible.

If a person insults another he must not only *ask God's forgiveness*, he must also ask pardon of the one he has insulted. If someone appropriates another's property it does not suffice to feel *sorrow and remorse*; he must, as far as he can, make good the harm caused. The will to make *satisfaction and restitution* is a touchstone of *conversion*.

A Christian must also be ready to forgive someone who asks his pardon. A person who has experienced God's forgiveness also pardons his fellow-men. That is why Jesus teaches his disciples to pray: 'Forgive us our trespasses as we forgive those who trespass against us'. Christians should not harbour grievances. The Letter to the Ephesians gives this advice: 'Never let the sun set on your anger' (Ephesians 4:26). Not many words are needed to grant *pardon*; sometimes a gesture of reconciliation suffices.

The *Church* devotes certain *times to penance*: Lent in preparation for Easter and the time of Advent. They serve for the practice of good and turning away from sin. For this reason in many parishes the faithful are invited to take part in *penance services*.

The following words from Paul's Letter to the Romans may serve to encourage us in our daily lives:
Resist evil and conquer it with good.   *Romans 12:21*

Penance or **Penitential service:** A Liturgy of the Word (→ 27.1) at which it becomes especially clear that not only is reconciliation with God necessary but also reconciliation with the Church, the community of the faithful. Those present ask one another's pardon and forgive one another. Together they ask God for forgiveness for their own sins and the sins of the whole Church. If someone has estranged himself from the Church he may, through a penance service, find his way also to the reception of the sacrament of penance.
Satisfaction and restitution: A readiness, according to one's ability, to make good the harm caused (this is part and parcel of penance).
Penitential acts: Conversion makes one want to express one's sorrow in action. One who is forgiven will want to respond to God's generosity. As every sin removes us from God, so everything that is good (our thoughts and our actions) brings us nearer to him. In practice, the forms of penance are as varied as life itself. Since earliest times the following have been considered especially important: prayer, fasting and other good works. In all that we do, it remains a fact that we are dependent on the mercy of God and on pardon from our fellow-men.

30.4   Various kinds of forgiveness
→ 7.2 a God who forgives; 27.3 the Lord's surrender; 22.1 being reconciled

The Church offers us many possibilities for asking *forgiveness for our sins*: for example, reading Holy Scripture; this is why the priest, after reading the gospel, says: 'May the words of the gospel wipe away our sins'. Someone may refuse to help another and later do his best to help him (1 Peter 4:8), or as he goes into church, a person takes holy water and renews the thought that he is baptised — all these are ways to conversion and forgiveness of sin. Above all, participating in the celebration of the Eucharist has power to forgive sin; for it is a celebration in the belief that the blood of Jesus is 'shed for you and for all men so that sins may be forgiven'. Another way is a penance service; it shows that the Church, *community* of the faithful, is a place of reconciliation.

In the Our Father the Christian prays: 'Forgive us our trespasses as we forgive those who trespass against us'. Anyone who at the end of the day looks back and says an *act of contrition* expressing his sincere will to be converted and make a fresh beginning can be confident that he is forgiven by God. Anyone who overcomes his pride and *asks forgiveness* of another person receives not only his forgiveness but also God's.

The *sacraments* have special significance: in baptism Christ brings people out of their involvement in the sin of the world and places them on God's side. So we say in the Nicene Creed: 'We acknowledge one baptism for the forgiveness of sins'. Faced with death, the faithful are forgiven their sins by the anointing of the sick. Between baptism and death our lives as Christians are accompanied by God's standing invitation to conversion and reconciliation in the *sacrament of penance.*

In the Old Testament the works of mercy are considered very important; in the Book of Tobit the angel Raphael says:
Almsgiving saves from death and purges every kind of sin.
Tobit 12:9

Indulgences: In the early Church sinners had to take upon themselves, for serious sins, long public acts of penance before they received absolution and were received back into the community of the Church. If a fellow-Christian, who had suffered in the times of persecution on account of his faith, interceded for a sinner, the sinner's penance could be remitted. Later, this remission of public penance (not remission of the sins) was called 'indulgence'. Even later this practice became widespread in the name of the 'merits' of Jesus Christ and the saints. Finally, it became a pious practice to obtain 'indulgences' for the 'poor souls' in 'purgatory' (to shorten the time of their purification). In the Middle Ages the practice of indulgences became very offensive (above all in connection with the payment of money which was regarded as equivalent to doing penance); this was one of the external causes of the Reformation. In today's religious practice indulgences play only a very small role. But, because unease is felt over the word 'indulgence', it is as well to know what is meant by it. — The teaching of the Church says: By indulgences temporal punishment is remitted for sins already forgiven. To gain an indulgence one must be 'in a state of grace', that is, free from serious sin, and carry out the prescribed good works or prayers.

30.5 The sacrament of penance

→ 22.2 power of sin; 8.2 not succumb to temptation; 16.3 we are redeemed; 21.1 Church as community; 26.4 sacraments

What a Christian does always concerns the community of the faithful — for good or for ill. If someone has sinned, he has simultaneously offended *God* and the Church, the *community* established and *sanctified* by God. Therefore he must confess his sin in the community of the Church. According to the traditional practice and teaching of the Church, *individual confession* is necessary for the forgiveness of serious sin. In the name of Christ and of the community of the Church the priest receives the *confession of sins* of the sinner and gives him in God's name *absolution*, that is: God grants forgiveness through the services of the Church. Absolution in the sacrament of penance pre-supposes, like all forgiveness, *contrition* on the part of the sinner, his *good resolution* and his will to *make satisfaction*.

The sacrament of penance is the opportunity for forgiveness offered us by God, especially in the case of serious sin. One who has excluded himself from the Eucharistic community finds in this sacrament reconciliation with God and with his fellow-Christians. He may once more take part in Christ's sacrifice and the *Eucharistic meal*. The congregation thus shows him their faith in God's forgiving love, not by condemning him, but by meeting him in forgiveness and encouragement. The sacrament of penance is the sign that God never gives man up, he offers him a new beginning (Matthew 18:18; John 20:20–23). He remains turned towards man, even if man turns away from him. God, in his generosity, does not merely disregard man's sins — as it were, forgiving but not forgetting — when God forgives sins they are for ever obliterated. Even more: Luke's gospel gives us these words of Jesus: With God 'there is more rejoicing over one repentant sinner than over ninety-nine virtuous men' (Luke 15:7). This knowledge may compensate for much unease that many have to overcome because they do not find confession of sin easy.

Even a person who has no serious sin to confess can receive the sacrament of penance meaningfully. In so doing he acknowledges that he belongs to a *community of sinners*. The sacrament of penance helps him to be clear-sighted about himself and to gain a fresh impetus to do better. Therefore the Church recommends to all the faithful regular reception of the sacrament of penance.

The priest gives the absolution in the following words:
God, the Father of mercies,
through the death and resurrection of his Son,
has reconciled the world to himself
and sent the Holy Spirit among us
for the forgiveness of sins:
through the ministry of the Church
may God give you pardon and peace,
and I absolve you from your sins
in the name of the Father, and of the Son,
and of the Holy Spirit.
The penitent answers:
Amen.

Sacrament of penance: The Catholic Church teaches that in this sacrament, through an authorised priest, God gives to the baptised sinner (who is sorry for his sins, confesses them and is prepared to make satisfaction) pardon and power to make a fresh beginning (cf. Matthew 18:18; John 20:20–23). For a person who has committed serious sin, reception of the sacrament of penance is an obligation, but all others are also invited to receive it regularly: the sacrament of penance is an important help in one's life as a Christian.

Confession of sins: There is a general confession of sins at the beginning of every Mass (→ 30.1; 30.2). Personal confession is part of the sacrament of penance; at least all serious sins of which one is conscious must be named.

Individual confession: Confession, exhortation and absolution follow one after the other in the context of a confession 'conversation', usually in the confessional or a room suitable for confession.

Absolution: This is given in the name of Christ and emphasises the certainty that God forgives the guilt.

Secret of confession (or seal of confession): Strict obligation on the part of the priest to silence concerning everything confessed as a sin with a view to absolution, even if it is a question of a crime which is juridically punishable or if the priest himself, through remaining silent, finds himself in great difficulties.

Confession room: The *confessional* in the church, or an adjoining room where confession can take the form of a conversation between priest and penitent.

30.6　Guilt — sin — self-knowledge

→ 36.2 freedom; 7.1 no one is without sin; 39.6 making decisions

Exteriorly no one can judge what, for an individual, is *sin*. Each one must look into his life, question his *conscience*, examine his actions and omissions before God. By doing this people come to very different conclusions. Someone with a delicate conscience may feel that some little attention he has neglected is selfish and sinful, even though those around him may not have noticed any fault. Another has *unintentionally* done considerable harm so that all say 'You're guilty', while the person, knowing his inner self and his intentions, is at peace before God. When faith grows stronger, one's awareness of sin is keener.

There is no list of sins, no examination of conscience which fits every occasion; on its own, the fact of an action done says nothing of the circumstances, the intentions, the motives and lack of love which come into play. Even if a deed causes loss of human life, we have to distinguish: (a) cold-blooded murder with *clear knowledge*, freely *decided on*, (b) reckless killing (manslaughter) but without full intention to kill, (c) carelessness with fatal consequences, (d) a complete accident, or (e) a justified or perhaps an overhasty act of self-defence. Sin is not in the first place an isolated action; much more crucial is the *attitude* and out of this attitude a specific action arises. Only God knows the heart of man. 'God is greater than our conscience and he knows everything' (1 John 3:20) — for our happiness and salvation.

An *examination of conscience* (for confession and at other times) can, if correctly used, help towards *self-knowledge*. It reminds one and makes one acutely conscious of much that one would like to refuse to believe.

A conversation with a friend, with an experienced person, with a priest, is often even more helpful. A person who continually examines his life in God's presence acquires, in time, a delicate sensitiveness. He learns how to *pass judgement* more accurately on his deeds and the motives for his thoughts, words and actions. He knows where and when his conscience accuses him. He learns to understand what God wills of him.

In the Old Testament one of the psalmists begins his prayer with the words: 'Lord, you search me and you know me'. He ends with the following request:
O search me, God, and know my heart.
O test me and know my thoughts.
See that I follow not the wrong path
and lead me in the path of life eternal.
Psalm 138(139):23–24

---

31 Serious illness and death: the anointing of the sick

→ 17.1 he has preceded us

Everyone's life is limited: his years, days and hours are counted. The end, *death*, is signified in the impairment and gradual *diminution* of life. These experiences of weakness, helplessness and pain are a trying test for us. But there is no need for them to withdraw us from God. In the sacrament of the *anointing of the sick, God's closeness* is given to us precisely because of our special need.

However, it is also the strengthening and consoling nearness of the community of the faithful that the sick and dying should be enabled to experience in this sacrament. The Letter of James bears witness to this (5:14–15). Even if the priest comes — perhaps only once — the sick can hardly feel that the parishioners share sympathetically in their illness if no one else from the *parish* visits them. The faithful in a parish must therefore ask what they, as *believers*, can do to support the sick and dying in their loneliness.

31.1 Praying and caring in the parish

→ 21.1 Church as community; 39.10 praying to God; 34.1 people of God; 29.2 service in the world; 37.1 loving one's neighbour

It can be distressing enough to be alone and to have no one who cares, but if a person is so ill that his life is in danger, he suffers acutely if he is left alone. He feels 'abandoned by God and the world', already 'written off' by those who are in good health. Therefore, visiting the sick is one of the seven corporal *works of mercy* (cf. Matthew 25:36, 43).

In a world where sick people tend to be excluded from society, the Church has a special duty to stand by them and care for them; this she has taken upon herself as fraternal charity. The first hospitals were monasteries and convents and even in our day Christian nursing Sisters care for the sick and, with doctors, nurses and others, bear witness to the *loving kindness of God* which motivates these people. There are places in the Christian world — for example, in Lourdes — where the sick are considered God's 'privileged children'. Many Christian parishes arrange various services for the sick: helping with their meals, visiting them and taking them flowers, writing to them and undertaking their household chores.

Medical care is not of itself sufficient. What anyone who is seriously ill needs above all is a *caring* person *close at hand*. Bidding prayers can be a particularly helpful sign of our union with the sick: that God may help them interiorly and exteriorly and console them. The sick person himself will often pray to be restored to health. Perhaps he will learn too to pray for strength to accept his illness and thus be more like *Jesus* along the way of the cross.

For Christians illness can become a conscious sharing in Christ's redeeming passion; with Paul they can say:
If we live, we live for the Lord; if we die, we die for the Lord, so that alive or dead we belong to the Lord. *Romans 14:7–8*

Works of mercy: In addition to the corporal works of mercy (→ 37.2) Christian tradition lists the spiritual works of mercy (→ 39.10).
Care for the sick: The motive behind care for the sick has its origin in the

commandment to love one's neighbour; at the deepest level it is seeing the person of Christ in the least of his brethren (cf. Matthew 25:36). The earliest hospitals in Western Christendom in the Middle Ages were founded by the Church; the first organisation founded especially to care for the sick was that of the Knights Hospitaller.

31.2   The sacrament of the anointing of the sick

→ 23.2 faith gives courage; 39.9 com-passion; 26.4 sacraments

There is, among the seven sacraments, a *symbolic action* especially appropriate for those who are ill: the anointing of the sick. The sick person himself, a relative or someone else in the parish calls the priest to the sick person's bedside when the illness is critical or when — for example on account of age — the strength of a sick person is considerably weakened. With the relatives the priest *prays* for the sick person. He *anoints* his forehead and hands with blessed oil, saying as he does so: 'Through this holy anointing may the Lord in his love and mercy help you with the grace of the Holy Spirit. Amen. May the Lord who frees you from *sin save* you and raise you up.'

If the sick person is conscious, in addition to the anointing of the sick he may receive the sacraments of *penance* and the *Eucharist* (*Viaticum*). The anointing of the sick may be repeated every time a person has a fresh illness that is serious.

> The anointing of the sick is first mentioned in the Letter of St James:
> **If anyone of you is ill, he should send for the elders of the church, and they must anoint him with oil in the name of the Lord and pray over him. The prayer of faith will save the sick man and the Lord will raise him up again; and if he has committed any sins, he will be forgiven.**   *James 5:14–15*

Extreme Unction (Lat. = last anointing): Former name for the sacrament of the anointing of the sick; it comes from the fact that in practice the sacrament was administered only when a person was dying. Reception of this sacrament more than once is still not very common.

Viaticum (Lat. = food for the journey): The name Holy Viaticum was used for

Holy Communion when the person was dying (about to set out on his last 'journey').

Preparation for the anointing of the sick: Many fail to let the priest know at the opportune time so that he can administer the sacrament to a relative who is ill. They are unsure what to prepare (table covered with a white cloth, a crucifix and, if possible, candles and holy water) and sometimes afraid that the patient may be alarmed by the celebration of the sacrament, still known to many as the 'last rites' or 'last sacrament'.

31.3   Christian death and burial

→ 18.2 judge the world; 16.2 power of death; 16.4 basis of our faith

A sick person close to death has a very special need of sympathetic help. Many are afraid of offering this last act of charity to a human being; modern organisation in a hospital sometimes makes it well-nigh impossible. In our times, therefore, many die lonely and abandoned. This is unbefitting human dignity and a sign of impoverishment, a reproach to our society.

Christians who support a *dying person* should let him feel that he is not abandoned. In this case words are often less important than a silent presence, affectionate contact and a sympathetic *caring*. As long as it remains possible to speak to the dying person, Christians can strengthen him in hope in God's fidelity and help him to suffer in faith his death-agony. Like Jesus they can pray with the dying person: 'Father, into your hands I commit my spirit' (Luke 23:46); I place my life in your hands. In this way a Christian dies full of *hope*. Many Christians anticipate preparation for their death by asking the special help of Our Lady, Mother of Jesus: 'Pray for us sinners now and at the hour of our death' (the Hail Mary).

On the day of the *funeral* the parish assembles for a Requiem Mass with the relatives and friends of the dead person. They accompany the deceased person to the graveside. The *prayers* and hymns at the burial express that, despite all the sorrow felt over the loss of a loved person, Christians hope in eternal life, because they know the dead person is with God and because they believe in the *resurrection* from the dead. The early Church used to celebrate the day of death of their saints as their birthday into the new life without end.

> Prayer for the dead:
> **Eternal rest give to them, O Lord,**
> **and let perpetual light shine upon them.**
> **May they rest in peace. Amen.**

All Souls: On this day (2 November) the Church remembers her dead in a special way. By going to Mass, by praying and by visiting the cemetery the faithful show their union with those who have gone before them (→ 27.6).

Requiem (from Lat. requies = rest): Mass for the Dead, so called from the first Latin word of the prayer: Requiem aeternam dona eis, Domine (= Lord, give them eternal rest), with which the Mass for the Dead begins.

Funeral: In her faith in the resurrection the Church honours even the body of a deceased person. The body is buried in the earth, in the cemetery, like the 'grain of wheat'. At the graveside the priest or deacon proclaims the promise of the resurrection in the words of Jesus: 'I am the resurrection. If anyone believes in me, even though he dies he will live. and whoever lives and believes in me will never die' (John 11:25).

Cremation: Burning the corpse and placing the ashes in an urn. Until recently, cremation was forbidden for Catholics: it was regarded as a sign of denial of belief in the resurrection; since 1964 it is permitted for Catholics, provided they do not thereby expressly deny the resurrection.

Prayers for the dead: 'To pray for the living and the dead' (→ 39.10) is one of the seven spiritual works of mercy. — There is no passage of time where God is concerned — events which are past for us, as well as those which are yet to come, are present for God. Prayers offered around the time of death, as well as those offered long after, are alike present in God's mind when that person comes to judgement — and so we can help by praying for the souls of the departed.

32   Companionship for life: the sacrament of matrimony

→ 39.1 loving life; 26.2 images of the Church

Marriage is a *life-long* union. This union is a source of permanent protection for the two partners and offers shelter and security for the children who may be born to them. Because society and the state have a natural interest in marriage and the family, they protect and support it.

Even in earliest times people placed this *union* of husband and wife under the special protection of the gods. In the Old Testament marriage is an image of the covenant which God formed with his people. In the New Testament marriage is compared with the bond between *Christ* and his Church. Marriage contracted between Christians is a sacrament: this means that it is the sign through which Jesus Christ himself is present in the *love* of the two partners.

Are these the reasons why, according to the teaching and practice of the Catholic Church, a marriage cannot be dissolved? And we might also ask: Is a marriage between Christians less threatened than that of non-Christians? Civil law allows divorce; what are the consequences of this for Catholics?

Monogamy: One husband, one wife: the legal form of marriage among nations bearing the imprint of Christianity. Other religions (e.g. Islam) allow a man to have more than one wife (*polygamy*).

32.1 Man and woman
→ 37.4 physical expression of love; 37.5 learning to love; 37.6 ability to practise self-denial

A human being exists either as a man or as a woman. A person is characterised by his/her sex. A strong power of attraction results from this difference between the sexes. Man and woman feel drawn towards one another, they are delighted to be together, see one another, talk to one another, touch and caress one another. They experience their *togetherness* as an enhancement of their lives, as happiness. By many signs and gestures they show and affirm their affection and love. Their sexual union surpasses all other gestures in intimacy and passion; it calls for final *choice and acceptance* of one another, for lasting fidelity. Sexual surrender is the highest expression of *trust*. Marriage is the *bond* of this trust.

Marriage as a bond for life is the strongest acceptance which a person can experience through another and at the same time give to the other. In giving themselves to one another in marriage man and woman publicly *promise* lifelong partnership and love. Henceforth they share not only 'bed and board' but their possessions, their cares and their joys. They lead a life together, go through their crises and help one another reciprocally in all their difficulties. In every marriage there are greater and smaller annoyances, failings, guilt and pardon. Their union and their growing together are seen in their *children*. They rejoice and are deeply touched by discovering themselves in their children with all their many talents and weaknesses. It is through children that a family is built up. Because father and mother are united for ever, the children can feel secure and protected in the family.

The book of Genesis says of the relationship between man and woman:
God created man in the image of himself . . .
male and female he created them.
God blessed them, saying to them, 'Be fruitful, multiply, fill
the earth and conquer it'.   *Genesis 1:27–28*

Sixth commandment: 'You shall not commit adultery' (→ 35.5 Ten commandments).

Ninth commandment: 'You shall not covet your neighbour's wife' (→ 35.4 Ten commandments).

Adultery: A husband or wife who, by a free decision, is unfaithful to his/her marriage partner, leaves and turns to another, disrupts the marriage. The person is guilty before the marriage partner, because the promise to be faithful is broken, before the children, because the protection necessary for them is endangered, before the community, because harm is done to a situation that is of importance in life, before God, because there is disruption of the life together willed by God.

Chastity: The right ordering of sexual behaviour in thought, word and action, inside and outside married life (→ 37.6 modesty).

Contraception: To avoid a pregnancy there are various methods, about the right and wrong of which, even among Christians, there is confusion and difference of opinion. The teaching of the Catholic Church distinguishes between methods that are permissible and those that are not. 'Artificial means' are not allowed; only the 'natural' method of choice of time is allowed. The words *'responsible parenthood'* express positively what is meant. They give the parents not only a certain freedom but lay upon them the obligation to consider carefully, in conscience, their decisions in favour of new life. The decision of Catholics must, in conscience, in the sight of God, take into consideration the teaching of the Church.

Divorce: A marriage validly contracted can, according to the teaching of the Church, not be dissolved. According to civil law it is possible. If husband and wife separate, it is very hard for all concerned. For Christians this holds: it is true that God has at heart the welfare of those who have separated; they can find his mercy. They can obtain, in faith, confidence and encouragement for a new beginning. They should above all experience help and strength in the Christian community. But fundamentally the Church maintains the words of Jesus: 'What God has

32.1   **200**

united, man must not divide' (Matthew 19:6). So, even in the case of separation of the partners, the marriage validly contracted remains; no church re-marrying is possible. But the Church is bound, in whatever way she can, for the sake of the gospel, to support those separated.

Marriage impediments: A circumstance that prevents one from entering upon a Church marriage, e.g. difference of denomination. From some impediments dispensation can be obtained.

Dispensation (Lat. = remission): Being freed from an obligation of ecclesiastical law, e.g. from the commandment to fast or from a marriage impediment.

Mixed marriages: Between Christians of different denominations; related to the problem of lack of unity on important issues of life, religious upbringing of the children and the danger of one's own straying from the faith. Mixed marriages demand from the partners great respect for the other's belief and a strong attachment to one's own faith.

32.2   The sacrament of matrimony

→ 38.1 the family; 26.2 images of the Church; 39.5 trustworthiness;
26.4 sacraments

As a social and legal contract, marriage exists independently of whether the marriage partners believe in Jesus Christ or not.

But for one who believes in *Jesus Christ* and lives within the *Church*, marriage is more than 'the most natural thing in the world'. When two baptised Christians marry their marriage is a *sacrament*. This means that not only do they make a gift of their human love to one another, but God's love is central to the marriage. In married love between man and woman God's love for these two people — and through them for many others — is present. So the sacrament of matrimony is an *effective sign* of the acceptance and fidelity that God gives to us human beings.

The expression *'Church wedding'* is misleading. The bridal couple administer the sacrament of matrimony to one another provided they say their 'yes' in the presence of a priest and two witnesses. A valid marriage becomes indissoluble when it has been consummated. To conform with the provisions of civil law in Britain, a registrar or a duly appointed 'authorised person' must also be present. In Catholic parishes it is not uncommon for the priest to be an authorised person ('authorised person' is a legal technical term).

The effect of this sacrament is not limited to the wedding ceremony. During the whole of their married life the couple in their *love* and *fidelity* share God's love and fidelity. From their conviction that God never refuses his fidelity, Christians find courage to enter upon the bonds of marriage 'till death do us part'. In the covenant with Israel and finally in Jesus Christ and his Church God has united himself with man: *God's fidelity* is the source of fidelity for human beings.

The bridal couple administer the sacrament of matrimony to one another with the following words:
I call upon these persons here present to witness
that I, N. . . . . ,
do take thee, N. . . . . ,
to be my lawful wedded wife/husband
to have and to hold from this day forward,
for better for worse, for richer for poorer,
in sickness and in health,
to love and to cherish,
till death do us part.

Nuptial Mass: Mass which includes the rite of matrimony; the rite takes place after the Liturgy of the Word, before the beginning of the Liturgy of the Eucharist.

Celebration of a mixed marriage: Where both parties are committed members of their respective churches the marriage is further defined as an 'inter-church marriage'. Where one of the partners is a baptised Roman Catholic, recognition of the marriage as valid requires that it be performed by a Catholic priest according to the rites and ceremonies of the Catholic Church. However, a local bishop, if he considers that he has sufficient reason, may dispense from this requirement and allow a Catholic to marry before a non-Catholic minister, in a non-Catholic church, according to the rites of that Church, and without any participation by a Catholic priest. Shared participation by clergy of the respective churches involved (subject to the provisions of canon and civil law) is increasingly common, and the joint pastoral after-care of couples in mixed marriages is to be encouraged.

33   Serving God's people: priestly ordination: the sacrament of Holy Orders

→ 34.1 people of God; 34.2 leadership in the Church; 30.2 work of the Spirit

The Church as community of the faithful needs fixed *structures*, a pattern easily seen, a clear distribution of duties and well-defined *leadership* so that the appointed end may be attained. This end is formulated for the Church: to be at the service of the coming of God's kingdom for all. All members of the Church are called upon and qualified to contribute to the attainment of this *end*.

The parish needs the most varied talents and services to do justice to the commission given by Jesus and to be aware of the *tasks* in the parish. Three directives in the New Testament make this commission especially clear: 'Do this in memory of me' (cf. Luke 22:19) — 'Make disciples of all the nations' (Matthew 28:19) — 'If anyone wants to be first, he must make himself last of all and servant of all' (Mark 9:35). All in the Church should know that they have an obligation with reference to this commission. But it holds good above all for those who bear an official responsibility for leading the parish and for teaching, those who hold an *ecclesiastical office* in the Church.

Many Christians find it difficult to distinguish this special office from the general commission given to all Christians. In what does the special commission of priests consist? Haven't all the faithful a share in the priesthood common to all?

33.1   Offices and services in the Church

→ 34.1 people of God; 28.2 member of the parish; 29.2 service in the world

Among the many people who followed Jesus there were some to whom he allotted specific assignments: his *disciples*. He sent them ahead into all the towns and villages where he himself intended to go, asking them to 'cure those in the town who are sick, and say, "The kingdom of God is very near to you" ' (Luke 10:9).

Among the disciples were the Twelve whom Jesus called and

sent out: the *apostles*. Within this group of the Twelve three were even more significant: Simon, James and John. Finally Jesus called Simon to be *Peter*, which means 'rock', the rock on which he wished to build his church (Matthew 16:18).

The various duties assigned to the group of disciples found their counterpart in *Church history*. As the Church spread she needed men and women to undertake specific services. These services can be grouped according to three basic tasks in a parish: as a teaching body the parish needs a *preacher*, catechist and missionary (messenger). As a group that 'celebrates', the parish needs an authorised *president for the liturgy*. A 'serving' parish needs *deacons* and others commissioned to carry out various *charitable works*.

But the work in the parish is not the duty only of those who hold special offices. Every Christian has a vocation, a charism, in the parish. A parish is more obviously at the service of God's kingdom in proportion to the recognition by its individual members of their vocation and of their opportunities to exercise it.

There are many offices and services in the Church. St Paul writes:

There is a variety of gifts but always the same Spirit; there are all sorts of service to be done, but always to the same Lord. . . . All these are the work of one and the same Spirit, who distributes different gifts to different people just as he chooses. *1 Corinthians 12:4, 5, 11*

Apostolate (Gr. = sending): Sharing by all the baptised in the mission of the Church (→ 26.1) (*Lay apostolate*).

Charism (Gr. = gift, grace): Special aptitude given by the Holy Spirit for the service of others. Each one has his own charism.

Parish council: A group chosen by the parish which, together with the parish priest, other clergy and helpers, looks after the needs of the work and life of the parish; the rights and duties of the parish council vary in each diocese.

Catechist: A teacher responsible for religious education in parish or school. May also be someone who helps to prepare small groups for first communion, confession or confirmation.

Laity (Gr. laos = people): Originally a title of honour for all who form part of God's people (or the Church). Later, the name for those members of the Church who do not belong to the clergy or a religious order.

33.2 The sacrament of Holy Orders

→ 34.2 leadership in the Church; 34.8 Church organisation; 34.1 people of God; 26.4 sacraments

The sacrament of *Holy Orders* has a special significance for the many services needed in the parish. In the Acts of the Apostles we are told that one day the local church, in order to ease the burden falling on the apostles, selected seven men 'of good reputation, filled with the Spirit and with wisdom' as deacons in the parish. 'They presented these to the apostles, who prayed and laid their hands on them' (Acts 6:6). We also learn from the letters to Timothy (1 Timothy 4:14 and 2 Timothy 1:6) that the duty of leadership was conferred by the laying-on of hands. So today this happens in the same way as in the early Church. Men who feel themselves called to serve in the parishes are commissioned for this service by the *bishops*, successors of the apostles; by *prayer* and *laying-on of hands* the bishops administer to them the sacrament of Holy Orders, priestly ordination. Many years of study lead up to this step. A person who carries out priestly service in the Church does not do so for himself but for the Church. Such a service naturally affects the life of the one who carries it out: his life-style is dictated by the priest's readiness to serve.

When a priest is ordained, as far as possible the priests of a diocese come together. They too lay their hands on the one being ordained — a sign of the close relationship between all those called and ordained for an office in the Church. With the consecrating bishop they celebrate Holy Mass together. In this way it is obvious that, in their service, those ordained are the bishop's representatives, are *commissioned* by him and are answerable to him. The bishop for his part has their welfare at heart. In this way they share in the commission and authority of the bishop.

The *bishop*, who thus works with the *priests* and *deacons* of his diocese, is ordained and receives his authority as bishop through the prayers and laying-on of hands of other bishops. This college of bishops, in union with the Bishop of Rome, is in a line of unbroken succession with the apostles. The sacrament of Holy Orders is administered, then, to those who are to serve the Church as bishop, priest or deacon.

The bishop is a member of the college of bishops and successors of the apostles. He leads his diocese. He is responsible for teaching, for the liturgy and care of his brethren and their service in his diocese, but also in the universal church. He confirms the faithful, he ordains deacons, priests and other bishops; he consecrates new churches.

Priests, commissioned by their bishop, lead a parish in the diocese or work in some other special service for the Church. They preach and teach. They have authority to celebrate the Eucharist and administer the sacraments of penance and anointing of the sick. They also have authority to administer solemn baptism and receive the marriage promises of bridal couples (a deacon also has authority to administer the last two sacraments). They have a duty to care for all, especially those in need, the sick and the dying. They must strive to maintain unity in their parishes.

Deacons serve the parish in the Liturgy of the Word, in preaching, teaching and in the care of the sick and those in need. In parishes where no priest is available they conduct Bible services and distribute Holy Communion.

The apostle Paul says of the priestly office:
We are not dictators over your faith, but are fellow-workers with you for your happiness. *2 Corinthians 1:24*

Clergy (Gr. kleros = share): Like the tribe of Levi, the clergy have service in the presence of God as their 'portion and inheritance' (Numbers 18:20); a general term for all men sacramentally ordained in the Church: deacons, priests, bishops. — Women are not allowed to assume office in the Church; this gives rise to much discussion (in some non-Catholic churches the regulations are different).

Priest (Gr. presbyteros = elder): In the Church a word for ordained leaders of the parishes and presidents at the celebration of the Eucharist. The Second Vatican Council says: 'By the power of the sacrament of orders, priests are consecrated to preach the gospel, shepherd the faithful and celebrate the divine worship as true priests of the New Testament' (*The Church*, para. 28). The Catholic Church does not see the priesthood as an entry into an office, possibly for a time, but as a vocation, expressed once and for all, with a validity that is unlimited and comes from God. Therefore priestly ordination cannot be repeated or revoked (→ 28.1 and 29.2).

First Mass: The first Mass of a newly-ordained priest is normally celebrated in his home parish.

Concelebration: Celebration of the Eucharist by several priests together, above all the Mass celebrated by the bishop with his priests. Sign of the brotherhood that exists among the priests and with their bishop, successor of the apostles.

Celibacy (Lat. caelebs = unmarried): By ecclesiastical law, priests of the Western Catholic Church are bound not to marry. This obligation is freely taken upon themselves by those concerned. It is the expression of whole-hearted service for God and man. Celibacy was an obligation as far back as the fourth century.

Lack of priests: In most countries there is a fall-off in the number of priests so that, in the foreseeable future, parishes may well be without a priest. There is a need for more vocations to the priesthood so that the Church may be adequately served.

Deacon (Gr. diakonos = servant): The office of deacon is found established in the Acts of the Apostles. For many centuries the diaconate was merely a step to the priesthood. Only in recent years has it been once more recognised in the Catholic Church. The deacon is to be seen as a direct helper of the bishop, not as a subordinate of the priest. Ordination to the diaconate does not empower a deacon to celebrate Mass or to administer the sacrament of penance.

Religious vocation: Under this heading vocations to the diaconate, priesthood and to the religious life are included. Efforts to interest people in vocations must be the concern of the whole Church.

Reader: Performs the duty of reading at Bible services and at Mass and may also help the priest by taking part in the bidding prayers. The office of reader goes back to the early Church.

Letters to Timothy: The two New Testament letters to Paul's companion Timothy (Acts 16:1–3) and the one to Titus are called the Pastoral Letters. They testify to the respect in which Paul was held in the early Church and are concerned above all with trustworthy handing-on of the apostolic tradition in Pauline churches at the end of the first century.

34 The Church in the concrete

→ 20 Catholic Church; 26 sign of salvation

When we speak of the Church it is not enough to know her most important doctrines. We must know too how the *Church* in the concrete lives and works, what *forms of organisation* she has developed in order to fulfil her duty of service to the coming of God's kingdom.

The Church is a *community* of people characterised by a common faith, carried along by hope and conscious that they are called upon to love God and man. The Church is a movement begun by Jesus Christ himself, an organism which lives through Jesus Christ; the Church is his body. In the power of his Spirit she extends throughout the whole world.

A movement needs external structures if it is to remain at all times effective; so too with the Church. Yet one should recognise that much in the *structures of the Church* is conditioned historically and can therefore also be changed. That this 'was always so' — accurately, perhaps for 'only' 500 years — is in itself no reason that it must remain so 'for ever'. Only the basic form of the Church cannot be called in question. It is a community commissioned by *Jesus Christ* and in his *Holy Spirit*, provided with authorised leadership appropriate to the preparation of the coming of the kingdom of God. This can lead to a host of questions. Above all, each generation must ask itself afresh: How can the concrete Church today be what she should be, a living movement in the Spirit of Jesus Christ corresponding as far as possible to God's promises? What can the individual Christian contribute to bringing this about?

34.1 Responsibility in the people of God

→ 38.4 the whole world; 29.2 service in the world; 33.1 offices and services; 30.3 sin and community; 31.1 praying and caring

In the course of nearly two thousand years a variety of institutions and structures has been established in the *Church*; the rights and duties of church officials have been laid down in detail. This external *organisation* of the Church can easily be described, but it would give a false picture if one wished the Church to be defined solely by those who have been ordained and given official standing in the Church. What the Church is and should be is entrusted to the whole *people of God*. In making the Church a reality one cannot proceed according to one's own discretion. For essential elements, for example the basic meaning of Holy Scripture, the sacraments, and the significance given to the offices set up for service (Pope, bishops, priests), have been established for the Church by Christ. Within this framework much can change in the course of history. But the essentials of the form of the Church cannot be changed. In each age the whole people of God must be careful that the life of the Church is so structured that it corresponds as well as it possibly can to the commission given by Jesus Christ. All members of the Church bear *responsibility* for this, even if in different ways. The Church does not remain alive and active through organisation, administration or laws — although these are indispensable for a living *community*. The real life of the Church comes from the devotedness of the faithful in the home and at work, in the parish and in their public life in the world.

Readers, choir and ministers of Communion feel joint responsibility for arrangements for the liturgy, others are concerned for the sick and old or for people in need. Others again are active in work for children and young adults, or preparation for various parish celebrations, etc. Mothers and fathers prepare children in small groups for the reception of the sacraments of penance, the Eucharist and confirmation. Nowadays there is sometimes a tendency to make of each *duty* newly recognised one's own personal 'business', a special office, a new commissioning. In this way a considerable number of the laity have taken over responsible tasks in the Church. Yet this development can also bring with it a certain danger; it may lead to inactivity on the part of the 'average' member of the parish. Each one of the *faithful* in a parish should do something on his own initiative; for the life of the Church depends on the living sense of faith of her members — and she is as active or as lame as her members. This sharing by every Christian in the mission of the Church is called the *apostolate* of all the faithful. It is based on the common priesthood of all (1 Peter 2:9).

The following is a prayer for the parish:
Lord Jesus Christ,
you are the head of our parish.
Give us the grace to love one another,
to say the right word
and to give one another a helping hand.
From the German prayer book *Gotteslob*

34.2 Leadership in the Church

→ 21.1 Church as community; 20.1 work of the Spirit; 33.2 priestly ordination; 20.2 tradition; 34.8 Church organisation

'But the Advocate, the Holy Spirit, whom the Father will send in my name, will teach you everything and remind you of all I have said to you' (John 14:26). These words give the Church confidence that the *Spirit of God* strengthens her in *fidelity* to God's word, and as the people of God she remains preserved from error. Individuals or groups may deviate and err; yet the Church believes that the faithful as a body do not err in important questions of faith. This 'sense of the faith' has been given to God's people by the Holy Spirit.

The *bishops*, as successors of the *apostles*, have been called to *lead* God's people. They bear the burden of care for the visible *unity* of the Church. In the practice of this office they are bound to be faithful to *Holy Scripture* and to the *tradition* of the Church, but also bound to the people entrusted to them. Their duty is to see that the *gospel* is correctly preached, that *fraternal charity* is a reality and that *church services* and the sacraments are fittingly celebrated. All the bishops of the Church together form the college of bishops.

The Bishop of Rome is the successor of the apostle Peter. He is called *Pope* or 'Holy Father'. At the time of St Peter, Rome was the capital of the known world. Peter received from Jesus the promise: 'You are Peter and on this rock I will build my Church. And the gates of the underworld can never hold out against it. I will give you the keys of the kingdom of heaven: whatever you bind on earth shall be considered bound in heaven; whatever you loose on earth shall be considered loosed in heaven' (Matthew 16:18–19). Catholics are convinced that this promise is effective not only for Peter but also for his successors. This means that the Pope is not only the first among the bishops according to rank, but that he also has *supreme authority* over them. The Pope is the guardian of unity and the promoter of the life of the Church throughout the world.

So that the gospel may be handed on intact and that the faith entrusted to the Church may be preserved from error, distortion, additions, restrictions and abbreviations, the bishops in union with the Pope exercise the *office of teaching* (magisterium) in the

Church. Normally this is done by the fact that each bishop in his own diocese has at heart the true, living teaching of the Church — in union with the other bishops and the Pope, through intercessory prayer and by exchange of questions and answers concerning their *common faith*. But there is also an extraordinary way in which the teaching office of the Church is exercised: namely, by a *General Council of the Church*.

The Church believes that the Holy Spirit preserves her from error when the bishops in communion with the Pope reach a solemn decision concerning the faith — in spite of all human limitations on the part of individuals taking part in the Council.

The First Vatican Council (1869–70) decided that such a decision about the teaching of the Church in matters of faith or morals could also be made by the *Pope alone*, acting as president of the universal college of bishops and in fidelity to the tradition of the Church. He must do this publicly and make it binding on the whole Church. Such decisions, or definitions, are for Catholics part of the fundamental faith of the Church.

The second Letter to Timothy, drawn up about the year 90 A.D., shows us the significance even then of the bishop's office. The letter exhorts the bishop:
Proclaim the message and, welcome or unwelcome, insist on it. Refute falsehood, correct error, call to obedience — but do all with patience and with the intention of teaching. The time is sure to come when, far from being content with sound teaching, people will be avid for the latest novelty and collect themselves a whole series of teachers according to their own tastes. . . . *2 Timothy 4:2–3*

Teaching, priestly and pastoral office: Description of the threefold office of the bishops united with the Pope (in the life of the Church often closely interrelated). It is their duty to be watchful that the whole Church proclaims the gospel and passes on correctly the teaching of the Church; that she administers the sacraments in the approved manner and that she follows the precepts of Christ according to the gospel. Priests and deacons, in a lesser degree, share in the episcopal office (→ 33.2). In fulfilment of these three basic duties of the Church — which are the foundation of these offices — every Christian is expected to play a part (→ 28.3 priesthood common to all).
Primacy (Lat. = first position): The supreme position of the Pope in the Church.

It is not just a *primacy of honour* but implies full authority to make regulations binding on the whole of the Roman Catholic Church (*primacy of jurisdiction* = authority to make legal decisions). The Bishop of Rome is not, in the usual sense, the senior bishop or president of the college of bishops, but as Pope he is the universal bishop of the whole Church (→ 34.8 college of bishops).

Synod: Assembly of about two hundred bishops from all parts of the world; chosen from the bishops' conferences in the different countries; held, since Vatican II, in Rome every three years.

Council (Lat. concilium = synod): Assembly of bishops. The words 'council' and 'synod' mean the same; however, council has become the official word. The bishops of the whole world assemble under the presidency of the Pope to advise about matters concerning the whole Church; it is sometimes called an *ecumenical council* (from Gr. oikumene; = covering the whole world).The last general or ecumenical council (the 21st) was held in the Vatican in Rome (1962-65); it is called the *Second Vatican Council* (the first was held 1869-70).

Infallibility: A concept often misunderstood. The Church believes that she as a body is through the Holy Spirit preserved from teaching anything contrary to divine revelation. When in matters of faith for the whole Church a decision has to be made, by a Council or by the Pope alone, such a decision, through the assistance of the Holy Spirit, is 'infallible' (i.e. it is preserved from falsehood).

Definition: Solemn decision in matters of faith or morals, through which a fundamental statement of the faith (dogma) is formulated as binding for the whole Church.

Apostolic succession: Technical expression for the fact that the bishops of the Catholic Church trace their office back in unbroken line to the apostles.

Encyclical: A circular letter from the Pope to the whole Church in which he speaks of important problems of faith and the Christian life.

Imprimatur (Lat. = let it be printed): Ecclesiastical expression used for the bishop's permission to publish a book concerned with matters of faith or the Christian life.

Pastoral care (or care of souls): The Church's care for the salvation of man and for everything important for salvation. This takes place chiefly through preaching, administration of the sacraments and fraternal acts of charity, but also through conversations with individuals and in many other ways.

Theology (Gr. = study of God): From the beginning in Christianity it was considered important to reflect diligently about the faith. A person whose main concern is theology is called a *theologian* (→ 11.2).

Exegesis (Gr. = interpretation): Explanation and interpretation of biblical writings; research into content, literary forms, meaning. — Important branch of theological studies.

Sermon or homily: A 'speech' or talk in which the word of God is explained. In the Catholic Church only a person appointed by the bishop is commissioned to do this.

Catechesis (Gr. = oral instruction): Instruction in the faith, also as introduction to specific sacraments. The preparation of a young person or an adult preceding reception into the Church is called the *catechumenate.*

34.3 Precepts of the Church

→ 35.4 ten commandments; 30.5 sacrament of penance; 27.5 each week Easter

The Church wants to *help* the faithful to remain united with God in their following of Jesus and within the *community of the Church*. The most important precepts, or commandments, of the Church enjoin on all Catholics to celebrate Sunday as the Lord's day, to participate in the Eucharist on Sundays and Holydays of obligation, to keep the laws of fasting and abstinence appointed by the Church, to receive the sacraments of penance and the Eucharist regularly, at least in paschal time, and to contribute to the support of their pastors.

Part of the 118th psalm, the longest in the psalter, helps us to see what our attitude in these matters should be:
You have laid down your precepts
to be obeyed with care.
May my footsteps be firm
to obey your statutes.
Then I shall not be put to shame
as I heed your commands.
I will thank you with an upright heart
as I learn your decrees.
I will obey your statutes.   *Psalm 118(119):4–8*

Sunday as the Lord's day: On this day the Church reflects in a special way on the death and resurrection of her Lord Jesus Christ. Christians keep it as a day of celebration, rest from work, a day for the community of the faithful and for the family (→ 35.4).

Celebration of the Eucharist on Sundays and Holydays: From early times Christians have assembled on Sundays to celebrate the Eucharist. It is an expression of their faith in, and adoration of God, but at the same time it is the source of their strength to live a Christian life. Anyone who, without sufficient reasons, absents himself from Mass, bypasses the centre of the Church's life. He withdraws from the community of the faithful, rejects God's offer to come close to him (→ 35.4) and thus fails seriously before God and the parish. Therefore since ancient times the Church enjoins on the faithful to take part in the Sunday Mass (so-called 'Sunday obligation').

Friday self-denial: Christians make efforts on this day freely to deny themselves something in order to give concrete expression to their union with their suffering

Lord and their suffering fellow-men. They deny themselves something at table (e.g. meat — formerly a precept of the Church) or some enjoyment, or they do something special in order to help others (→ 39.9).

Reception of the sacraments of penance and the Eucharist: To receive the Eucharist, at least during Paschal time, is a minimum precept, for the Church says that going to Holy Communion is an integral part of every Mass. She also recommends all Christians regularly to ask forgiveness of their sins in the sacrament of penance. Anyone conscious of serious (mortal) sin is bound by the Church to receive the sacrament of penance (→ 27.5 and 30.5).

Responsibility for Church and parish: Each Christian is responsible for helping the Church to spread the message of the coming of the kingdom of God, for celebrating the Eucharist and for helping people in need. An individual Christian can take over various duties in the parish and in the Church (e.g. individual services, financial support of good works, etc.). Each one should place at the disposal of the Church some of his free time (→ 34.1; 33.1; 34.5).

Paschal time: Liturgically the time from the Easter Vigil till Pentecost. According to ecclesiastical law the time from Ash Wednesday until the feast of the Blessed Trinity. During this time each Catholic should receive the Eucharist and (in case of serious sin) must receive the sacrament of penance prior to receiving the Eucharist: it is in this sense that penance is one of the so-called 'Easter duties'.

34.4   Religious orders and congregations

→ 35.2 the God worthy of our love; 37.6 self-denial; 36.1 necessary; 38.2 friends and groups

Since the time of the early Church there have been men and women who consider they have a vocation to live a life entirely for the *gospel*. In order to do this more easily they have joined a *religious order* or *congregation*.

Life in community is characterised by the three 'evangelical counsels' which are traced back to the gospel or to Jesus himself. They are intended to help people to be completely free for God and their fellow human beings: through *poverty, chastity* and *obedience* for the sake of the kingdom of God. A person who, of his own free will, in faith and love, lives poorly, expresses his union with the poor and God's promise to be close to them. One who renounces married life with this attitude shows himself drawn to all those who are lonely and abandoned. The one who, trusting in God, gives up his own power, places himself consciously in God's name on the side of the helpless and lives with and for them. So religious communities anticipate and are a pattern of God's future world, where it will be clear that all men are loved equally.

When candidates enter a community of this kind their preparation lasts for several years — at first they are postulants, then novices. Only after a time are they allowed to take *vows* to live according to the rule of their order. At first these promises are only for a time; after further years of probation (and not in all congregations, even then) perpetual vows, binding for life, are made. In the course of the centuries new orders and congregations have repeatedly been established because, in different conditions, new challenges have been presented to the faith of Christians. As examples for the whole Church, religious do their best to respond to these challenges.

The different orders and congregations have taken on responsibility for different *duties* which are characteristic of them, for example, prayer and liturgy, preaching, missions, care of the sick, education. Many are named after their founders, e.g. Benedictines, Franciscans, Dominicans. Many founders of religious orders were later honoured as saints.

According to their duties, a distinction is made between '*active*' and '*contemplative*' orders, that is, between those who are above all active in the service of their fellow-men and those who devote themselves especially to prayer, meditation and the celebration of the liturgy.

Most orders have their own houses and some form of religious dress for their members. There are also communities called secular institutes, similar to religious communities, whose members wear no distinctive form of dress and who live in the world, not in a *convent*; they are engaged in a profession in the '*world*'.

At first some of the churches of the Reformation rejected religious life, but in recent times new groups have been formed in these churches. The best-known is the brotherhood of Taizé in France.

Each new age needs individual Christians and Christian groups who live the faith in such a way that God's world can be concretely expressed as an alternative to our world. Just as Abraham set out on his wanderings *at God's bidding*, departing from his usual, familiar circumstances, so even now these Christians seek a new form of life.

> Jesus says to those who, for his sake, live differently from the majority of people:
> **Everyone who has left houses, brothers, sisters, father, mother, children or land for the sake of my name will be repaid a hundred times over, and also inherit eternal life.**
>
> *Matthew 19:29*

Evangelical counsels (or gospel counsels): The name given to the religious vows of poverty (renouncing personal possessions), chastity (renouncing sexual relationships, marriage and a family) and obedience (subjecting oneself to superiors). With reference, for example, to Mark 10:17–31, these are counselled, but not explicitly demanded in the gospels.

Vows: Solemn promises, of poverty, chastity and obedience, made to God by members of a religious order; they either bind for a time (temporary vows) or for life (perpetual).

Convent or monastery: A dwelling set apart where a religious community lives. Those who ask for admission into a convent are called *postulants*; while they are seeing whether they are suited to the life they are called *novices* (= newcomers). In many orders the novices receive the religious dress (or *habit*) only when they take vows. 'To enter the monastery' (convent) = to enter an order or congregation.

Order (Lat. ordo = rule, regulation): Whether one speaks of an order or a congregation depends on the rule, the degree of *enclosure* (how much the members are confined to the monastery), and on the date of the foundation of the order. The Benedictines are an example of an order in the strict sense of the word. Communities very recently established, whose members live in the world and follow a profession, are called *secular institutes*. Members of the older orders are called monks or nuns; the terms brothers, sisters, friars, etc. are also used. In many men's orders some are priests (they have studied theology and been ordained) and others are brothers (members of the order who have not been ordained).

Enclosure: That part of the monastery or convent into which outsiders, even guests and visitors, are not admitted.

Abbot: Superior of an abbey of monks, usually elected by the monastic community. In many orders the leader is called Prior, Guardian or Superior.

Taizé: Place in France; site of an ecumenical brotherhood founded in 1942 by Brother Roger Schutz. Most important duty: work for Christian unity. Has great influence on the spiritual renewal of young people (Youth Council). Prayer and social commitment: meditation and community life.

Asceticism (Gr. askesis = training): Forms of self-control and self-denial for Christ's sake practised by many Christians, not only by religious.

34.5   Good works

→ 26 sign of salvation; 6.2 bread for others; 37.2 loving in deed;
29.2 service in the world

Within the Catholic Church there are associations which people
freely join according to age, profession and social interests. They
have various names, e.g. *societies*, *groups*, etc. They take over
— usually by arrangement with the bishop — duties in the social
or educational spheres or they help in spreading the gospel. Many
of these organisations extend to other countries and are international. It is clear from them that the faithful are *co-responsible*
for the work of the Church, not only in their own parish but also
on the national and international levels.

Side by side with them are *charitable organisations*, usually
arising from the initiative of the faithful: they are often begun
'from below' and are then given approval by Church leaders.
They are signs of Christian *solidarity* and have given people
confidence in the Church, enhancing her credibility.

Paul writes to the Galatians about the way in which
Christians can give help:
**You should carry each other's troubles and fulfil the law of
Christ. . . . While we have the chance, we must do good to
all, and especially to our brothers in the faith.**
Galatians 6:2, 10

Missions: To the Church is given the commission to proclaim the gospel all over
the world (→ 26.1). Each Christian, each parish, each diocese must collaborate in
the carrying out of this task.

Societies, groups, etc.: Numerous associations are established in most countries –
professional, social, charitable, etc. Some are international, others diocesan
and/or parochial. Parish priests can usually help people to find one or more
organisations in which they can be of assistance and help the Church. Detailed
information about them is also to be found in annual publications like *The
Catholic Directory*.

34.6 Christians in the service of peace

→ 5.2 God's will; 37.3 taking the world seriously; 38.4 the whole world; 38.3 society and state

Our world is beset with conflicts. War-like disputes repeatedly rear their ugly head. The distribution of arms assumes gigantic proportions, the power of weapons to annihilate is so far beyond our imagination that one is easily inclined to be resigned and to give up all hope of peace.

Individual *Christians* and the Church as a whole are bound to *serve the interests of peace*. Such efforts are difficult, for peace is not a fixed state of affairs which can be reached once and for all. It is continually threatened afresh. The Church, not confined to state interests and national frontiers, has special opportunities for devoting herself to peace. In the service of peace the Catholic Church collaborates with other churches; she makes use of her world-wide opportunities, and the Vatican diplomatic service is available for this purpose. In conflicts she decides unequivocally for non-violent solutions.

Christians devote themselves to the cause of peace when everywhere they uphold *human rights* and the just claims of the poor and oppressed. The interests of peace are served by efforts to overcome *prejudice*, by learning to master hatred, envy and distrust, by developing the skills required to protest against injustice, by courageous support for the deprived and by *non-violent opposition* to injustice. The cause of peace is furthered when Christians show one another signs of reconciliation and aim at collaboration with the various groups.

Much *smaller steps* are equally necessary in the cause of peace, steps that can be taken by individuals. Christians must learn so to deal with conflicts that solutions are reached that give satisfaction to all concerned.

Sometimes Christians draw different conclusions from the gospel and the teaching of the Church. Some say that military service is necessary in order to preserve peace; others say peace will be maintained only if no one has recourse to arms. In such a situation both groups are called upon to show, in *dialogue* and in practice, that they have peace seriously at heart. In any case, the one anxious to perform military service is right only if he intends

34.6

to serve the cause of peace, and the conscientious objector is right only if he is prepared to *serve society*.

The Second Vatican Council makes it clear:
It is our clear duty to strain every muscle as we work for the time when all war can be completely outlawed by international consent.
The Church in the Modern World, para. 82

Pax Christi (Lat. pax = peace): Catholic movement for peace established in Lourdes 1944/45. Makes special efforts for peace among nations by making people conscious of what it means. Calls for prayer and political initiative.

34.7 The Church in the world
→ 38.3 society and state; 38.4 the whole world; 39 do likewise

The Church lives in the world, she arouses expectations and she experiences rejection. Even when she strives after *justice*, peace and the lessening of human distress, she is not infrequently blamed and in many countries even persecuted. At no time have so many Christians, for the sake of their faith, been discriminated against, imprisoned and even put to death as in this century. Yet the Church, following Jesus, may not cease to make herself the advocate of human *dignity* and *freedom*, even if this should cause her exterior harm.

It is grave that the credibility of the Church should be weakened so frequently by the attitude of many Christians who act selfishly and unthinkingly, seeking only their own advantage and gain, thoughtlessly ranging themselves on the side of the rich and powerful. This is in contradiction to the gospel.

Because Christians are citizens, members of the state, there are many points of contact between *Church* and *state*. In several of their tasks they work together, in other matters Church and state are interested in different aspects, e.g. marriage, family, school, social affairs. The New Testament accepts civil authority and sees obedience to its laws as a duty before God (Romans 13:1-7), but it places the *decisions of one's conscience* above all claims of those who govern the state: 'Obedience to God comes before obedience to man' (Acts 5:29).

In the course of history the relationship between church and state has changed in various ways. In modern times an attempt is made in many countries to find a solution by collaboration; state and church try to work together for man's welfare. In other countries, e.g. the USA, great stress is laid on separation of church and state without, for this reason, completely excluding co-operation. In many countries there are contractual agreements, so-called *concordats*, between the government and the Vatican. This means that there is reciprocal agreement concerning rights and duties.

There are important spheres of collaboration between church and state in *social* and *educational* policies. Here, by suitable laws, Christians try to bring about *social justice* and to ensure policies that correspond to, and are effective for a Christian concept of man. However, where politics are concerned, different solutions are acceptable even for Christians. Therefore, fundamentally all parties whose basic laws are compatible with a *Christian conscience* are available to Christians.

On the other hand, Christians must be critical towards and oppose those parties whose policies and efforts are contrary to a Christian conscience. Christians may not remain silent even if their silence proves detrimental.

The commission to make known to all nations the message of the coming of God's kingdom includes doing everything one can in order that life in the world may be more human and more just. How much the Church knows that she has an obligation in this matter is clear above all in her *social teaching*.

When asked if it was permissible for believing Jews to pay taxes to the heathen emperor in Rome, Jesus answered:
Give back to Caesar what belongs to Caesar — and to God what belongs to God.   *Mark 12:17*

Catholic social teaching: Summary of the statements of the Catholic Church about the attitude of the individual towards society or towards problems of social justice. Catholic social doctrine is based on three principles: persons, solidarity, subsidiarity.

Person (as principle of social doctrine): Society and state exist for man, not vice versa.

Solidarity (as principle of social doctrine): There are reciprocal relationships between person and society; the individual has duties to society and is responsible for the well-being of society, and vice versa.

Subsidiarity (as principle of social doctrine): What the individual (or a specific group) can do on its own initiative should not be taken away and off-loaded on to the — greater, higher — community. But the 'higher' or more important community must so support the 'lower' that it can cope with its duties (i.e. helping others to help themselves).

Educational policy: A term used for the efforts of different groups to make their educational ideals publicly effective; Catholic educational policy attempts to make the Christian image of man recognised in matters of formation; Catholic schools, institutes of Higher Education, etc.; working with and in political parties can also make its contribution in this matter.

Social policy: Collective term for the efforts of different groups in society to make their social proposals effective and negotiate them by contract. Christian social policy is under obligation, from a gospel viewpoint, to help the poor, sick, helpless, immigrants, etc.

Concordat (Lat. = agreement): Contract between a state and the supreme ecclesiastical authority (Vatican) concerning reciprocal rights and duties.

Established or state religion: One which exists as part of the political system of the state and is to be distinguished from one which is allowed to operate freely without actually being established by law.

34.8   Structures of Church organisation

→ 21.1 Church as community; 26 sign of salvation; 33 sacrament of Holy Orders

The smallest unit of organisation in the Church is the *parish*. It is led by the parish priest. Sometimes a curate or chaplain, a deacon or lay helpers assist him. Often a sacristan and organist provide important professional services.

In addition to the chief officials there are many assistants in a parish. The parish council participates in the co-ordination of the various parochial activities and advises the parish priest with regard to pastoral work; someone may be responsible for administration of property and for finances. The visible centre of the parish is the church with its altar and lectern, tabernacle and sanctuary lamp, baptismal font and facilities for confession. Other buildings (e.g. parish hall, etc.) make it clear that in a parish devoted to the service of Jesus Christ it is not only the church services that are of importance.

Several parishes form a *deanery*, with a dean in charge, but the oldest and most important unit of the Catholic Church is the *diocese* of which the bishop is the leader. The bishop's jurisdiction is sometimes known as that of the *Ordinary*, in so far as it arises from his very office and is not merely granted him by law. Under him is a Vicar General.

Several dioceses form a *province*, of which an archbishop is in charge. The bishops of a country are united in a Bishops' Conference.

At the head of the bishops is the Pope, the Bishop of Rome. He is the successor of St Peter, the visible head of the *whole Church*. He is supported by the Roman Curia, who are responsible for all ecclesiastical administration. Every three years the Bishops' Synod meets in Rome. It is an assembly of elected representatives of the Bishops' Conferences and advises the Pope in the government of the Church.

The cardinals have a special duty. They are named by the Pope and support him — if they are in Rome — in the government of the Church. Those not in Rome work as bishops in the different dioceses of the world. All the cardinals together form the College of Cardinals. After the death of a Pope they meet together in Rome and elect his successor. This regulation dates back to the year 1059.

The officials in the Church are there to serve the people of God. The words Jesus addressed to his disciples are appropriate:
Anyone who wants to become great among you must be your servant, and anyone who wants to be first among you must be slave to all. For the Son of Man himself did not come to be served, but to serve, and to give his life as a ransom for many. *Mark 10:43-45*

Parish: Community of Catholics who live in a specific place (village, town or part of a city); sometimes a group of specific people distinguished not on a territorial basis, but on the basis of something else they have in common (e.g. status as students, nationality, etc.).
Parish priest: The one who presides over a parish. This duty is entrusted to a priest who is commissioned by the bishop. He often has chief (or lesser) assistants — they may be numerous.
Curate: A priest, usually a younger one, who helps the parish priest.

34.8

Chaplain: A priest specially trained for specific work; he may assist a parish priest in pastoral work or may work in a school, an institution, etc. (e.g. youth work).

Deacon: By ordaining deacons the bishop assigns them to special services in the Church. There have been deacons since the early days of the Church (→ 33.2).

Dean: Several parishes (originally ten) form a deanery. This unit is administered by one of the priests of the deanery, whose election (appointment) to this office must be confirmed by the bishop. This office is more correctly termed rural dean, to distinguish its holder from the person who heads a cathedral chapter, sometimes called Provost, often Dean.

Diocese (also called 'see'): The oldest and most important division of the Church. Also called 'seat' in reference to the bishop's 'throne'.

Vicar General: Authorised personal representative of the bishop in the sphere of ecclesiastical law; appointed by the bishop, but receiving much of his authority from the universal law of the Church; his office is terminated when the bishop's office is terminated.

Canon law: The precepts and law valid in the Church. It regulates the life of the community of the Church; e.g. rights and duties of parish priests, of bishops, etc. The regulations are found in the book of canon law (codex).

Curia: A group of officials who administer a diocese, under the authority of the bishop; for the whole church there is the Roman (or papal) Curia, which does this administrative work. The Roman Curia is divided into sections (congregations), each of which is generally governed by a cardinal.

Bishop: → 34.2

Auxiliary bishop: Chosen to help the bishop either by carrying out certain functions (e.g. confirmation, consecration of churches), or by representing him at certain functions throughout the diocese, or by undertaking responsibility for one area within the diocese.

Cathedral chapter: College of priests called together by the bishop (an individual is called a cathedral canon because the canons belong to the cathedral). The chapter advises the bishop, like a senate, and, when the bishop dies, it takes over the administration of the diocese.

Bishops' Conferences: National or international assemblies of bishops under the leadership of a president. They deal with questions of the care of souls and the liturgy, with general ecclesiastical problems and policy. A national conference may make decisions binding for the country concerned. The role of an international conference is consultative.

College of bishops: All the bishops assembled under the presidency (primacy) of the Pope. It is most clearly seen when all the bishops meet in Council. A Council can be convoked only by the Pope.

Cardinal (Lat. cardo = hinge): The highest dignity (after the Pope) in the Church. Cardinals are chosen by the Pope. Usually a cardinal either is a diocesan bishop or administers an office in the Roman Curia. Since the eleventh century cardinals have elected the Pope.

Pope (Lat. papa = father): The Bishop of Rome and therefore successor of St Peter and leader of the whole Church. He is in a special way the sign and guardian of unity in the Catholic Church.

Apostolic See: Name for the papal government (lit. seat of the successor of the apostle Peter).

Hierarchy (lit. priestly government): Ordered grades of ordained persons in the Catholic Church.

Patriarch: Certain episcopal sees had, even in the first century, greater importance and influence than others (Antioch, Alexandria, Jerusalem). In addition there were the two seats of government: Constantinople and Rome. Distinct from the four patriarchal sees in the East was Rome in the West (other 'senior' bishops in the West were not influential). As long as East and West were not separated, these five patriarchates were considered the most important bishoprics in the Church. Until the separation a certain primacy of the Bishop of Rome was recognised. In the Eastern Church even today the title of patriarch has significance. In the West its significance is less (although it is a title of honour, e.g. Patriarch of Venice), because the 'chief patriarch of the West' is the Pope (→ 20.2).

Vatican: Since the fourteenth century the *home* of the Pope; it also houses the offices of the Roman Curia. Famous all over the world are the *Sistine Chapel* (place where the Pope is elected during the conclave) and the *Vatican Museums*.

Conclave (Lat. = a space that is locked away): The meeting place of the cardinals when they assemble to elect a Pope. The meetings are held in complete seclusion from the public so that the choice of the Pope may be completely free from outside influence; introduced in 1274.

Vatican City State: Established in its present form by the Lateran Treaty of 1929. Independent city state in the western part of the city of Rome (¼ square mile approximately). It includes St Peter's Basilica, St Peter's Square, the Vatican palace and gardens. The Pope as head of the state enjoys complete independence and full sovereignty.

Church finance: In different countries ecclesiastical finances are arranged in various ways. The faithful in Britain contribute to the maintenance of the Catholic Church by the Sunday collections. They obviously have a definite duty to contribute generously to the various needs of the Church.

34.9   Work for Church unity

→ 20.4 unity in diversity; 20.2 tradition; 1.2 following; 1.4 read the Bible; 9.2 Jesus teaches us how to pray

It is scandalous that the one church of Jesus Christ is divided into many churches. *Christian unity* no longer exists. At a certain period in her history the opinions prevalent at the time came so much to the fore that unity in faith was lost sight of. Christians sometimes proclaimed their own opinion rather than their Lord Jesus Christ and his message.

The institutional unity of the Church as community of the bishops among themselves and with the *Bishop of Rome*, the

Pope, was shattered and was no longer recognised by everyone. Christians could no longer celebrate the Eucharist together. The credibility of their faith was in this way lessened; they often set their own opinions above the claims that Christ makes on all men.

Christians cannot, of themselves, find the strength necessary to bring about unity; it comes from Jesus Christ and his *Holy Spirit*. Therefore all Christians have a duty to *pray* that the unity of the Church and through it the unity of the world may become more and more a reality. And they have the duty to do all in their power — given plurality and variety in forms of expression — to give more credible testimony to the world and to live out the *unanimity* of the Christian faith.

In our age there is a growing conviction that *separation* into different denominations and sects contradicts the will of Jesus Christ. The *Ecumenical Movement* works for the unity of all Christians. A first step towards this is to stress what unites us instead of what divides us: faith in God the Father, in Jesus Christ and the Holy Spirit; the *Bible* as a common foundation, *baptism*, *prayer* and waiting for the coming of the *kingdom of God*.

Certainly one must continue to be realistic: unity in faith cannot be dictated from above; it must grow from the grass roots. For unity is first and foremost the honesty and *determination* with which Christians and the various churches must strive to live according to the gospel. Therefore ecumenical efforts do not take place 'at the highest level'; they are fostered above all in active parishes. In ecumenical services, held regularly, Christians *pray* for unity. In theological dialogue they try to learn to know, and to have a better understanding of their own faith and other Christian convictions. Christians together perform *services for their neigh-bours*. In *missionary territories* Christian unity is felt to be especially urgent. Therefore in many countries there have been experiments in new forms of collaboration between the churches. The more intensively all Christians are centred on Jesus Christ and prepared to give up their prejudices, the better placed they will be to build bridges and *overcome their divisions*.

This hymn helps to sum up what our attitude should be:
**The Church's one foundation
is Jesus Christ, her Lord;
she is his new creation,
by water and the Word;
from heaven he came and sought her
to be his holy bride,
with his own blood he bought her
and for her life he died.**

**Elect from every nation,
yet one o'er all the earth,
her charter of salvation
one Lord, one faith, one birth;
one holy name she blesses,
partakes one holy food,
and to one hope she presses,
with every grace endued.**   *S. J. Stone*

Orthodox Churches (Gr. = correct belief): Between the two parts of the Roman empire (with the capitals of Rome and Constantinople) increasing rivalry arose even in the fourth century; this had its effects in ecclesiastical circles. The Church of the East (nowadays, especially the Greek and Russian Orthodox Churches) held fast to the traditions of the original Church. It was above all ecclesiastical-political conflict that led to separation. Many short-lived schisms were tolerated until the schism of 1054. Since the Second Vatican Council (1962–65) efforts at a rapprochement have been intensified (→ 16.2).

Roman Catholic: The Orthodox churches are also called Catholic (outside England). When we say 'Catholic Church' we mean the Western Church (as distinguished from the Eastern) or also the 'Latin Church' (as distinguished from the Greek or Russian), or more accurately the 'Roman Catholic Church', i.e. the Christians who acknowledge the Pope as the supreme authority in the Church (primacy of jurisdiction). The Second Vatican Council says of the relationship between the Catholic Church and the other churches: 'This Church, constituted and organized in the world as a society, subsists in the Catholic Church, which is governed by the successor of Peter and by the bishops in union with that successor, although many elements of sanctification and of truth can be found outside her visible structure. These elements, however, as gifts properly belonging to the Church of Christ, possess an inner dynamism toward Catholic unity' (*The Church*, para. 8; → 20.1).

Reformation: Discussions about the reform of the Church in the sixteenth century, which led to a division in the church. From that time there were Catholics and 'Protestants' (who protested against the decisions made at the Diet of Speyer in 1529). Some Protestants are called Evangelicals (i.e. they rely wholly on the gospel).

Denomination: Since the sixteenth century there are two main denominations (as above).

Martin Luther (1483–1546): The man who 'set the Reformation in motion'. Founder of Protestantism, well-known theologian and translator of the Bible; first printed Bible in German 1552. There are many of his followers in Germany.

Church of England: The established church in England; arose in 1534 when Henry VIII separated himself from Rome because the Pope refused to grant him an annulment of his marriage. In most points the church retained Catholic doctrine. Now there are three groups: 'High' Church, those closest to Catholic doctrine and customs, 'Low' Church, those who lay emphasis on deeds, and 'Broad' Church, a group somewhere between the previous two groups. The following are some of the other Christian Churches in Britain:

Presbyterians: Founded at the time of the Reformation. They have no bishops but are ministered to by *presbyters* (Gr. = priests) very similar to the clergymen of the Church of England. The Church of Scotland is Presbyterian.

Congregationalists: 'Free Churchmen'. Founded in the seventeenth century. Beliefs largely those of other Christians. The local congregation is the basic unit of their churches.

United Reformed Church: In 1971 the Congregationalists and the Presbyterians in England united, retaining some of the individual characteristics of each.

Baptists: Were first established in England at the beginning of the seventeenth century. They have baptism by immersion (i.e. the whole body dipped in water) and, following the example of Christ's baptism, they baptise only adults. To them belief in the Bible and the New Testament are more important than ceremonies. Bunyan, the author of *Pilgrim's Progress*, was one of their members.

Society of Friends (or Quakers): Sometimes described as a 'do-it-yourself' religion. No priests or ministers. They are people who think for themselves and they usually hold strong religious convictions; they help one another (friends) by praying together at meetings, either in silence or by sharing their experiences, religious or otherwise. They were founded in the seventeenth century.

Methodists: Founded by John Wesley in the eighteenth century. Emphasis on Christian living rather than on doctrine. Governed by an annual Methodist Conference which ordains ministers of the church, including women. Lay preachers also a feature of Methodism.

Sects: Many small church groups who have become separated from a larger church: e.g. Jehovah's Witnesses, Adventists, etc.

Ecumenism (from Gr. oikumene = the inhabited part of the world; = general): A word for all the work done for Christian unity. The modern ecumenical movement began in the present century in Edinburgh in 1910. In 1948 the World Council of Churches was established in Amsterdam; its general secretariat is in Geneva. Nearly all Christian churches (90%) are members; the Roman Catholic Church is not a member but is represented by observers. The Second Vatican Council strongly encouraged further efforts towards unity by its decrees on Ecumenism. A week of prayer for Christian unity is held every year around the feast of the Conversion of St Paul (25 January).

Part IV: The greatest commandment

You must love the Lord your God
with all your heart,
with all your soul,
and with all your mind.

This is the first and greatest commandment.
The second resembles it:

You must love your neighbour
as yourself.

Matthew 22:37–39

Introduction

'What must we do?' (Acts 2:37) — after Peter's sermon those struck by his words ask the question. It is prompted by the insight that *faith* in God, in Jesus Christ, must be worked out in what a person *does daily* and in what he refrains from doing. The believer asks himself what kind of life is in accordance with *God's will*.

How is he to discover what God does want of him? First, his reason and his *conscience* help him to know what is good and right; what fits in with circumstances; what the situation demands; what makes for peace; what brings about justice; what makes people happy — in doing this he comes to recognise God's will.

A person learns much too from what he experiences from day to day as his duty. Jesus summarises this experience by quoting an ancient saying — called the 'golden rule' — 'Always treat others as you would like them to treat you' (Matthew 7:12). This means that everyone knows precisely what he personally needs, what does him good, and how he would like to be treated by others. And this is exactly what others expect of him.

However, what makes a Christian a Christian goes beyond an attitude based solely on reason. The *attitude of Jesus* is the norm for a Christian: 'I give you a new commandment: love one another; just as I have loved you, so you also must love one another' (John 13:34). Jesus lived wholly for the Father. He lived wholly for others — paradoxically, living for others implied a readiness to die for them. 'A man can have no greater love than to lay down his life for his friends' (John 15:13). A person who, according to the example of Jesus, tries to live for others, is living according to God's will, as Jesus has revealed it to us; he loves God. To love God and one's neighbour — this is the *'greatest commandment'* the essential commandment for a Christian, the one that includes all other *commandments*. It is the basic law of Christian life.

Matthew's gospel hands on to us the greatest commandment as the answer given by Jesus to the scribe's question concerning the most important commandment in the law (Matthew 22:34-40). In Luke the wording of the greatest commandment is quoted by the scribe in answer to the question asked by Jesus (Luke 10:27), and Jesus confirms it: 'You have answered right, do this and life is yours' (Luke 10:28). Then, as explanation of the commandment to love one's neighbour, he tells the *parable* of the good Samaritan: 'Who is my neighbour?' (cf. Luke 10:29).

The basic structure of Part IV of this catechism is Luke's version of the great commandment, together with the key sentences of the parable of the Samaritan: 'Who is my neighbour?' (Luke 10:29) and 'Go and do the same' (Luke 10:30).

The 'greatest commandment' in the Old Testament: The commandment concerning the love of God is found in Deuteronomy 6:5; the commandment concerning love of one's neighbour in Leviticus 19:8. The passage in Deuteronomy 6:4–9 is the first part of the so-called 'Shema, Israel' (Hebr. = hear, O Israel). Even today the orthodox Jew begins his daily prayer with these words (second part: Deuteronomy 11:13–32). Mark begins his version of the greatest commandment (Mark 12:28–34) with the previous verse from Deuteronomy (8:4) 'Hear, O Israel! The Lord our God is one Lord, and you shall love the Lord your God . . .' (Deuteronomy 6:4–5, RSV translation; → 35.3 love God).

35 You must love the Lord, your God

→ 37 love your neighbour as yourself

I can love only when I myself am loved. Love gives rise to love from another; *love* demands a response. This is what the Bible says: God loves us. Before we begin to love God, we are already loved by him, and he never ceases to love us. A *message* not without its consequences if we are prepared to accept it. For if he loves us — has he not merited our love in return?

But can one love someone he does not know? I know God only from hearsay. How then can I love him — and be commanded to do so? On the other hand there is *experience*: only when I love someone do I learn really to know him; only then is there intimacy between us. Perhaps the reason why we do not know God is that we love him too little?

35.1 God first loved us

→ 23.3 sign of hope; 24 eternal life; 2.3 God, Father of all; 10
I believe in God

I live because God wills me to exist. I exist because God says 'yes'
to me. Christians and Jews alike believe this. What God
announces to the people of Israel through the prophet is valid for
each one: 'I have called you by your name, you are mine' (Isaiah
43:1).

I am free because God made me free. That I act in this or that
way, or that I am like this or like that, that I can take my life in my
own hands, all this I owe to God. It was one of the basic experiences among God's people in the Old Testament that *freedom* had
been received as God's gift to man: 'I am Yahweh, your God, who
brought you out of the land of Egypt, out of the house of slavery'
(Exodus 20:2). This experience of being set free by God shows the
nature of his *love*. In his love he does not give *life* and freedom
once and for all, but is always with man and repeatedly opens up
for him a new *future*. The believer knows: I have a future, because
God has promised it to me.

This *hope* has become stronger in the new people of God in the
Christian era. Paul says: 'The present given by God is eternal life
in Christ Jesus our Lord' (Romans 6:23). God's love, revealed in
Jesus Christ, gives us hope against all despair. Christians in all
ages testify that a person who *believes* can experience the love of
God in what happens to him, and therefore he can have hope.

John, in his first Letter, speaks of God's love for us:
God's love for us was revealed
when God sent into the world his only Son
so that we could have life through him;
this is the love I mean:
not our love for God,
but God's love for us.   *1 John 4:9–10*

35.2   The God worthy of our love

→ 2.1 God is close to us; 13.1 Christ; 15.1 who so lives; 24.1 metaphors for eternal life

Many do not in any way doubt that God sets men free and they are very willing to believe that he opens for them an eternal *future*. Yet God remains for them only a concept, which they perhaps explain, but not a person whom they can love.

God seems to be distant — yet he has come close to us. He seems to be invisible — but he has let us see him: in Jesus *Christ*. 'No one has ever seen God; it is the only Son, who is nearest to the Father's heart, who has made him known' (John 1:18); this is what, together with the Christians of the first century, contemporary Christians dare to say. In Jesus God has been given a face and a form. Just as Jesus looked on men, just as he turned to them in love, so is God's goodness focused on us. The gospels have preserved the memory of how worthy of love Jesus was and how he went about doing good. In him, in human form, God became lovable.

In the following conversation John's gospel keeps alive the knowledge of *God's nearness* brought by Jesus: 'Philip said, "Lord, let us see the Father and then we shall be satisfied". "Have I been with you all this time, Philip," said Jesus to him "and still you do not know me? To have seen me is to have seen the Father, so how can you say, 'Let us see the Father'?" ' (John 14:8-9).

A hymn may help us to understand this:
Jesu, the very thought of thee
with sweetness fills my breast;
but sweeter far thy face to see,
and in thy presence rest.

Nor voice can sing, nor heart can frame,
nor can the memory find,
a sweeter sound than thy blest name,
O Saviour of mankind.   Translated by *Edward Caswall*

35.3 Loving God in all things

→ 37.1 loving one's neighbour; 37.3 taking the world seriously; 21.2 Church of saints; 34.4 orders

Man needs a purpose for his life. He would like to see in his existence and in the whole of the world a *meaning* with which he is in agreement.

The person who believes that the God whom Jesus calls his Father has created the world and its inhabitants, remains near them and will bring them to fulfilment, sees in God the meaning of the whole and of his own life. To love God means to make a *commitment* to this faith and, once one is committed, to make an attempt to live it out: 'You shall have no gods except me' (Deuteronomy 5:7).

To love God is not only an affair of the heart. To love God means to bring one's *life* into line with him, to act, as *commissioned* by him, according to his word, and to shape the world according to his meaning. In this way everything done by one who believes can be an expression of his union with God. This means loving God in all and above all.

For the Israelites the whole of life was determined by this relationship with God and with his bidding. In the book of Deuteronomy we are told that the words in which we are commanded to *love God* should be written on our hearts: 'You shall repeat them to your children and say them over to them whether at rest in your house or walking abroad, at your lying down or at your rising; you shall fasten them on your hand as a sign and on your forehead as a circlet; you shall write them on the doorposts of your house and on your gates' (Deuteronomy 6:7–9).

When the scribe asked which was the most important commandment Jesus answered by quoting a passage from Deuteronomy (6:4–5). Today this is still part of the daily prayer of a pious Jew:

Listen, O Israel, the Lord our God is the one Lord, and you must love the Lord your God with all your heart, with all your soul, with all your mind and with all your strength.

Mark 12:29–30

Deuteronomy (Gr. = second law or repetition of the law): The first five books (the Pentateuch) of the Bible are also called the books of Moses; Deuteronomy is the fifth; it contains exhortations, collections of laws and explanations, many of which are already treated of in the earlier books of the Pentateuch, thus making the book to a certain extent a repetition of the law.

Prayer tassels: The orthodox Jew wears two prayer tassels (called phylacteries) throughout the day — cases are attached to the forehead and upper left arm. Each contains four passages from the Bible written on parchment (Exodus 13:1-10; 13:11-16; Deuteronomy 6:4-9; 11:13-21). By the wearing of these phylacteries, these passages, all of which allude to the keeping of Yahweh's law, before one's eyes and in one's heart, are literally fulfilled. At the time of Jesus the ten commandments were included.

35.4   God's precepts: the ten commandments

→ 5.2 God's will; 39 do likewise; 34.3 precepts of the Church

In many places in the Bible there are *commandments* and challenges. They contain a summary of what the faithful have recognised as *God's will*. Here and there such commandments have been collected in list-form. The most familiar of them are the 'ten commandments' (Exodus 34:28). They are found twice in the Old Testament: in the book of Exodus (20:2-17) and in the book of Deuteronomy (5:6-21). In the New Testament various references are made to them, for example in the *Sermon on the Mount* (Matthew 5:21 and 5:27), in the story of the rich young man (Mark 10:19) and in the Letter to the Romans (13:9); nowhere, however, in the New Testament do we find a complete list of them.

These *ten commandments* have special significance for Jews and Christians, who see in them a summary of God's most important instructions for life and for the general conduct of God's people. Therefore, since earliest times, the ten commandments have been handed down in Christian preaching and instruction as a rule of life for the faithful.

The ten commandments give basic conditions for the preservation of the life-long union between God and his people. They invite the faithful to collaborate with the liberating work which God himself has begun so that all human beings, as images of God, may receive their rights and be able to live as free persons.

The list of commandments begins with God's self-portrait: he has concern for his people and has shown himself to be their deliverer. Because he is the God of his people and has brought them out of Egypt, Israel will honour no other gods. Because the Israelites are indebted to him for their *deliverance*, they will not crush other people; they will devote themselves to obtaining human rights for the weak and the oppressed. The 'you shall not' of the commandments is therefore really a 'you shall (no longer)' act thus, because you have had experience of God.

This is the short form of the ten commandments based on the wording of the book of Exodus:
I am the Lord your God who brought you out of the land of Egypt, out of the house of slavery.

1. **You shall have no gods except me.**
2. **You shall not utter the name of God to misuse it.**
3. **Remember the Sabbath day and keep it holy.**
4. **Honour your father and your mother so that you may have a long life in the land that your God has given you.**
5. **You shall not kill.**
6. **You shall not commit adultery.**
7. **You shall not steal.**
8. **You shall not bear false witness against your neighbour.**
9. **You shall not covet your neighbour's wife.**
10. **You shall not covet your neighbour's house, or his servant, or his ox, or his donkey, or anything that is his.** cf. *Exodus 20:2-17*

The first commandment forbids the worship of false gods. For the Christian this means a challenge unwaveringly to acknowledge the God who truly sets free and to trust in him alone. Power, success, fame, money and pleasure are examples of the false, enslaving gods of our times (→ 10.2).

The second commandment warns us not to call on God in the wrong way. If a person calls on God to do harm, in God's name, to a person's life and freedom, he is misusing God's name (→ 3.1).

The third commandment warns man to free himself from slavery to his profession, occupation, job, etc. On every seventh day he is to share in the creative rest of his God, to take time for God and for himself and to let himself be renewed, re-created by God (→ 39.5; 27.5).

The fourth commandment is a warning that there can be no stability where the younger generation no longer honour their parents (→ 38.1).

The fifth commandment protects human life, especially that of those who cannot defend themselves. In this commandment Christians see not only a prohibition to kill but also a challenge to devote themselves to safeguarding the right to life of all, especially the weak, and to bringing about healthy conditions for life (→ 39.1).

The sixth and ninth commandments have as their object the safeguarding of married love, the shared life of man and woman — an image of God's fidelity — against its destruction by selfishness (→ 32.1; 37.6).

The seventh and tenth commandments point out that safe and orderly conditions for possessions are an indispensable element of social life. God wills that people should live in freedom. That is why he gave them the promised land. It is not just a matter of protecting one's property. A person who possesses property must look after it conscientiously; it is not only for himself, he is obliged to use it in such a way that it is beneficial for others too (→ 39.9; 37.2).

The eighth commandment expresses the experience that no society can last if freedom and human rights are destroyed by deceit, lies and treachery; these vices ruin confidence (39.5).

36 With all your heart, with all your soul, and with all your mind

→ 1.2 following Jesus; 21 communion of saints

To love 'with one's whole heart' is not merely to obey commands: it is to respond freely and joyfully to the love already given by God. The *'commandment of love'* is not a commandment in the sense of a legal precept. It is a testimony of the centuries-long experience of Israel and is handed on as a directive for life: a man who has experienced who God is will love him wholeheartedly. The people of God know by experience that this is the only way in which we can survive.

The challenge to love 'with all our heart, with all our soul and with all our mind' means that the whole person is concerned. There is no part of us excluded from *loving God*.

Only God can be loved so unconditionally, so radically and so unreservedly, and this is how the faithful should love him. But who can really say that he loves God in this way? And doesn't the person who attempts to do so lose sight of the *world*? Are there people who have been able so to love and what is the pattern of their lives?

36.1 Only one thing is necessary

→ 6.1 do not worry; 23.3 sign of hope; 21.2 Church of saints

The person who believes that God loves him can entrust his life to him. To love God means living a life of complete *trust*. Jesus has encouraged us to do this: 'So do not worry; do not say, "What are we to eat? What are we to drink? How are we to be clothed?" It is the pagans who set their hearts on all these things. Your heavenly Father knows you need them all' (Matthew 6:31–32).

The person who trusts in God must certainly also be concerned about things necessary for *life*, but he can do so conscious that his life does not consist only in these and that his *happiness* is not dependent on them. The believer experiences that he should not be anxious about himself. This relieves him from always thinking about his own affairs. True, he remains subject to the many necessities inherent in life in this world, but they do not dominate him. He knows that they are temporary and will come to an end. This makes him independent with regard to earthly powers and forces. He obeys God rather than men.

One who lives for God has no need to fear that unbearable burdens will be imposed on him. Jesus says: 'My yoke is easy and my burden light' (Matthew 11:30). In the Letter to the Galatians Paul warns the community not to allow themselves to submit to the yoke of the prescriptions of the law: 'When Christ freed us he meant us to be free' (Galatians 5:1). It is not obedience to laws and prescriptions that is to determine the life of a Christian but solely the '*new commandment*' (John 13:34), the power of the *love* of Jesus. Because, through Jesus, we have become sons of God, we too share in 'freedom and glory as the children of God' (Romans 8:21).

The following is a version of a hymn attributed to the Jesuit St Francis Xavier expressing his love for God:
At such love, my love I kindle;
   Was there no heaven, still must I love!
Were there no hell, sin would I shun!
   Were heaven and hell to pass away,
With their rewards and punishments,
   In me would love for love endure.

Christian mysticism: A state of life characterised by prayer and an immediate knowledge of God reached through personal religious experience. As distinct from mysticism found in other religions, the Christian form preserves the transcendence ('apartness') of God the creator, who always remains distinct from the creature. And in an area of the spirit where there is a risk of self-deception, the test of authenticity lies in the fruits to be found in the lives of genuine mystics — e.g. love, humility, patient endurance of suffering, etc.

36.2 Freedom of the children of God

→ IV greatest commandment; 37.3 taking the world seriously; 30.6 guilt/self-knowledge; 39.6 making decisions

If anyone thinks that a free person can do, or not do, as he likes, or what suits him, he has misunderstood *freedom*. Freedom is something different from arbitrary and unrestrained behaviour. It is harder and more challenging than unthinking obedience to commandments and precepts.

If a person is not told or clearly commanded what he is, or is not to do, he must find out for himself what is right and good. He is *responsible* for what he does: to himself, to the community and to God. From what he knows and has experienced and from what others have told him, he must try to recognise what his situation demands of him.

In general, people have a right feeling, a kind of sense, for what is good and what is evil: their *conscience*. We speak of a bad conscience and say that conscience 'pricks' when we take a wrong step or do evil. And conscience is drawn to what is good — irrespective of blame or reward for the good we do.

Certainly, our conscience must be 'formed'; commandments can help us, from childhood onwards, gradually to learn to distinguish between good and evil. The more mature and self-reliant a person is, the more closely he is attuned to what he recognises as the *will of God*. Freed to be a child of God (Romans 8:21) he will become a person as he makes wholehearted and free *decisions* that spring from conscious awareness of reality and its source, God.

In his first Letter Peter exhorts people to the right use of
freedom:
**You are slaves of no one except God, so behave like free
men, and never use your freedom as an excuse for
wickedness.** *1 Peter 2:16*

Obedience: 'Right listening' to the needs of one's fellow-men, to commandments, laws and instructions, and acting according to what comes from the heart.
In this way obedience contributes to a circumspect life. One speaks on the contrary
of 'blind obedience' (cf. the obedience of a corpse), when someone carries out
each command from another, without adverting to his conscience.

Conscience: Even if the boundaries between good and evil — influenced by the
circumstances of one's life, upbringing, environment and history — are sometimes differently decided, nevertheless there is overwhelming agreement that each
one must do — after careful consideration — what he holds as good, and refrain
— according to his convictions — from what is evil. Cardinal Newman said:
'Conscience is the aboriginal Vicar of Christ, a prophet in its informations, a
monarch in its peremptoriness, a priest in its blessings and anathemas' (*Difficulties of Anglicans*, Vol. II: Letter to the Duke of Norfolk, chapter 5).

Freedom of conscience: One of the fundamental human rights: the right, after
examining one's conscience, to do or to leave undone a specific action without
being, for that reason, subjected to external force.

False conscience: A conscience which, according to objective standards of values,
is wrong; morally a person who acts according to his conscience cannot be condemned, even if his conscience is false.

Lax conscience: An easygoing or indifferent conscience; a person makes a
decision according to his own whim or one that is, at the moment, an advantage
for him.

Scruples: Unfounded or exaggerated pressures of conscience. Such over-anxious
people are described as *scrupulous*. A person who acts without consulting his conscience is considered *unscrupulous*.

36.3 Signs from God: the Saints
→ 3.2 the all-holy One; 21.2 Church of saints; 35.2 the God worthy of
our love; 37.8 rejoicing with others; 27.6 the liturgical year

Paul has called all Christians *saints* because through faith and
baptism they are set apart and belong to Christ (Romans 1:7).
When we speak of saints today we mean those extraordinary
people who take their Christian faith very seriously and model
their lives unreservedly on it.

There are saints in all ages, among all peoples, in all professions: men and women, married people and priests, statesmen and peasants. They are very diverse in origin and character, gifts and temperament, destiny and importance.

Many withdraw from the world and devote themselves wholly to the service of God and to *prayer*. Others stand at the focal point of public life and devote their ability and strength to bring about greater *justice* and *peace* in the world. Among them are people who, unobtrusively, care for children and old people, the poor and the sick, those imprisoned and persecuted, outsiders and outcasts, and thus give proof of God's love for little ones, for those who are weak and despised. There are others again who as missionaries preach the gospel of salvation to the uttermost bounds of the earth, or those who as 'God's rebels' stir the *consciences* of those responsible for Church and state, or who, as *witnesses*, unafraid, pay with their lives for their *fidelity* to Christ.

Saints offer an alternative to the standard descriptions of happiness in their times. They show that possessions and prosperity, power and pleasure do not allow men to be truly human; they set different norms and have other objects in life.

For all that, saints are not demi-gods. They remain human. They have their faults and weaknesses, their doubts, and their struggles. They fail and incur guilt. But they are sinners open to conversion; they know their limitations but they come to terms with them; they acknowledge their guilt but remain continually open to something better and greater.

However different the saints may be, they have two things in common: their awareness that they owe everything to God, and their efforts to respond, throughout their lives, to the *love God has for them*. Saints are models of Christian life.

The following hymn would seem appropriate if applied to the saints, but its words may also help the 'average' Christian:

Happy the man who wanders with the Lord.
Happy the man who knows how to live.
Happy the man who never seeks reward,
giving because he loves to give.
He seeks no gold, he wants no gain. . . .
This man has found his own soul.
Happy the man, happy the man of the Lord.

Sebastian Temple

Saints: Christians whose lives were recognised as a special way of following Christ and who were therefore honoured. Since the tenth century this has been solemnly confirmed by a papal document. At the beginning, only martyrs were honoured as saints; since the fifth century also those who — without suffering martyrdom — publicly professed their faith (confessors), people who, so to speak, 'lived for Christ' without having to 'die for Christ'.

Honouring the saints: Saints are not adored; they are honoured as examples and invoked by the faithful who ask them to pray to God for them (Litany of the Saints). Honouring the saints is a form of piety practised above all in the Catholic (and Orthodox) churches (as distinct from Protestant churches).

Canonisation: A solemn declaration on the part of the Church that a dead person may lawfully be honoured as a saint and therefore his intercession may be asked in public. Through this declaration he is inscribed in the register of saints (the first canonisation was that of Ulrich of Augsburg on 31 January 993). Canonisation is preceded by beatification (= authorisation for a more restricted local veneration of a holy person — called 'Blessed' at this stage). The whole process leading up to declaration of sainthood is conducted with the most careful and thorough examination of the person's manner of life, death, writings, etc. and is called the *'cause'*. Those honoured by the first nine centuries of the Church's history were not expressly 'canonised'. Essentially, honour is paid to the dead by the community of the faithful and this nowadays is confirmed by canonisation. The Church acts on the firm conviction that, through Christ, the saints live in complete union with God.

36.4 Queen of all saints — Mother of the faithful

→ 14.3 mother of our Lord; 21 communion of saints; 17.1 he has preceded us; 27.6 liturgical year

Among all the saints in the Church, *Mary*, mother of Jesus, has pride of place. She is also called *Queen of all saints*.

We know few details of her life, but above all we do know that she said an unconditional 'yes' to what she recognised as the *will of God*. She believed what was said to her by the Lord (Luke 1:45) and she entrusted her whole life to God. Even what, in the message, must have seemed strange and incomprehensible to her, she accepted: 'I am the handmaid of the Lord; let what you have said be done to me' (Luke 1:38) was her answer. According to John's gospel Mary was the cause of the first 'sign' performed by Jesus, a sign of God's glory which shone out for the disciples (cf. John 2:1–12). John also writes that Mary endured to the end at the foot of the *cross* when nearly everyone had abandoned Jesus (John 19:25–27).

Because Mary was chosen to be *Mother of God*, the Catholic Church believes that God sanctified her from the beginning of her life. He excepted her from involvement in sin. Therefore on 8 December the Church celebrates the 'Solemnity of Mary, virgin mother of God, conceived without original sin'.

As with the beginning, according to the conviction of the Catholic Church, so with the end of her life: God fulfilled in Mary all the promises he has given to man: Mary was assumed (taken up) into heaven body and soul. This mystery is celebrated on the 'feast of Mary's assumption' (15 August).

Because Mary lived the *faith* fully, she is also called 'mother of the faithful'. In prayers and hymns we ask for Mary's *intercession*. People go to places of pilgrimage, trusting, through her prayers, in God's help.

Luke explains what Jesus sees as the significance of his mother. He tells how a woman in the crowd following him cried out: 'Happy the womb that bore you and the breasts you sucked!' The answer of Jesus provides food for thought: 'Still happier those who hear the word of God and keep it!' (Luke 11:27–28). This means that Mary's faith is more important than her motherhood.

36.4   244

The best-known prayer to Our Lady is the Hail Mary. It connects the angel's greeting (Luke 1:28) and that of Elizabeth (Luke 1:42), with a request to Mary to pray for us:
Hail Mary, full of grace, the Lord is with thee;
blessed art thou amongst women and blessed is the fruit of
thy womb, Jesus.
Holy Mary, mother of God, pray for us sinners
now and at the hour of our death. Amen.

Honouring Mary: Mary is honoured in the Catholic and Orthodox churches more than in other Christian churches. However, growing devotion to Our Lady in Protestant churches is one important feature of the Ecumenical Movement. Forms of Marian devotion: feasts of Our Lady, the rosary, May devotions, pilgrimages to shrines of Our Lady.

Hail Mary (also known by its Latin name **Ave Maria**): Beginning of the prayer which Catholics use most frequently (after the Our Father) (→ 13.3 rosary).

Immaculate Conception: Name given to the feast of 'Mary, Virgin Mother of God, conceived without original sin', celebrated on 8 December (often confused with the virgin birth of Jesus → 14.1). Meaning: According to the teaching of the Catholic Church Mary was from the first instant of her life (i.e. when she was conceived by her mother) free from stain of original sin; God's grace preserved her from it because she was chosen to be the Mother of God, and thus redeemed her by anticipating Christ's redeeming work.

37   You must love your neighbour as yourself

→ 35 love the Lord, your God

Many think they are pious but fail to notice the person next to them. 'Pious' people of this kind have often brought the *Church* into discredit. This is bad enough, but even worse evil is done to others 'in God's name', when they are rejected and even persecuted because they are 'different': members of sects, heretics, 'pagans', people of other nations and races. All this has happened many a time and still happens today.

On the other hand there are 'non-believers' who do not bother about God and religion, and yet — humanly speaking — they are real friends. In cases like this it can be hard for *Christians* to know what attitude to adopt. Are such people on the right path although, as far as they are concerned, God does not exist? What is the relationship between *love of God* and *love of our neighbour*; does the one exclude the other? Does a person who turns his attention to his neighbour necessarily lose sight of God? And vice versa; does loving God above all else mean that everything except him is no longer of importance?

37.1 Loving one's neighbour

→ 18.3 norm for judgement; 1.5 through the eyes of Jesus; 39.10 praying to God; 31.1 praying and caring

When asked about the most important commandment Jesus names not one but two equal commandments. He has linked *love of God* and *love of one's neighbour*. The 'second commandment' is just as important as the first. This is a new *life-style*. The relationship between man and God is determined in a new way. Love for one's neighbour is part of the fundamental principle of the Christian life. The Christian can be a Christian only if he thinks, feels and acts with human sympathy. There is therefore no incompatibility between love of God and love of one's neighbour. No one can say: 'I love God' if he is not concerned for his neighbour. And vice versa: the person who, in accordance with the mind and heart of Jesus, is available to his fellow-men will find God. The more someone considers another as his neighbour, the nearer he is to God. God wants to be loved in our neighbour. The individual is judged before God according to this norm. Matthew's gospel describes the *last judgement* in picture-form (Matthew 25:31–46). The 'good' will be separated from the 'wicked', just as in the evening a shepherd drives his sheep and goats — after they have grazed together all day — into separate pens. The good are those who have served the hungry, the homeless, the sick and prisoners. Their astonished question betrays that in so doing they did not think at all of God; they helped because human beings needed help. Now they are invited to take possession of what God has prepared for them.

> The first Letter of John repeats the fact that love of God and
> of our neighbour should not be separated:
> **Anyone who says, 'I love God',**
> **and hates his brother,**
> **is a liar,**
> **since a man who does not love the brother that he can see**
> **cannot love God, whom he has never seen.**   *1 John 4:20*

37.2   Loving in deeds

→ 37.8 rejoicing; 39.9 com-passion; 38 my neighbour

Love of one's neighbour, as Jesus sees it, is not a sublime feeling
nor is it sentimentality. 'You must love your neighbour' means
literally: 'Act lovingly towards your neighbour'. This is directed
towards deeds rather than feelings. We find many of these deeds
mentioned in the New Testament: feeding the hungry, clothing
the naked, healing the sick, sheltering the homeless, consoling the
sorrowful, being *peacemakers*, having patience and being
generous. These are examples, not precepts. Each must discover
for himself what his neighbour needs and how he can *act lovingly*
towards him. Whether one's love is genuine is seen by an awareness of the needs of others.

Love your neighbour 'as yourself' means 'as if it were you
personally'. Transfer yourself to the other's position and try to
see things with his eyes. Give him what you would like if you were
in his place. Act lovingly towards your neighbour in the way in
which you personally would like to experience love.

> John's first Letter exhorts us to practical love:
> **If a man who was rich enough in this world's goods**
> **saw that one of his brothers was in need,**
> **but closed his heart to him,**
> **how could the love of God be living in him?**
> **My children,**
> **our love is not to be just words or mere talk,**
> **but something real and active.**   *1 John 3:17–18*

Tenth commandment: 'You shall not covet your neighbour's goods' (→ 35.4 ten commandments).

Envy: Displeasure at the more favoured state of another person, sometimes, though not necessarily, accompanied by a sense of having been deprived personally.

Corporal works of mercy: Associated with Matthew 25 and Tobit 2 are the 'corporal works of mercy' which are part of Christian tradition: to feed the hungry, to give drink to the thirsty, to clothe the naked, to shelter the homeless, to visit the imprisoned, to visit the sick, to bury the dead (→ 39.9).

37.3 Taking the world seriously

→ 1.5 through the eyes of Jesus; 12.1 the world; 14.1 he became man; 34.7 Church in the world; 23.2 sign of hope

People often reproach Christians by saying that they despise the world, that they never really come to a correct knowledge of it because their thoughts are already 'in heaven'. The existence of such *Christians* does not mean that their attitude to the world is Christian. For there should be no one who takes the world more seriously than a Christian. He believes that God created the world and entrusted it to human beings, and he believes that the *world* is destined to have a good *future*. Therefore he can see things as they are, inclusive of all their imperfections; he has no need to seek an escape in daydreaming in order to be able to bear with life.

Precisely because the Christian sees things in the light of their future, from God's viewpoint, he has no need to be deluded. His faith in God makes him sensitive to the high-handedness of the world, to the idolising of men and things, achievements and success, money and power. His *aim* is to do justice to things and to people. A Christian tries to bear this in mind in his actions, for only in this way can he really practise love of his neighbour. This neighbourly love will make him want to help the other to live his life well; this is possible only for a person who himself knows how to live and who knows too what is characteristic of a life worthy of human dignity and worthy of life itself.

In order to *distinguish* what is correct or false, good or evil, *experience* is necessary. A person must know what happens when he acts in this, or in some other way. By evaluating the consequences what is right in this situation or that becomes clear to him. So love for one's neighbour does not consist merely of goodwill. Experience and knowledge, *conscience* and rules are also needed.

Basic attitudes — that are lasting — are developed in one who is experienced in the right kind of action. The moral effect of these is an inclination to do good and to devote oneself to renewing the face of the earth (Psalm 104(105): 29).

> The following is a prayer for God's help with regard to our responsibility for the world:
> **Lord, show us the world as it really is, show us the duties which await us. Let us know where you need us.**
>
> *Felicitas Betz*

World (Gr. kosmos): Totality of all that has been created by God (= creation). We are told: 'God saw all he had made, and indeed it was very good' (Genesis 1:31); and 'God loved the world so much that he gave his only Son' (John 3:16). But in John's gospel the same word is used in a negative sense: 'world' as a concept for lack of faith, distance from God, Satan's sphere of influence (John 17:14). With this world the kingdom of Christ has nothing in common (John 18:36); Jesus says of this world that he has overcome it (John 16:33) and that the prince of this world is already condemned (John 16:11).

Cardinal virtues (Lat. cardo = hinge, i.e. basic virtues): Basic attitudes which were recognised by the ancients in pre-Christian times as necessary for a human being: *prudence* = to know what is good and to recognise what is appropriate; *justice* = to give to each one what is his due; *fortitude* = to remain faithful to what is right even in difficult circumstances; to remain firm in hope, even in face of overwhelming threats to one's well-being and peace of mind; *temperance* = moderation in the control of one's appetites and passions according to reason. The other virtues are derived from these four.

Human dignity: Foundation of (or reason for) the respect due to each human being as a person.

Basic values: Values that are derived from human dignity, above all because they they concern a person precisely as a person (e.g. justice, love, truth, fidelity, peace).

Natural rights: Rights based on the nature of man and the order of creation, irrespective of time, place and legal arrangements. In moral theology they are a foundation of the 'natural moral law' which everyone can understand via a certain degree of self-reflection.

Human rights: Inalienable and inviolable rights and freedoms of the individual which ought not to be interfered with by others. In 1948 the United Nations drew up a 'Declaration of Human Rights' which was taken over by many countries. It is the duty of the Church and of Christians to act decisively for the implementation of human rights.

Humility (from Lat. = lowliness): Although today this is not a greatly respected virtue, it is nonetheless an important Christian virtue; it arises, not from a consciousness of inferiority to other people, but from a knowledge of one's own worth and one's own imperfection. Humility is fostered by encountering God, and this attitude is maintained in one's contacts with people (Matthew 11:29); humility is essentially different from diffidence (or even timidity) and has nothing to do with submissiveness, or feeling that one is of less value than others.

37.4   Physical expression of love

→ 32.1 man and woman; 37.5 learning to love; 37.6 ability to practise self-denial; 12.3 God's creature; 23 resurrection from the dead

If a person fails to give visible, tangible form to his feelings, his sympathy and his love for another, he is not sharing and he is left without any response. If he is not ready to soil his hands or to walk his feet sore, to smile with those who are cheerful, or if he refuses to hold the hand of a dying man, he cannot speak of *loving his neighbour*. Where affection and love have no physical dimension, they become stunted and wither. Love of one's neighbour concerns the whole person.

Can this statement be maintained unchallenged? Hasn't Christianity often been reproached with concern, fundamentally, only for the 'immortal soul'? Isn't the *body* regarded only as a necessary evil which, with its pleasures and its desires, holds the soul imprisoned? Isn't the *soul* the better half of man?

There certainly are such attitudes among Christians; there were even times when this way of thinking was widespread in Christian circles. Yet it is not Christian teaching and Christian faith, and it is not in keeping with the witness given in the Bible. For the Bible is concerned with the whole person whom God created in his likeness. And we believe in the *resurrection* of the dead, that is, we believe in the fulfilment of the *whole* person. The first of those risen from the dead is Jesus Christ himself. Christian faith emphasises that God did not only take home his soul but his body too after raising him from the dead.

As the body belongs indispensably to man, it is true that, for a Christian, the body also is an indispensable part of the new man. In consequence, a Christianity opposed to everything physical is as wrong as a Christianity that totally disowns the material world. So neighbourly love must be concerned with the whole person. This is as true for the actions of the individual as for those of the whole Church.

> Because the whole person is destined for eternal life, the body too is to be glorified. Paul writes this to the Corinthians:
>
> **Your body, you know, is the temple of the Holy Spirit, who is in you since you received him from God. . . . That is why you should use your body for the glory of God.**
>
> *1 Corinthians 6:19, 20*

Hostility towards the body: Considering the body as the 'prison of the soul' goes back to the Greek philosopher Plato (about 400 B.C.) and his school. Related to this is an image of the division of the world (*dualism*) into good and bad, light and darkness. These thoughts are also contained in a philosophical trend of the so-called *Gnosis* (Gr. = knowledge) which had many supporters in the first centuries of the Christian era; Christianity had hard struggles with Gnosis, which valued everything to do with the mind as much 'higher' than everything material (→ 12.3 soul; 23.1 immortality; 27.2 body).

37.5 Learning to love
→ 32.1 man and woman; 32.2 sacrament of matrimony; 39.1 loving life

A tiny child is surrounded by the 'basic school of love' in the person of his mother and father; they feed the child, keep him clean, caress, cuddle and embrace him. In this intimate affection a small child experiences what it means to be loved. Although he cannot yet speak, he has already experienced for his whole life: it is good to be alive. If this is lacking it may be very difficult to compensate for the *experience* later.

An older child makes his own first steps in *love*. He expresses his *affection* by embracing his mother and running into his father's arms, by sharing with other children, letting them play with him, by giving things away and by caring for pet animals. Later still, boys and girls discover one another. They are, in a puzzling way, drawn to one another. They are on friendly terms, 'go around' together, exchange little kindnesses and even tenderness. They experience in a new way what 'loving' means.

A person who loves also tries to express this love and it can happen in many ways. One can say: 'I like you'. But a glance, a movement of the hand, a nod of the head, a smile can be equally full of meaning. One cannot be *close* to everyone to the same extent. One's marriage partner is a neighbour in a different way from the next-door neighbour, the postman or a colleague at work. In one case a greeting or a handshake suffices to show the other that one is well-disposed to him; in the other one needs time for conversation. A friendship calls for more varied signs of '*togetherness*' than everyday contact with neighbours. Friends need time for each other, they must be able to discuss mutual interests, to be concerned for one another's worries and to be faithful even if there are disagreements. All this goes to show that people learn to love and form relationships other than sexual relationships.

The first meeting between boys and girls is seldom serious love; while they are still young their relationships often change rapidly, most of them without inner compassion for one another, but sometimes in great interior suffering. From a first falling in love they may grow in love for one another; in the end 'the heart beats more quickly' for some one person. Both feel a reciprocal *responsibility*, acknowledge to one another their weaknesses and failings and love one another in spite of all limitations. They want their love to become permanent. From affection and *love* grows the will to be *faithful*: you alone and you for ever.

This unreserved 'yes' leads to new, more all-embracing forms of affection between two people. A man and woman come closest to one another in physical union. Their marriage is a natural way of life for them. When they give themselves completely to one another the deepest form of *physical love* is reached. This is the most intimate expression of the fact that they belong to one another. This love of man and woman can grow literally in physical form: in the child which owes its existence to their union.

Learning to love is a lifelong process. It is not primarily a matter of sexual relationships, although this is a powerful human characteristic, but it is above all the strong affection which binds the partners ever closer together. However, such *union* does not mean being linked together at the expense of *freedom*. Union with one another and freedom grow simultaneously into an unfolding of their true selves in love. This too comes only with practice.

Many people remain single by choice or through force of circumstances (e.g. caring for an aged parent, being homosexual, etc.). They too learn throughout their lives how to love and to grow in the strength of their affection for others. A person who is prepared to place his talents disinterestedly at the service of God and his fellow-men can experience the fulfilment of his wish for a life of happiness.

> A whole book of the Old Testament deals with love in poetic language:
> **Love is strong as death,**
> **jealousy relentless as Sheol (= the underworld).**
> **The flash of it is a flash of fire,**
> **a flame of God himself.**
> **Love no flood can quench,**
> **no torrents drown.**   *Song of Songs 8:6–7*

37.6   Ability to practise self-denial

→ 34.4 orders; 32.1 man and woman; 38.1 the family; 39.8 living differently

In matters of *sexuality* the Church is thought by many contemporaries to be prudish and old-fashioned. Her demands seem inexorable and far removed from reality. The obligation of a celibate priesthood gives rise to the same estrangement as does the Church's attitude to contraception. And when someone tries to stimulate understanding for the religious vows of *chastity*, poverty and obedience, he is often met by a shrug of the shoulders. Is Christianity really as far *removed from the world* and as averse to sex as the reproaches of many would lead one to suppose?

Perhaps the '*evangelical counsels*', on which the religious vows are based, are, in fact, appropriate to clarify the basic principle which the Church has at heart and which seems to many contemporaries so strange. The promises made by individuals to renounce private possessions, live without physical intimacy and to be subject to authority serves to draw attention to a danger that exists for everyone: namely, that, for Christians, *possessions,* sexuality and *power* can become more important than concern for the kingdom of God. The first concern of Christians must be that *God's kingdom* may come into its own in the world (Matthew 6:33).

In the case of sexuality this does not in any way mean that a Christian life is determined by prohibitions; it is rather that a Christian is challenged not to lose sight of the greater object of his life. The rules which are established for Christians in questions of sexual morality are intended to strengthen their *conscience* and at the same time lead to sexual behaviour *worthy of human persons*. This means, among other things, the practice of self-denial. A Christian is someone who is capable of *self-denial,* even in sexual 'possession' and 'sexual power'. However, self-denial as such is no virtue. Motives for it may be very superficial and selfish; sometimes self-denial is practised for reasons of strange or self-imposed compulsion (e.g. excessive dieting for reasons of vanity). Self-denial can be called Christian only if it comes from 'greater love' and sets us free for a new freedom.

Changes of opinion are the reason for moral criticism of specific questions with reference to sexual behaviour. What seemed quite natural at one time is considered at another immoral — and vice versa.

At certain times in one's life, for example, during adolescence, sexuality has high priority. An almost unquenchable thirst for *love* breaks out and grasps at everything promising satisfaction. Hardly anyone is spared from taking wrong paths and detours — and not only at this particular time in life. It is important that a Christian should have a clear, basic orientation. It is a question of understanding sex in the wider context of a love prepared to give and to serve, instead of isolating it and being dominated by it. Acquiring the necessary self-control is often difficult, but it is important for a fully human relationship between persons.

A German bishop in his pastoral letter says:

In our times it is very difficult for people to find the right path through life. In many respects they no longer have clear guidance by norms and universal values. Many ways are offered them. Our world has become richer, but also more complicated. Personal decisions are questioned.

Johannes Joachim Degenhardt

Modesty: Natural reserve about surrendering one's own privacy and invading that of others; one's intimate, personal sphere is limited not only to what is sexual; often described in everyday speech as 'decency' (→ chastity 32.1).

Masturbation: Especially during adolescence, boys and girls are exposed to very marked changes of mood. At times of discouragement or depression they may seek to compensate their lack of self-confidence by sexual satisfaction without a partner. But because sexuality concerns one's relationship with another, masturbation is basically not 'in order', i.e. it is sinful. In most cases it is merely a passing occurrence and it should not be made too important, but if it is represented as completely a matter of personal choice, there is a danger of promoting selfish behaviour.

Pre-marital intercourse: Sexual intercourse between a man and a woman who love one another but who are not (yet) married. In our society pre-marital intercourse is no longer felt to be shocking, if the couple have decided to get married, but Christians are obliged in their lives to correspond with the Church's ruling. The Catholic Church has always considered pre-marital intercourse as a serious offence against the natural, moral and sacramental ordering of marriage, not because she considers sexual intercourse — as such — to be sinful, as is often said, but because she ascribes to sexual intercourse special significance as a sign and expression of a lasting union (cf. 32.2).

37.7   The gift of oneself

→ 6.1 do not be anxious; 37.6 ability to practise self-denial; 15.1 who so lives; 39.9 com-passion; 39.10 praying to God

There is a proverb: 'Everyone is a neighbour to himself'. Usually we think first of ourselves, even when we intend to do good to someone else.

Jesus calls for a reversal of this order. The other person should come first. In the gospel there are hard, unequivocal *demands*: 'Sell your possessions and give alms!' (Luke 12:33). The disciple of Jesus must choose the last place (Luke 14:10); he must deny himself (Mark 8:34).

Only one who entrusts himself, his *future* and his *happiness* to God can understand such words and act on them. Such a person can refrain from always thinking first of himself. For him it is possible to be free from himself in order to be free for others. Because God 'provides' for him, he can concern himself with the happiness of others.

It would be good to live in a world where people generously forget themselves and are friendly to others, help without expecting a return, where they do not serve only where their *sympathies* lie, where they do not even allow themselves to be discouraged and disconcerted by lovelessness and hostility. Jesus speaks of such a world when he challenges us to set our sights on the love of God, who 'causes his sun to rise on bad men as well as good, and his rain to fall on honest and dishonest men alike' (Matthew 5:45). Jesus even says: 'Love your enemies and pray for those who persecute you; in this way you will be sons of your Father in heaven' (Matthew 5:44–45).

One needs to commit oneself to Christ's *directives* in order to experience that they are not inhuman. They make it clear what it means to be human. A person who gives himself to others is not lost, it is only thus that he truly comes to himself. If anyone thinks this is not so, he should beware lest, by considering only himself, he 'withers and dies'. So it is true that a person who does not spare himself but commits himself fully and retains nothing for himself, will discover the real meaning of life (cf. Matthew 8:35).

In following Jesus a person must be ready to give him his life:
Come, Lord Jesus, come.
Come, take my life,
take it for your own.
Take it for your service, Lord.
Take it for your glory, Lord.
Come, Lord Jesus, come.
Come, Lord Jesus, take my life.   *Kevin Mayhew*

37.8 Rejoicing with others
→ 23.3 sign of hope; 6.1 do not be anxious

The happy hours of our lives are characterised by sharing our cheerfulness and our laughter with others. They give us a glimpse of the fact that man was created for *joy*. But joy can also be selfish if someone seeks it for himself and begrudges it to others. And when someone is unhappy, another person's laughter can be painful for him. *Happiness* and success make the one who has them happy; but they may easily be painful and cause sadness or envy in an onlooker. Christians are not preserved from this, nor is it surprising; they do not live in another world.

And yet there is something in the life of a Christian which can change his point of view and open out a fresh horizon: the *hope* given through Jesus Christ. This can transform one's *life*, making it free from compulsion, from chasing one's own happiness and seeing in achievements and success the *meaning* of one's existence. This hope enables one to be light-hearted, relaxed and patient in the face of misfortune and of the injustice one suffers, but also in face of one's own inadequacies. It relieves one from regarding others as burdensome and dangerous rivals in the competition for fame and happiness instead of seeing them as brothers and friends over whose success one can rejoice whole-heartedly. Such rejoicing shows more clearly than mere pity the depths of one's love for one's neighbour.

The apostle Paul exhorts the Christians in Rome:
If you have hope, this will make you cheerful. Do not give up if trials come; and keep on praying. Rejoice with those who rejoice and be sad with those in sorrow.
Romans 12:12, 15

---

38 Who is my neighbour?

→ 1.1 a Christian; 14.1 he became man; 18.3 norm for judgement

We too ask the same question as the scribe: Who is my neighbour? (Luke 10:29). Whom do I mean — only those nearest to me; parents, brothers and sisters, friends, companions in school, colleagues at work? Are those of whose fate I read in the newspaper, or learn about on radio or television, included? Is a foreigner or stranger, someone of a different denomination, a personal *enemy*, my neighbour too? How far must I go in calling people my *neighbour*?

From my own viewpoint my neighbour is always the person closest to me. The measure of my concern decreases in proportion to his distance from me. Is this Christian? On the other hand, many are strongly committed and very active for far-distant world problems, while they can watch their own aged parents declining and do nothing. Is this Christian? It would seem necessary to translate the scribe's question into terms of our *everyday life.*

38.1   The family

→ 32.1 man and woman; 32.2 marriage; 39.3 acting in a spirit of solidarity

In a family the members are intimately united. Therefore it is in this most important sphere that *love of one's neighbour* is put to the test. Anyone obliged to grow up outside a family circle suffers the consequences of this deprivation, sometimes throughout his life. The *family* can become a first school in loving one's neighbour, where all learn to share in the fate of the others. In a *community* or group as closely knit as a family there has to be 'give and take' on the part of the individuals, no one can be preoccupied only with having and 'holding on' to things.

A family has no right to shut itself off from the outside world; it must be open to many other people. Parents must be prepared gradually to see their children emancipated as they grow up and allow them to go their own way. This transition brings difficult stress and strain for many families. Tensions, clashes and disappointments are unavoidable for both parents and children. Unjust and bitter words escape them; suddenly those who are closest become estranged from one another.

For the parents love of their neighbour means: showing fresh *confidence* and *trust* in their children, even if they have already been disappointed in many ways; it means not demanding from the children at any price an obedience — which may be justified — even though a reasonable degree of consistent strictness is necessary as the young are growing up. For the children, love of their neighbour means: recognising the worries and *responsibilities* of their parents, even if they find this burdensome;

accepting the weaknesses and faults of their parents and never showing disdain for them. The 'mantle of Christian love of one's neighbour' should not cover up clashes; on the other hand, removing tension should not lead to an unhealthy mania for always being in the right. Bearing with one another reciprocally, without grumbles or reproaches, reveals a deep love for one's neighbour — and this can be learnt in the family.

The Letter to the Colossians contains good advice for this relationship between parents and children:
Children, be obedient to your parents always, because that is what will please the Lord. Parents, never drive your children to resentment or you will make them feel frustrated.

Colossians 3:20–21

Fourth commandment: 'You shall honour your father and your mother' (→ 35.10 Ten commandments). In the Old Testament this commandment is not intended in the first place to make disobedient children 'good'; it is intended primarily to emphasise the duty of 'grown-up' children to care for their aged parents, a social duty arising from family circumstances; the commandment includes appreciation, obedience and responsibility.
Rights of parents: Parents have rights and duties, some of them laid down by law, with regard to the upbringing of their children.
Independence: Capacity to make one's own decisions and to be responsible for oneself; dependent on the age and degree of maturity of a person.
Being 'of age': Having reached the age at which the law allows full independence and ability to conduct business; in Britain the eighteenth birthday.

38.2   Friends and groups
→ 37.8 rejoicing with others; 37.7 gift of oneself; 39.3 acting in a spirit of solidarity

'True human love must grow from practice.' These words of Cardinal Newman are relevant also with regard to friendship. We often make *friends* through inclination or sympathy without any specific action on our part; friends are a gift. Whether such friendship lasts does depend on us; friendship has to be cultivated.

Therefore good friends do as much as possible together. They give and take; they talk and listen to one another; reciprocally they point out one another's failings; they are discreet and trust one another. Good friends, however, are not self-sufficient; they find, through their friendship, strength for other meetings.

People who are united by a common interest are often found in a *group*. Usually personal involvement for one another is less here than among friends. Objective discussion and argumentative rivalry about specific roles are as characteristic of a group as is a natural spirit of comradeship when one needs company.

The Christian finds himself involved in many kinds of groups. *Objectivity*, fair play, *readiness to help* are expected of him as of everyone else. Could it be that words spoken by Our Lord to his disciples run counter to this 'cut and thrust' process commonly found in a group? Matthew's gospel says: 'Anyone who wants to be great among you must be your servant, and anyone who wants to be first among you must be your slave' (Matthew 20:26–27). One is not asked to 'knuckle under', to be afraid to hold one's own or to *decline* to take over the leadership of a group. The words are directed towards the strength implicit in *yielding* for the sake of another; Our Lord is speaking of generous willingness to give oneself. This must be the real motive for our actions.

The Book of Ecclesiasticus contains much wisdom for our lives:
A faithful friend is a sure shelter,
whoever finds one has found a rare treasure.
A faithful friend is something beyond price,
there is no measuring his worth.
Ecclesiasticus (Sirach) 6:14–15

Group: Coming together in a manageable number of people who have a common interest. (There are quite specific patterns of 'interaction' in a group.) The word is also used for larger groups, especially in society: e.g. the Church, political parties, trade unions, but also housewives, taxpayers, pensioners, etc.

38.3 Society and state

→ 34.7 Church in the world; 39.2 responsibility; 39.4 work —
celebrate; 29.2 service in the world

There is a widespread opinion that a person who goes regularly to church and is in other ways a 'respectable' person is already a good Christian. It never occurs to many Christians that love for one's neighbour includes *responsibility* for the *state* and *society*. Morally, they live according to double standards: love of their neighbour is considered important in the private sphere; a thoughtless struggle for human advantage characterises their social, political and professional life.

Anyone who takes Christian love of his neighbour seriously knows that the obligation is universal. Therefore Christians have to share responsibility for human order in society and state, and be involved in the cause of *freedom* and of the right of all to voice their opinion. They must be concerned for industrial arrangements serving the common good and help to spread *peace* and *non-violence*. This presupposes their collaboration in social groups, political organisations, parties and trade unions. Here Catholics represent the basic principles of the Church's *social teaching*. Concrete conclusions are drawn from this teaching on the commandment to love one's neighbour, conclusions which affect social and civic arrangements. In these matters it is the Christian's duty not so much to maintain legal rights where there is a clash of opinions as to uphold the dignity of the human person which is his concern.

Repeatedly in society and state one sees the danger of over-organisation and bureaucracy. Even 'organised love of one's neighbour' in state, society and Church treats those seeking help merely as 'cases', as statistic material, and no longer as persons. To correct, as far as possible, wrong developments such as these is an obligation for every *Christian*. The initiative of individual citizens can often be more effective than an administrative body — and less expensive.

> Faith cannot exclude anything in the world:
> **To look away from the world does not help one to find God.**
> **To stare at the world does not help one to find him either.**
> **But the one who looks on him in the world stands in his**
> **presence.** *Martin Buber*

Social encyclical (Gr. = circular letter): A papal document sent to the whole Church or to 'all men of goodwill' in which the Church's attitude towards social or industrial questions is stated.

Communism: Description of an industrial and social order where everything social and political has to be on equal footing. There is to be no more private property or private means of production. No one is to become rich at the expense of another. Communist teaching, developed by Karl Marx and continued by Lenin, is based on the foundation of militant atheism.

Class conflict: Expression of enmity between different groups and levels of society, one (at least) of which has a sense of grievance and (often) a feeling of being exploited. The words (used also in ecclesiastical documents) describe the situation prevailing in many countries. Through her social teaching the Church tries to work to remove the tensions between the social 'classes' by peaceful means and to improve the living conditions of those socially deprived.

Marxism: A view of the world which has spread in various forms. It goes back to Karl Marx (1813–83), who maintained that society progressed by means of a continual struggle between social classes and their ideas. As soon as one class established itself in power, opposition would arise and the result of their conflict would be a step forward in human society. So Marxism would like to establish a 'fraternal world' through violent upheavals which would eventually lead to overcoming social differences by a 'dictatorship of the proleteriat' (i.e. the ordinary wage-earner). Actual attempts to do this have so far led to totalitarian systems characterised by inhuman oppression of and encroachment on the essential freedom of human beings.

Capitalism: An economic system based on a recognition of private property in which a minority of people controls the means of production and the profits from them. The system presumes that most of the workers do not possess capital. In its extreme form this would mean that the employer thought only of the greatest possible gain to increase his fortune. In fact, consideration given to the worker and the influence of governments and trade unions often serve to lessen its influence. But the danger of its degenerating into something inhuman must always be energetically counteracted (→ 39.8).

Revolution: Violent change in civic relationships. Paul VI says in his encyclical concerning the progress of nations: 'A revolutionary uprising — save where there is manifest, long-standing tyranny which would do great damage to fundamental personal rights and dangerous harm to the common good of the country — produces new injustices, throws more elements out of balance and brings on new disasters. A real evil should not be fought against at the cost of greater misery' (*The Great Social Problem*: CTS, 1967). On account of the problems which

38.3

revolution brings in its train, the Church involves herself, where change is urgently needed, by non-violent methods. These can be very effective, but they demand courage and discipline (→ 39.1).

38.4   The whole world
→ 39.2 responsibility; 39.3 acting in a spirit of solidarity; 12.1 the world; 24.2 the last days

In a technological age the whole *world* has shrunk. Radio, television and means of transport make of all the nations of the earth our neighbours. The happiness and misery of our friends come into our homes, as does a far-distant theatre of war. This brings with it both opportunities and dangers: our *responsibility* and readiness to help can grow, but we can also become indifferent when faced with the flood of new catastrophes. The same is true for development in all spheres of industry and technology: side by side, opportunities for good and for danger increase. Chaos can be averted only if all are *very much aware* of the responsibility that new knowledge and fresh skills bring with them. Atomic energy and pest control might serve as examples. Whatever promotes the cause of *peace* and health can equally well be abused for war and for the destruction of the human dignity of man.

There is no point in closing our eyes to future problems and weeping over the world of yesterday. Christians must accept the commission to 'renew the face of the earth' and try to unite love of their neighbour with love for those most distant from them: concern for a sick neighbour with concern for the next generation; care for the little plot of earth where we live with protection of the environment and the struggle against the thoughtless exploitation of the earth's energy-supply. Responsibility for the whole world is not merely the concern of politicians. In a democracy they can only carry out what is supported by the broad sweep of the population. All must bring into play their convictions and all are called upon to form public opinion, to give encouragement and also — when necessary — to protest or disclaim.

The urgency of such an appeal to a Christian conscience is shown by the astonishing objection that one often meets: No doubt this is an important problem but it has little to do intrinsically with being a Christian — If this is not intrinsic to the will of God, what is? Some Christians appear to accept a dichotomy between the world in which we live and the world with which Christ is concerned, as if, indeed, there were two distinct and separate worlds. In recent years the Church has stressed Christians' responsibility to carry on Christ's redeeming love by transforming the world in which they live.

The following words are attributed to St Francis of Assisi:
Lord, make me an instrument of your peace:
 where there is hatred let me sow love,
 where there is injury let me sow pardon,
 where there is doubt let me sow faith,
 where there is despair let me give hope,
 where there is darkness let me give light,
 where there is sadness let me give joy.
O Divine Master, grant I may
 not try to be comforted but to comfort,
 not try to be understood but to understand,
 not try to be loved but to love.
Because it is in giving that we receive,
it is in forgiving that we are forgiven,
and it is in dying that we are born to eternal life.

Love for those most distant: A concept formed by the philosopher Friedrich Nietzsche parallel to 'love of one's neighbour'; positive (including everyone) or negative (an excuse for failing to love one's neighbour); in the latter sense people sometimes say reprovingly 'Charity begins at home'.

Environment: The surroundings of a person, shaped by him, and on which he has an influence. The continuing pollution of the natural environment is a far-reaching problem. Everyone can, and should contribute to its protection (initiative on the part of citizens, laws for the protection of the environment). God has entrusted the world to man to be developed, not to be exploited and destroyed (cf. Genesis 1:28).

Progress: Step-by-step improvement of living conditions, technology, scientific knowledge, etc. What is progress in one sphere often brings disadvantages in another sphere. True progress is successful only when motivated by sensitive foresight, consciousness of one's own responsibility and fitting moral standards. Naïve belief in progress does more harm than good.

38.5 The person who crosses my path

→ 37.1 loving one's neighbour; 37.3 gift of oneself; 39.10 praying to God

It would seem quite clear who 'our neighbour' is: literally, the *ones nearest* to us — the farther away people are, the less the measure and degree of our *responsibility*. Therefore there would appear to be a kind of graded 'order of love'; and from this it appears that normal relationships must retain their validity and what calls for neighbourly love must not be allowed to blur into a pale love-of-those-distant.

A glance at the classical biblical text about love of one's neighbour suddenly makes us question this simple solution. Why doesn't Jesus take up the scribe's simple question? Instead of doing so, he tells the story of a man who has fallen among thieves; a priest and a Levite pass him by and eventually he is cared for by a foreigner, a member of another religion. Then Jesus returns to the original question, but with a different emphasis: Who made himself a neighbour to the man who had fallen among thieves?

By this question Jesus draws attention to the crucial point: it is no good asking if our neighbour belongs to this or that circle of people when we want to know who our neighbour is. The person who is crucial is the one who crosses *my path*, the one who needs me here and now. I cannot foresee whom I shall meet today or tomorrow, the person to whom I shall have to be a neighbour. They may be people with whom I live or work, or they may be unknown to me or even opponents and *enemies*. They can all become my brothers and sisters. For my neighbour is the person who crosses my path and who has need of me.

Jean-François Six has this to say: 'The Psalm, you know, is the prayer of the poor in exile. Life is not easy for them under the invader's yoke, stripped of all they had. Day by day they proclaim their suffering and their revolt, their despair of everything. As you pray the psalms today, think of the Third World; read the psalms as they can be read and understood by the men and women who live in India or Brazil, China or Cuba' (*Prayer and Hope*, pp.27–28, Fontana Books).

> In Luke's gospel Jesus enjoins on us this unreserved love of our neighbour and gives the reason:
> **Love your enemies and do good, and lend without any hope of return. You will have a great reward, and you will be sons of the Most High, for he himself is kind to the ungrateful and the wicked. Be compassionate as your Father is compassionate.**
> *Luke 6:35–36*

39 Go and do the same

→ 35.1 God loves us first; 1.5 through the eyes of Jesus; 37.3 taking the world seriously

The Christian is faced daily with situations in which he has to adjust his actions to the example of Jesus. Not infrequently he has to depart from what is common practice: thinking of others when he would prefer to think first of himself; allowing the opinions of others to count when he would like his own to prevail; *sharing* with those who have less, even when it gives him no pleasure; being good to others even if he himself has experienced evil at their hands.

A key sentence in the *Good News* is the following: Because God has first loved us (1 John 4:10), we too can love. We cannot repeat often enough that God's *gift* of love to us always comes first. If we begin to do good, it is only our response to his love. But since love needs to be shown in concrete form, how does our response appear in our everyday life? We may proclaim the principle in a general way while our love makes little impact on the one in need of it. How can this love be translated into our daily lives? Are there attitudes in our conduct which correspond to the *commandment of love*? Can one conclude how a Christian should act in specific situations? Can rules be established or examples given?

39.1   To love life

→ 24 eternal life; 37.4 physical love; 12.3 God's creature

'Everyone clings to life.' This would seem to be taken for granted. Yet suicide statistics show how many people put an end to their life because it has become a burden, an intolerable torture to them.

Christians believe that *life* is a gift from God — every life; therefore in every case life is worth living. A Christian will love life, his own and that of others, even if many people fail to find it worthwhile. For 'we are already children of God but what we are to be in the future has not yet been revealed' (1 John 3:2). The final *meaning* of life, as yet still concealed from us, lies in the *future* which God has promised us.

Because life is a gift from God, in all circumstances it must be protected and safeguarded. For the people of Israel this is part of God's law: 'I am Yahweh your God . . . you must not kill' (Exodus 20:2, 13). This prohibition is intended to prevent the worst from happening. But even the person who shrinks from taking the life of another is not necessarily an enthusiast for life. I can make life hell for a neighbour who has to put up with me day after day.

To protect life when it is endangered and to heal it when it is wounded is according to the mind and heart of Jesus. The Christian will devote himself to making life worthy of human dignity and worth living for the greatest possible number of people. To love one's neighbour means also to contribute to making life worthwhile for him and for seeing that he can *enjoy* life.

The following hymn is full of praise of the God who gives us joy:

Praise, my soul, the king of heaven!
To his feet thy tribute bring.
Ransomed, healed, restored, forgiven,
who like me his praise should sing?
Praise him! praise him!
Praise him! praise him!
Praise the everlasting king!   *Henry Francis Lyte*

Fifth commandment: 'You shall not kill' (→ 35.4 Ten commandments)

Death penalty: To take someone's life for a crime committed is the worst punishment that can be inflicted. It has been abolished in Britain apart from some very rare exceptions (e.g. treason). So far the Church has not pronounced a ban on the death penalty.

Euthanasia (Gr. = 'good' death = helping a person to die): Painless killing of persons who are old, or suffering from incurable and painful diseases. Not natural death (it is murder or akin to murder). The Catholic Church approves of all means of help in the framework of a natural death.

'Doing away' with people 'unfit' to live: Although sometimes wrongly called euthanasia, it is a form of murder specifically distinct from euthanasia, by virtue of its subject and its purpose. It is rejected by the law and by the basic instincts of mankind.

Suicide: Usually takes place for reasons of depressive mental illness (despair). Taking one's own life of one's own free will is, according to the teaching of the Church, a grave sin; for no one is justified in taking the life God has given him. Responsibility and therefore culpability for suicide are nevertheless difficult to assess.

Abortion: Putting an end to a pregnancy by surgical or medical means. Provided certain conditions are met, this is legally permissible in Britain, but it does not alter the serious duty of Christians to protect unborn life. Every form of intentional death of the 'fruit of the womb' (the foetus) is forbidden by the Catholic Church.

Self-defence: Protection against an actual, unlawful attack on life and limb, honour or fortune (one's own or another's) for which one is responsible. The person defending himself must make efforts to confine to the least possible harm the damage done to his assailant. Self-defence may never be an act of revenge.

Killing in wartime: The responsibility of the individual for a decision concerning life and death in exceptional circumstances, as presented by war, is very much diminished. Military action always includes danger to human life. But even if the question of responsibility is difficult to answer, it cannot lightly be laid aside. Much depends on whether it is a matter of attack or defence. Orders from higher authority cannot fundamentally remove an individual's responsibility. In every case the conscience of the individual must be respected (→ 36.2).

Murder of a tyrant: A subject repeatedly discussed, although for an individual it is hardly ever a burning issue. Deliberately to kill a dictator who, by his rule, does grave harm to his country and despises the life of its citizens, is a very serious decision to make and entails a heavy responsibility. According to general interpretation such a decision is considered morally justified if there is a probability of thereby preventing greater harm and of re-establishing well-ordered relationships. General judgements of this kind — however they turn out — can never do justice to the seriousness of such a decision (→ 38.3).

Death due to 'social' conditions: That old people in our neighbourhood die lonely and abandoned is a disgrace. It is as disgraceful (or even worse) that everywhere in the world human beings die before their time because they have not enough to live on, because their work is inhumanly hard or underpaid, because of inadequate safety precautions, etc. Christian faith in an after-life should not blind us to the iniquity of 'social' death, whatever its form. Attempts to prevent this kind of death are an integral part of our faith.

39.2 Assuming responsibility

→ 34.1 God's people; 29.2 service in the world; 31.1 praying and caring; 38 who is my neighbour?

Wherever a person assumes *responsibility*, where one person tells another of his expectations and hopes, where each one contributes his talents to reach a common goal, there active, living communities are formed. Commandments, laws, rules — written and unwritten — can make their contribution to consolidate order in a *community* and to assure its continuance; but the order thus won remains a façade which sooner or later will collapse unless the members are prepared to assume responsibility. Responsibility for important matters presupposes readiness to practise responsibility in small things.

The older children are, the greater the responsibility they assume for the *family*. Even in case of crisis the mutual responsibility between parents, children and other relatives should not be too readily handed over to welfare institutions (children's homes, homes for old people, etc.).

Even in school and in the *neighbourhood*, later in the group, in the *parish* and in the place of work, it is right to recognise one's own talents and to use them for the welfare of others. A person who withdraws from all responsibility and hands over every problem to an impersonal authority has little understanding of Christian love for his neighbour.

The *state* too is dependent on the readiness of its citizens to assume responsibility. Christians are called upon to collaborate in the most varied spheres. They must try to make their *convictions* effective where the implementation of good laws is concerned. Only then have they the right to criticise and to be on their guard that the state does not exceed its powers.

Paul exhorts the community in Rome:
We who are strong have a duty to put up with the qualms of the weak without thinking of ourselves. Each of us should think of his neighbours and help them to become stronger Christians. Christ did not think of himself. *Romans 15:1-3*

Responsibility: Moral or legal obligation to account for one's actions. This assumes that one has the qualifications required for the actions in question, and is capable of acting rationally.

Samaritans: A round-the-clock service in Britain, especially in large cities, whereby people can ask, by telephone, for advice and assistance in their problems. The chief members are trained and have already helped many in situations of distress, and have saved several from despair/suicide. Requests for help are treated with complete confidentiality.

39.3   Acting in a spirit of solidarity

→ 34.5 good works; 34.4 orders; 31.1 praying and caring

Christians may not resign themselves to the world as it is now — in the hope that in the future world all will, of its own accord, become better. According to their abilities they must work for a more human world here and now. It is not sufficient to be enthusiastic about magnificent plans for the future, they must be concerned for the people with whom they live.

It is good to keep one's eyes open for the many lawful concerns of people in *society*, especially those who are at a disadvantage, like immigrants, the unemployed, old people, children, large families, the handicapped and the sick. It is important too to *oppose* the increasing claims of the state to make all problems and troubles the domain of officials and authorities.

On the other hand one cannot leave it to chance that a person in need of help may meet someone ready to help — he may also be left waiting in vain. *Love of one's neighbour* needs also to be so organised that each one is given what he needs. In addition to church organisations (e.g. Society of St Vincent de Paul and many others) there are nowadays welfare services (health, social provision, etc.) which may well be regarded as 'organised' charity.

In the history of the Church there have always been communities founded to give signs of their Christian *solidarity* with suffering humanity, and they have devoted their lives to the poor, the sick, the aged, orphans and prisoners (e.g. John of God, Don Bosco and others). They are examples for us in that they show how Christians try to keep close to those in distress and so to follow Jesus who gave his life that others might live.

For Christians solidarity means not only taking their share of caring for the people in our own society. Christians make great efforts to further the work in developing countries and to adjust the balance between poor and rich on a world-wide basis. This common action calls for more than an alms to appease our conscience. The problems of mankind demand doggedness and inexhaustible *patience*, above all a caring heart which seizes every opportunity for effective help.

Solidarity with the weak makes Christianity convincing today — perhaps more than anything else:
All things are connected like the blood which connects one family. All things are connected. Whatever befalls the earth befalls the sons of the earth. Man did not weave the web of life; he is merely a strand in it. Whatever he does to the web he does to himself. *Chief Seathl's Testament*

Solidarity: State of being bound to other members of a group (however large) by a common condition, e.g. shared human nature. Leading to a 'togetherness' with those who are at a disadvantage; active, helpful collaboration in favour of the weaker ones.

Civic initiative: Collective decisions on the part of citizens who devote themselves to improvements in social life: by meetings, petitions, demonstrations, proposals, actions. Such initiative is important for a group whose citizens know they are co-responsible for social and civic life, even if particular requests need to be looked at very carefully.

Those at a disadvantage: People mentally or physically handicapped or severely deprived in some way, who find it hard to cope with the normal demands made on their lives: the blind, deaf, lame, educationally sub-normal, etc. Christians know they have an obligation to help them so that they may, as far as possible, learn to help themselves and be fully accepted in society. Young people — individually and in groups — can give valuable help to such people.

39.4 Work — rest — celebrate

→ 12.3 God's creature; 34.6 Church in the world; 23.3 sign of hope

We spend much of our lives working. But — thanks to modern techniques of production — our free time is considerably increased. *Work* and *leisure* are slowly assuming more balanced proportions in our growth towards self-development and *self-realisation*. In both spheres pain and pleasure are connected: work can be unworthy of human dignity; it can alienate and bore us; it can be tiring and soul-destroying; it can be crippling and harmful to our health. Yet it can also be a source of great *joy* to know what we are working for; systematically to use and develop our talents; to see how something new arises and takes shape; to discover how we ourselves are transformed by our work and to experience that we can use our ideas and our strength for others.

What about our *free time*? For many it means a joyless evening out, just 'killing time', unimaginative expense. Yet it can also be used for real leisure, for well-deserved relaxation and for a healthy break which not only renews the *strength* for one's work, but is of value in itself; such free time could renew our appreciation of a celebration; it could be in itself an experience of 'celebration'. For we do not live just to work. The following are also an essential part of life: games, love, celebrations, dreams, conversation, music, walks, reading and even time to contemplate our world. Both work and leisure are important for human beings.

Our celebrations can be expressed in many ways. For a person who has discovered in Christ the object of his life the *Eucharist* can become the climax of all celebration in which every element of free activity is reflected. We do not pray in order to achieve something and we do not celebrate the Eucharist to fulfil a religious duty. The Eucharist gathers together all human talents into a 'sacred drama', in the presence of the living God, to praise him, thank him and to rejoice in him. Therefore a Eucharistic celebration can be a source of strength for our work and a stimulus for creative action.

The ten commandments emphasise the seventh day as a day of rest. Work and leisure both foster human self-development:
For six days you shall labour and do all your work, but the seventh day is a sabbath for Yahweh your God. You shall do no work that day, neither you nor your son nor your daughter nor your servants, men or women, nor your animals nor the stranger who lives with you. *Exodus 20:9–10*

Work: A term often confined to manual or physical labour, but may include mental effort. Its main aim is to provide a living worthy of human dignity (e.g. food, clothing, housing, etc.). Various kinds of distinctions are made (e.g. skilled/unskilled work; manual/blue-collar/white-collar work).

Profession: Generally an activity carried out in society, usually at the same time one's source of income. In the choice of a profession ideally a person takes into account his own bent, his calling, his talents and the needs of society. This is true too for a vocation in the Church: priestly, religious and lay vocations.

Right to work: A fundamental right of every human being, rooted in the 1948 Declaration of Human Rights.

Unemployment: Exists as a consequence of economic conditions.

Trade Union: A voluntary association of workers organised to protect its own interests and working conditions. Its most powerful weapon is the strike — but before taking this step every effort should be made to negotiate an agreement by which both sides will be satisfied.

Collective bargaining: Process by which agrcement is reached between trade unions and employers concerning wages and working conditions. Generally concerns a large number of workers in one or more unions.

Contract of employment: Agreement between employer and employee to regulate their reciprocal rights and duties (e.g. continued payment of wages during illness, pension contributions, hours of work, holidays, etc.).

Free time: Leisure hours of those engaged in work, important for health, family, friendships, further training, sharing in social, civic and church life. With advances in technology and a consequent extension of leisure the ability to develop a meaningful and worthwhile use of free time becomes ever more important.

The arts: The use of imagination and creative skill to make objects of beauty. This is a sphere in which human life is enriched with significance and meaning.

Third commandment: 'Remember the Sabbath day and keep it holy' (→ 34.4 Ten commandments).

39.5 Trustworthiness

→ 37.3 taking the world seriously

Every day of our lives we depend on the trustworthiness of others: on the mechanic who repairs our car; on the doctor who gives us a prescription; on the friend to whom we entrust some undertaking. *Life* in *society* would be impossible if we could not *trust* one another.

For a Christian there is a special duty in this matter, for the basic conception of Christian life implies that others can trust a person is telling the truth, that he does not maliciously deceive and that he keeps his promises. To be honest, truthful and reliable means putting into practice *love for one's neighbour*. There is an exhortation to Christian life in the New Testament which reads as follows: 'So from now on, there must be no more lies: you must speak the truth to one another, since we are all parts of one another' (Ephesians 4:25).

The life and death of many people may depend on the *trustworthiness* of a single individual. This is why in olden times God's people, in the ten commandments, included the statement of a witness before a court of law: 'You shall not bear false witness against your neighbour' (Exodus 20:16). Christian tradition sees in this a command from God which unconditionally obliges man to speak the *truth*.

One who is repeatedly disappointed in his *trust* in others can easily become suspicious. There should be no such thing as basic distrust among Christians. It is not naïveté and blindness to reality when, despite unfortunate experiences, we try to remain open to goodness in others. Above all, love calls for one to have an unwavering determination to remain honest and trustworthy. Love takes as its norm God himself who remains *faithful* — even towards those who are unfaithful.

A lie has a threefold consequence:
The lie . . . is a distortion of the truth. It makes a person unreliable. It destroys mutual trust and confidence.
cf. *A New Catechism* ('The Dutch Catechism'),
pp. 442–443.

Eighth commandment: 'You shall not bear false witness against your neighbour' (→ 35.4 Ten commandments).
Truthfulness: Condition in which one's attitude and words correspond to reality; they neither abbreviate nor falsify.
Lie: Deliberately false statement.
Error: Assent to a statement or opinion that is false. In matters of faith it can be difficult to judge: according to Catholic teaching the Church's interpretation of revealed truth is preserved from danger of error and therefore has to be given the assent of faith.
Trust: An attitude which arises reciprocally from an open and honest relationship with people; can be fostered or shattered by one's experiences; sometimes used to describe 'faith'.
Honesty: An attitude springing from value placed upon truth and trustworthiness (e.g. not cheating others).
Professional secret: A duty connected with a specific office or profession (e.g.

solicitor, doctor, priest, data-processor) not to reveal information about people which has been entrusted to them. To protect a professional secret one can refuse to speak in a law court.

White lie: An untrue statement made with the intention of freeing oneself (or others) in a difficult situation (a protective statement) or to spare another from a painful truth. In spite of the awkward situation it remains a lie.

Suspicion: Unconfirmed doubt of another's innocence/culpability.

Distrust: An attitude arising from the fact that one lacks confidence in another.

Hypocrisy: A pretence of virtue or devotion.

Calumny: Malicious, false report, intended to harm the subject of it.

Oath: Solemn calling on God to witness a statement or a promise ('so help me, God'). According to Matthew 5:34 a disciple of Jesus is forbidden to swear on oath — one may not do so except in a very serious case.

Perjury (false oath): To make an untrue statement in a court of law after calling on God to witness the truth of what one says; incurs severe punishment by law.

39.6   Making decisions and remaining open

→ 36.2 freedom; 30.6 guilt/self-knowledge; 22.4 God's love

There are continually situations where we expect clear information: what is right and what is wrong? Am I to decide for this or that? Is this opinion right or that one? This desire for an unequivocal answer is not always satisfied. To many of our questions there are various answers. This leads to a state of uncertainty, especially if people have not learnt to come to terms with the manysidedness of life and if no one has shown them that the richness of our existence lies in its variety.

The fact that there are many possibilities does not mean that we should let ourselves be manipulated by them; on the contrary, we must repeatedly face *decisions*. For many this may appear irksome; a person puts off his decision again and again and in the end he himself is 'put off'. Others are of the opinion that, after reflection, they can leave situations open as long as they like because there are always 'various possibilities'. This results in a certain vacillation, excessive tolerance, or even in dishonesty and lack of strength of character.

A fascinating aspect of our *life* lies precisely in the possibility and the necessity of making decisions. But it also implies that we must be ready to test our decisions and to face up to them again if they have proved to be wrong. This calls for openness, self-criticism and a readiness to begin each time to learn afresh. It often needs more *courage* to change one's opinion than to remain faithful to it.

A person who claims the right to make decisions must also be ready to respect those of others, even when they are contrary to his own convictions. This does not mean indifference with regard to recognised truth, with regard to acknowledgement of error. But it does demand a greater esteem for a person's serious struggle for *truth* rather than a passive acceptance of a truth with which interiorly one cannot agree.

For do we, as Christians, know whether we have always recognised as true, or always described, preached and lived what corresponds to God's truth? The fullness of life in Jesus Christ goes further than we understand. 'To make up one's mind' and 'to remain open' are not incompatible; on the contrary, both are necessary.

The relationship of love for the truth and love for one's neighbour was formulated by St Augustine:
Hate error, and love the one who errs.

Tolerance: To consider the unfamiliar opinions of others, their customs and their convictions as valid, unless human rights are violated. The Second Vatican Council (1962–65) stressed freedom of conscience and of the practice of religion for all.

World-view: General view of the nature and meaning of the world and of human life: component of every religion but also independently of religion, even in conscious opposition to religion, e.g. the world-view of dialectical materialism (→ 12.1).

Religion: General word for the many different ways in which men are related with the 'holy' and with the ultimate reason for their existence; in general, people join an existing religious group. In addition to the five main world religions there are a large number of other religions, some of them comparatively recent.

Religious freedom: A fundamental right of a human being. The Second Vatican Council spoke officially on this subject against intolerance (1965); today the Church sees it as a serious duty to foster unity and love among human beings and among nations.

39.7 Sharing

→ 18.3 norm for judgement; 37.7 gift of oneself; 29.2 service in the world

The Acts of the Apostles describe the life in community of the early *Christians*: 'The whole group of believers was united, heart and soul; no one claimed for his own use anything that he had, as everything they owned was held in common' (Acts 4:32). Is this a description of a reality or of an ideal? Are Christians being told here that the *ownership* of private property is forbidden? The passage from the Acts is a reminder always to be prepared to re-think these matters.

Each one can give of what he has. This is true not only of money and possessions but also of one's talents: kindness, a sense of humour, joy, serenity and patience. Everyone is concerned to make something of himself, to develop his *potential*. Whatever I achieve or acquire or possess, my material and intellectual skills, give me 'status' and are part of me. They belong to me and are like a 'second me'. This is why people are so hurt when another takes something away or disputes my right to these things. Two of the ten *commandments* are therefore concerned with possessions.

All property brings with it its own dangers: if I cling to it, set my heart on it and am 'obsessed with possessing', for the sake of what I possess, even at the expense of others, it possesses me rather than the reverse. The message of Jesus warns us insistently against this attitude: 'It is easier for a camel to pass through the eye of a needle than for a rich man to enter the *kingdom of God*' (Matthew 19:24). When the Church defends private property she does so to provide people with the opportunity to give, to make life worthy of human dignity. In no way does she intend to favour an industrial system established solely to make proprietors richer still.

Property always implies *social obligations* too: giving others a share of what one possesses. Every community is dependent on this: the family, friends, the group, the state. Christian *love for one's neighbour* also includes the challenge to work for a distribution of goods that is socially just: for example, for a right equilibrium between poor and rich in the world, for a share of profits with the workers, for the organisation and distribution of the goods produced. If rights and output are shared, duties and *responsibilities* must also be shared.

Where sharing remains a mere obligation it quickly becomes a burden. Implicit in Christian sharing there is a different experience: the more I give, the richer I become.

The experience of many generations is expressed in the following:

A trouble shared is a trouble halved;
A joy shared is a joy doubled.

Seventh commandment: 'You shall not steal' (→ 35.4 Ten commandments).

Tenth commandment: 'You shall not covet your neighbour's goods' (→ 35.4 Ten commandments).

Private property: Property of which a person can dispose personally and which he himself can use; in many countries his rights are legally protected; the Church emphasises the social obligation of private property. The power to dispose fully and freely of private property can easily lead to an unhealthy concentration of property in private hands, to the disadvantage of the poor and to the benefit of the rich.

Possession: The actual domination a person has over a thing (as distinct from legal domination over a thing = property). The words 'property' and 'possession' are often used without distinction.

Social obligation: Everyone has some responsibility for the general good by the use he makes of his property and possessions, his gifts and his talents. Nowadays many of these obligations are undertaken by civic authorities and financed by taxation, health insurance, etc. But even in a 'welfare state' charitable institutions are not redundant. Personal help is even more important in certain individual cases.

Co-responsibility: A general term for the shared responsibility of the individual in smaller or larger groups, as well as the larger and smaller groups themselves.

Participation in management: Sharing by the workers in decisions within their firm on matters affecting their welfare: conditions of work, organisation, appointments, transfers, dismissal; collaboration in basic decisions with regard to the extension, removal, or closure of a firm; all this may be partially regulated by law, especially in larger firms.

Theft: Illegal appropriation of the possessions or property of another; also false underpayment (e.g. of taxes), fraud, looting, robbing, petty pilfering. The catchword 'property is theft' is a criticism of capitalist control of the means of production; it implies that what the proprietor owns really belongs to the workers and has been stolen from them. Against this idea the Church upholds the right to private property but at the same time emphasises the social obligation incurred.

Robbery: Theft carried out with violence or threats of violence with danger to life and limb.

Receiving stolen goods: Accepting or paying for something that has been stolen.

39.8 Living a different kind of life

→ 34.5 good works; 34.7 Church in the world; 37.7 gift of oneself; 9.3 pray without ceasing

Young people today no longer wish to be resigned to having their lives too clearly determined by *society*. They want to take their own affairs in hand and seek out their own path.

For example, a few want to go and live in the country. They give up their work in a big city and a well-paid job. They seek a simple, unpretentious life as an alternative to the life-style accepted by most of their contemporaries. A number want to work directly, at least for a time, in and for the Third World.

Much that today seems unavoidable — people crowded together in high-rise flats and inner cities, air pollution caused by industry and traffic, waste of energy and raw materials spoiling the countryside — could be changed. If this is to happen, one must make a firm decision *to live a different kind of life* from that to which people are accustomed and to give up much that is taken for granted.

Christians are commissioned to seek new life-styles. 'Do not model yourselves on the behaviour of the world around you, but let your behaviour change, modelled by your new mind' (Romans 12:2) is what Paul writes to the church in Rome. In Church history there are many people who opted out of the life-style in their society and began to live a new kind of life. They were often mocked for this by the people around them; but their attitude soon proved that they were blazing a new trail for many.

The crucial question about a 'different life-style' is very important for us because our *prosperity* – often excessive – is responsible for much of the poverty and misery in Africa, Asia and Latin America. Here and now we must live simply that others may simply live (slogan of CAFOD, the Catholic Fund for Overseas Development). The will to do this may determine our choice of profession and it can change our *way of life*. 'Living a different kind of life' is also an important theme for Christian prayer. It is true that prayer alone will not alter conditions, but it modifies the attitudes that lead to action.

A prayer from Africa may be an example for us:
Lord, you know us all.
You know those who have nothing.
You know those who are oppressed by injustice.
And you know those who become ever richer
and more powerful at the expense of others.
All are your children.
We need your love,
so that we, in our turn, may love.
Rouse us, stir our hearts to love!

Third World: Collective term for the developing countries: Latin America, Africa and Asia, in contrast to the two powerful blocks in the East and West; nations express their social obligations towards each other by giving aid for development — aid intended to help the poorer nations to help themselves; it should not be a fresh form of exploitation.

Industrial systems: By industry we mean the production and distribution of goods designed to serve the needs of society. The aim is to do this at minimum cost. To achieve this aim the free market economy depends upon the profit motive while socialism uses central planning. A middle course (often called 'mixed economy') tries to combine both methods. The criterion by which a system is to be judged is whether or not it fosters the dignity and freedom of people.

39.9 Com-passion

→ 37.8 rejoicing; 37.7 gift of oneself; 1.2 following Jesus; 31.1 praying and caring

We find many people *sympathetic*: those who are cheerful, good-humoured, healthy and well liked on all sides. Those who are touchy, ill-humoured, quick-tempered, sour and sick, we find unsympathetic.

The word sympathy really means *feeling with* or suffering with, that is, being com-passionate; to be united with others in such a way that one feels and suffers with them. This is easy enough with someone we like, someone who is in good form and does us good. We are inclined to give the others a wide berth — closing our eyes and ignoring them: the person is just not there — as far as we are concerned.

But love of one's neighbour means: not closing our eyes, being *open* to everyone we meet. A *Christian* does not understand sympathy as beginning with himself, but as coming from another who is waiting for someone to feel and suffer with him. There are situations in which one can no longer change conditions. If, for example, someone is incurably ill, what can we do? A person who remains patiently faithful to another, supports him and, as far as he can, bears his suffering with him, does what only a lover can still do. John's gospel tells us that, near the *cross* of Jesus as he was dying, stood the mother of Jesus, the other women and the beloved disciple John (cf. John 19:25–27). They remained with him to the end; they stood 'beneath the cross'.

Catastrophes can neither be undone nor always warded off for the future. It is not possible to remove all the misery from the world; pain cannot be lessened in every case. Yet there still remains one thing: to continue to be present, to be compassionate and to allow our compassion to become *prayer — confident* in the One whose son has suffered for us.

Pascal (1623–62), a famous French scholar and Christian, spoke of the incomprehensible suffering of mankind as a continuation of that of Jesus;
Jesus is in his death agony until the end of the world.

Blaise Pascal

Sympathy (Gr. = suffering with): Com-passion; mental participation in the pain and suffering of another. Usually not commanded but instinctive. The opposite is antipathy which is an aversion — often without any reason — for another person (→ 37.1 corporal works of mercy).

39.10 Praying to God for the living and the dead

→ 9.4 kinds of prayer; 37.6 gift of oneself; 38.5 the one who crosses my path

Our love is not to be words or mere talk, but something real and active (cf. 1 John 3:18). It grows out of certain *basic attitudes* which enable us to step into the breach when someone is needed, when help is required. However, love of our neighbour does not consist in helping only when a catastrophe occurs — love of our neighbour is also a question of a *life-style*, and this calls for some re-thinking. If it is not enough for me to give out of my surplus possessions, I must begin to live differently, to plan less lavishly and to cut down expenses. And when my possessions are of no avail, I myself am demanded. Then I must give something of myself, my presence, my sympathy with those who suffer, and I must make their suffering my lot.

Anyone who has had experience of this — as the one helped or as the one helping — understands the wisdom of adding a second list to the corporal works of *mercy*. For the spiritual poverty and abandonment experienced by many call for the affection of *Christians* no less than hunger and thirst, nakedness and homelessness, imprisonment, sickness and death.

Courage and *determination* are needed to take to task someone who has done wrong; *patience* and time are required to instruct one less wise; vision and the *strength of one's convictions* are necessary to give helpful advice to one in doubt; only a person with imagination and a *loving heart* can comfort one in sorrow; much *serenity* and long-suffering are needed to support without resentment a person who is a burden to those around him; one has to have generosity and *kindness* to forgive someone who has offended us.

And when all this does not obtain our object, when everything done is to no avail, and we are at the end of our resources, then as Christians we still have a 'trump card': we can do what Christians have always done in their daily duties: entrust love of our neighbour to the *love of God*; we can *pray* to God for the living and the dead and surrender into his hands everything we ourselves fail to achieve.

In addition to the seven 'corporal' works of mercy, Christian tradition lists seven spiritual works of love for one's neighbour:
**To convert the sinner,
to instruct the ignorant,
to give advice to the doubtful,
to comfort the sorrowful,
to bear wrongs patiently,
to forgive injuries,
to pray for the living and the dead.**

Sympathy: → 39.9

Gracious Lord,
help us to accept each other
and learn how to give,
to be supportive and compassionate.
Give us understanding hearts
to perceive and discern what is real
and turn from illusions.
Grant your consolation to the sick
and to the dying your mercy.
Help us to centre our lives
on the things that matter,
truth and kindness,
Jesus and his gospel;
sharing your good earth
with justice and generosity.
Plant your peace in our hearts
and let it grow throughout the world.

Kevin Nichols

Index

(Section numbers in **bold** type indicate that the word indexed is explained in the Notes)

leadership (in Church) 33; 34.2
lectionaries 27.1
leisure 39.4
Lent 27.6; 30.3
Lesson 27.1
lies 39.5
life 23.1
   everlasting 23.1; 24; 24.1-2
   right to 35.4; 39.1
   value of 39.1
life-style (new) 37.1; 39; 39.1-10
litany 13.3
Litany of the Saints 36.3
liturgical year 27.6
liturgy 9.3; 9.4; 27; 27.1; →
   Eucharist
   reform of 27
Liturgy of the Word 27.1
'Lord' II; 13; 13.3; 14; 17; 17.1
Lord's Prayer → Our Father
Lord's Supper 27.2; 29
love 4.1; 4.4; 12.3; 12.4; 12.5; 18.2;
   22.1; 35; 37.5
   for God IV; 35; 35.3; 36; 37
   for our neighbour 21.2; IV;
     37-38; 39.3; 39.10
   God's 1; 5.1; 12.3; 12.4; 16.3;
     18.2; 22.4; 25.2; 28.1; 39.10
   → 'greatest commandment'
'love for those most distant' 38.4
loving kindness of God 7.2; 25; 31.1
'Low Church' 34.9
Lucifer 12.2
Luke's gospel 20.4
Luther, Martin I; 28.3; 34.9

magic 10.4
magisterium 34.2
Magnificat 9.1; 14.3
man as God's creature 12; 12.3;
   23.1
manna 27.2
manslaughter → killing
Marana tha 18.1
Mark's gospel 20.4
marriage 26.4; 32; 32.1-2; 37.5
   sacrament → matrimony
martyrdom 13.3; 21.2; 36.3
martyrs II; 16.1; 36.3
Marxism 38.3
Mary, Virgin 14; 14.1; 14.3; 36.4
   devotion to 36.4
   feasts of 27.6

Mass 27; 27.2-4
   structure of 27.4
masturbation 37.6
matrimony, sacrament of 26.4; 32;
   32.2
Matthew's gospel 20.4
maturity 29; → independence
Maundy Thursday → Holy Thursday
May devotions 36.4
meaning of life 10.1; 12.1; 39.1
meditation 9.4
memorial 27.2
mercy, corporal works of 31.1; 37.2
mercy, spiritual works of 31.1;
   39.10
message (Good News) 16.3; 35; →
   gospel
Messiah 13.1; 13.2; 20.4
Methodists 34.9
mighty deeds of God 20.2; 27.1
military service 34.6
miracles 4.3; 12.4
misfortune 5.3; 12.5
Missal 27
mission, Church's 18.1; 26.1
mission, parish 26.1
missionaries → missions
missions 26.1; 33.1; 34.5; 36.3
   methods 26.1
mixed marriage 32.1
   celebration 32.2
modesty 37.6
Mohammed 10.2
monastery 34.4
money (false god) 35.4
monks 9.3; 34.4
monogamy 32
monotheism 10.1
monstrance 27.4
morning prayer 9.3
mortal sin 30.2
Moses 2.1
Mother of God → Mary
   title 14.3
murder → killing
Muslims 10.2; 12; → Islam
mystery 4.1; 12.2; 25.2
mysticism 9.4; 36.1
myth 23.1

natural rights 37.3
Nazareth 15.1; 19.1

theological virtues 26.4
theology 10.5; 11.2; 34.2
third commandment 27.5; 35.4;
   39.4
'third day' 16.2
Third World 39.8
Thrones and Dominations 12.2
time, end of 18.1
Timothy, Letters to 33.2
Titus, Letter to 33.2
tolerance 39.6
tomb, empty 16.1
Torah 15.1
trade unions 39.4
tradition 1.3; 16.1; 20.2
traditional religions 10.2
transubstantiation 27.2; 27.5
trial of Jesus 15.1–2
Trinity 19.2; 25; 25.1
   images of 25.1
Trinity Sunday 27.6
trust 2.2; 32.1; 38.1; 39.5
   in God 5.1; 5.3; 6.1; II; 13; 19.3;
   36.1
   in Jesus 1.3; 4.3
trustworthiness 39.5
truth 39.5; 39.6
truthfulness 39.5
tyrant, killing 39.1

unbaptised 28.1
unchangeableness, God's 11.2
underworld 16.2
unemployment 39.4
'unfit to live' 39.1
Uniate Eastern Churches 16.2
United Reformed Church 34.9
unity
   Christian II; 20.4; 34.9
   of Church 20.1; 20.4

values, basic 37.3
Vatican 34.8
Vatican City State 34.8

Vatican Council
   First 34:2
   Second 10.2; 20.2; 22.2; 24.1;
   26.1; 27; 27.3; 28.3; 33.2; 34.2;
   34.6; 39.6
venial sin 30.2
Vespers 9.3
Viaticum 31.2
vicar general 34.8
Virgin → Mary
Virgin Birth 14.1
virtues
   cardinal 37.3
   theological 26.4
vocation
   Christian 8.2; 21.2
   religious 33.2
vows 34.4

war 34.6
   killing in 39.1
water (in baptism) 28.1
Western Church 20.4; 34.9
white lie 39.5
Whitsunday → Pentecost
will of God I; 5; 5.1–3; 9.3; 15;
   15.1; IV; 35.4; 36.2
Wisdom, Book of 12.4
witnesses 16.1
word of God 10.3; 20.2–4; 27.1
Word of God 10.3; 14.2
work 9.3; 9.4; 39.4
   right to 39.4
works of mercy → mercy
world 12.5; 37.3; 38.4
   Christian service in 29.1; 29.2
   origin of 11; 12; 12.1
   transformation of 23.3
World Council of Churches 34.9
world-picture 12.1
world religions 10.2; 39.6
world-view 12.1; 39.6

Yahweh 2; 2.1